Interpretive Conventions

Interpretive Conventions

THE READER IN THE STUDY
OF AMERICAN FICTION

Steven Mailloux

CORNELL UNIVERSITY PRESS

Ithaca and London

First published 1982 by Cornell University Press.
Published in the United Kingdom by
Cornell University Press Ltd., Ely House,
37 Dover Street, London W1X 4HQ.

International Standard Book Number 0-8014-1476-8
Library of Congress Catalog Card Number 81-70712
Printed in the United States of America
*Librarians: Library of Congress cataloging information
appears on the last page of the book.*

*The paper in this book is acid-free, and meets the guidelines for permanence and durability
of the Committee on Production Guidelines for Book Longevity of the Council on Library
Resources.*

For Edmund and Nell Mailloux

Contents

Preface

Readers approach prefaces expecting to find out how authors want their texts to be read. Such expectations and readings are what this book is all about. The following chapters present a general introduction to current reader-response criticism, a critical perspective that makes the reading experience the central concern in talk about literature. These chapters also propose a specific reader-oriented approach to the study of American fiction. I develop this approach while examining the activities making up the discipline: literary theory, practical criticism, textual scholarship, and literary history.

Chapters 1 and 2 analyze five influential theories of the literary reading process: those of Stanley Fish, Norman Holland, David Bleich, Wolfgang Iser, and Jonathan Culler. It turns out that none of these literary theorists provides the kind of reader-oriented approach most useful for studying American fiction. Only a reader-response criticism based on a consistent social model of reading can supply the required approach. Social reading models are based on sociological categories such as communities and conventions rather than psychological categories such as individual selves and unique identities. Chapters 3 through 7 develop such a social reading model, which owes more to the theories of Fish, Iser, and Culler than to the psychological reader criticism of Holland and Bleich.

Chapter 3 moves the discussion from theory to practice. A reader-response analysis of a Hawthorne short story tries to demonstrate the consequences of taking the reader's interaction with the text as the primary focus of practical criticism. The most important aspect of this interaction is its temporal dimension. In the Hawthorne interpretation, I describe the temporal structure of the reader's response using a combination of Fish's affective stylistics, Iser's phenomenological criticism, and Roland Barthes's concept of readerly codes.

But an emphasis on the temporal reading process is only part of the reader-oriented approach I wish to develop. Of equal importance is what produces and constrains the reader's response at any particular moment in the time-flow of reading. Focusing on this question, Chapter 4 emphasizes the social foundation of reading by developing accounts of authorial intention and communicative convention. The account of convention is preliminary, sufficient only to solve a specific problem in American textual scholarship: the definition and application of the concept of "author's final intention." This phrase has been left virtually unexamined even though it has been the governing slogan in the editing of American fiction during the last thirty years. Chapter 4 first defines "inferred intention" by using Culler's theory of reading conventions and the speech act philosophy of H. P. Grice and J. L. Austin. Then "author's final intention" becomes defined in terms of the intended structure of the reader's experience. I demonstrate the usefulness of these new definitions by examining textual problems in the fiction of Hawthorne, Melville, James, Norris, and others.

By the end of Chapter 4, I have developed a reading model that is temporal and convention-based and have applied the critical approach derived from this model to practical criticism and textual scholarship; but before the approach can be applied to American literary history, a more detailed account of convention must be given in order to focus more precisely on the interpretive work involved in reading and criticism. To develop this account, Chapter 5 builds on recent philosophy of language to present a general typology of conventions: traditional conventions that recognize past regularities in action and belief; regulative conventions that prescribe future actions; and constitutive conventions that describe conditions making present meaning possible. I apply this typology to the use of the term "convention" in literary study to get ready for my discussion of literary interpretation.

Chapter 6 begins with an examination of the ongoing debate over the nature of the interpretive process, which prepares the way for a working definition of "interpretation." This definition together with Chapter 5's typology forms the basis of a proposed theory of interpretive conventions. Chapter 6 defines "interpretive conventions" as shared ways of making sense of texts; they are group-licensed strategies for constructing meaning, describable in terms of conditions for intelligibility. My theory of interpretive conventions posits that traditional and regulative conventions become constitutive in interpretation, an assumption that is more fully explained through a discussion of related concepts in recent speech act philosophy.

With this account of interpretive conventions, I proceed to discuss American literary history in Chapter 7. I begin with an examination of how Stephen Crane used and modified traditional genre conventions, an examination that illustrates the established discourse of American literary history. This discourse is based on a production model of literature that usually ignores the important role played by the reading audience. German reception aesthetics, especially the work of Hans Robert Jauss, has recently presented an alternative model for doing literary history, one that is consistent with the reader-oriented approach I have been developing. Like traditional literary history, however, *Rezeptionsästhetik* tends to cover over the interpretive work of readers and critics that underlies all literary history. To uncover this interpretive work, I use the theory of interpretive conventions developed in the previous two chapters. A discussion of the contemporary reception of *Moby-Dick* demonstrates how traditional (genre) conventions became prescriptive and how this fact accounts for one difference between the American and the British evaluations of Melville's novel. In a second example of reception, the critical history of the Appleton *Red Badge of Courage* illustrates how traditional (genre, modal, and authorial) conventions became constitutive. *Red Badge* criticism is an especially clear example of disguised interpretive work because the published text was heavily expurgated and obviously had to be supplemented by its readers before its meaning could be discovered.

Throughout *Interpretive Conventions* I try to construct a spe-

Preface

cific reader-response approach to literature at the same time
that I illustrate what a focus on the reader can do in the context
of American literary study. Thus, each chapter adds to the developing model of reading as it attempts to demonstrate further
the use of reader-oriented criticism in solving problems and
achieving goals in the different activities making up the study of
American fiction. The final chapter examines the status of
reader-response criticism's discourse on "the reader," while an
appendix shows how reader-oriented approaches might bring
together literary study and composition teaching, the two tasks
assigned to most American departments of English.

A word about the subtext paralleling the main: The footnotes
are of two kinds, reflecting two types of readers whom this book
addresses. For the specialist in American literature who is not
familiar with all the recent activity in critical theory, textual
scholarship, or the philosophy of language, I have included basic
explanations and bibliographical references for the technical
concepts used in the main text. For specialists in these three
areas, I have footnoted discussions that develop technical points
glossed over in the main text. These two kinds of footnotes allow
the main text to be aimed at both types of readers as well as a
more general audience. The ideal reader for this book is simply
one interested in the different activities constituting the contemporary study of literature.

My attitude toward the American critical community remains
two-sided throughout most of *Interpretive Conventions.* On the
one hand, I attack the critical tradition for neglecting the reader
in its practical criticism and literary theory. On the other hand,
the specific proposals I make for using the reader are made
from *within* the traditional assumptions of American literary
study. For example, I propose reader-response criticism as a
useful corrective to the formalist interpretations dominating
practical criticism, but I do not call the activity of explication
itself into question. And I elaborate a new definition of authorial
intention grounded in a convention-based reading model, but I
do not reject reconstruction of the intended text as the proper
goal for textual editing. My purpose then is primarily to show
how a reader-oriented perspective can be used in performing
the traditional activities of American literary study. I hope the

12

achievement of this purpose will lead to a better understanding of both reader-response criticism and the framework for the study of American fiction. The next step is a thorough reexamination of that framework.

I begin to lay the groundwork for this reexamination in my Conclusion, where I attend to the institutional status of critical and theoretical discourse. The Conclusion focuses on a fact implicit in everything that has gone before: "the reader" is an interpretive (not a natural) category that functions (like "the text" or "the author's intention") as a hermeneutic device in practical criticism and the other areas of literary study. In one sense, then, the Conclusion provides a way of reading my book different from what I have just been suggesting. Most of this Preface asks that the book be read as an attempt to promote reader-response criticism as *the* most useful perspective for literary study and that the various chapters be seen as demonstrating the objective validity of this claim. In contrast, the Conclusion suggests that the book's descriptive claims be viewed as interpretations and that the various chapters be taken as persuasive attempts to illustrate how these interpretive constructs can affect institutional practices, practices that are always based on interpretive assumptions and strategies rather than on some bedrock of uninterpreted reality. The Conclusion does not reject the claims of earlier chapters but "undoes" them; it does not so much contradict the preceding claims as change their status from objective statements to persuasive interpretations—a new status that the Conclusion gives all practical and theoretical discourse, not just my own reader-response analyses and theory. Furthermore, I frame the Conclusion's "constitutive hermeneutics" as a series of questions that all reader-response critics should face by the inevitable logic of their arguments rather than as my definitive answers to all such questions. I believe finally that the questions and answers involved in a "constitutive hermeneutics" can prepare the way for a more general reexamination of American literary studies as an institution.

STEVEN MAILLOUX

Coral Gables, Florida

Acknowledgments

I thank the following people for the suggestions and encouragement that helped me write this book: Charles Altieri, Monroe Beardsley, Henry Binder, David Bleich, Roland Champagne, Michael and Thomas Clark, Jonathan Culler, Judith Davidoff, Hermione de Almeida, Stanley Fish, Walter Fisher, Gerald Graff, Norman Holland, Terry Lyle, T. Edith and Russell Mailloux, George McFadden, Guy Nishida, Hershel Parker, Adena Rosmarin, William Stockert, Susan Suleiman, Jane Tompkins, Alan Wilde, W. Ross Winterowd, and Mary Ann and F. Roman Young.

I extend special thanks to William Cain, Peter Carafiol, and Michael Sprinker for offering valuable criticism of a near-final draft. I am also grateful to Kay Scheuer of Cornell University Press for her close reading of the final manuscript.

A National Endowment for the Humanities Fellowship gave me the released time to complete the book, and the University of Miami provided funds for research, duplicating, and other expenses.

Portions of Chapters 1 and 2 appeared in *Genre*, 10 (1977), *The Journal of Aesthetics and Art Criticism*, 38 (1979), and *Centrum*, n.s. 1 (1981). Two sections of Chapter 7 were first published in *Studies in the Novel*, 10 (1978); and material in the conclusion appeared in *Centrum*, n.s. 1 (1981), and *Reader*, No. 5 (1978). An earlier version of the appendix was published in *College Composi-*

tion and Communication, 29 (1978). I am grateful to the publishers for permission to reprint.

Finally, I thank the person to whom I owe the most. I could not have written this book without Mary Ann Mailloux.

S. M.

Interpretive Conventions

CHAPTER ONE

Literary Theory and
Psychological Reading Models

> The Affective Fallacy is a confusion between the poem and
> its *results* (what it *is* and what it *does*). . . . It begins by trying
> to derive the standard of criticism from the psychological
> effects of the poem and ends in impressionism and rela-
> tivism.
> —Monroe C. Beardsley and W. K. Wimsatt,
> "The Affective Fallacy"

> However disciplined by taste and skill, the experience of
> literature is, like literature itself, unable to speak.
> —Northrop Frye, *Anatomy of Criticism*

American literary theory has seen an explosion of
interest in readers and reading. There is talk of implied readers,
informed readers, fictive readers, ideal readers, mock readers,
superreaders, literents, narratees, interpretive communities,
and assorted reading audiences. The term "reader-response
criticism" has been used to describe a multiplicity of approaches
that focus on the reading process: affective, phenomenological,
subjective, transactive, transactional, structural, deconstructive,
rhetorical, psychological, speech act, and other criticisms have
been indiscriminately lumped together under the label "reader
response." In these first two chapters I will bring some order
into this metacritical chaos by comparing the most prominent
models of reading and the critical theories based on those
models. To do this, I will investigate the work of the five
reader-response critics who have been most influential in the
United States: Stanley Fish, Norman Holland, David Bleich,
Wolfgang Iser, and Jonathan Culler. Out of this investigation

will come an agenda for developing a reader-oriented approach to American fiction study.

Reader-Response Criticism?

All reader-response critics focus on readers during the process of reading. Some examine individual readers through psychological observations and participation; others discuss reading communities through philosophical speculation and literary intuition. Rejecting the Affective Fallacy of American New Criticism, all describe the relation of text to reader. Indeed, all share the phenomenological assumption that it is impossible to separate perceiver from perceived, subject from object. Thus they reject the text's autonomy, its absolute separateness, in favor of its dependence on the reader's creation or participation. Perception is viewed as interpretive; reading is not the discovery of meaning but the creation of it. Reader-response criticism replaces examinations of a text in-and-of-itself with discussions of the reading process, the "interaction" of reader and text.

Stanley Fish's early essay, "Literature in the Reader: Affective Stylistics" (1970) presented one influential version of this reader-response criticism. Fish viewed a sentence in the text not as "an object, a thing-in-itself, but an *event,* something that *happens* to, and with the participation of, the reader." His claims were aggressively descriptive: "In my method of analysis, the temporal flow is monitored and structured by everything the reader brings with him, by his competences; and it is by taking these into account as they interact with the temporal left-to-right reception of the verbal string that I am able to chart and project *the* developing response."[1] And *the* developing response was that of the "informed reader," a reader with the ability to understand the text and have the experience the author intended.[2] In this

1. "Literature in the Reader: Affective Stylistics," *New Literary History,* 2 (1970); rpt. in Fish, *Is There a Text in This Class?: The Authority of Interpretive Communities* (Cambridge: Harvard University Press, 1980), pp. 25, 46–47.
2. See Fish, "Literature in the Reader," pp. 48–49; and two other articles by Fish: "What Is Stylistics and Why Are They Saying Such Terrible Things About It?" in *Approaches to Poetics,* ed. Seymour Chatman (New York: Columbia University Press, 1973), and "Interpreting the *Variorum,*" *Critical Inquiry,* 2 (1976), both rpt. in *Is There a Text in This Class?:* see esp. pp. 379–80 and 159–61.

"affective stylistics," Fish talked as if a text manipulated the reader—the text forced the reader to perform certain cognitive acts—and Fish, as practical critic, described that manipulative process. As a critical theorist Fish attacked formalist approaches, especially American New Criticism, for ignoring "what is objectively true about the *activity* of reading." He claimed that his own approach was in contrast "truly objective" because it recognized the "fluidity ... of the meaning experience" and directed our attention "to where the action is—the active and activating consciousness of the reader."[3]

In a major reversal, Fish rejects these claims in "Interpreting the *Variorum*" (1976), where he argues that all texts are in fact constituted by readers' interpretive strategies and that the process he formerly claimed to describe is actually a creation of his critical theory: "What my principles direct me to 'see' are readers performing acts; the points at which I find (or to be more precise, declare) those acts to have been performed become (by a sleight of hand) demarcations *in* the text; those demarcations are then available for the designation 'formal features,' and as formal features they can be (illegitimately) assigned the responsibility for producing the interpretation which in fact produced them."[4] This radical revision of Fish's theory has two consequences: a change in the relation of reader to text and a change in the relation of criticism to reading. Fish now claims that in reading the interpreter constitutes the text and that in reader criticism the interpreter's description constitutes the nature of the reading process according to his interpretive strategies.

Fish has moved from a phenomenological emphasis (which describes the interdependence of reader and text) to a structuralist or even post-structuralist position (which studies the underlying systems that determine the production of textual mean-

3. Fish, "Literature in the Reader," p. 44.
4. Fish, "Interpreting the *Variorum*," p. 163. The introduction and head-notes to the essays reprinted in Fish's *Is There a Text in This Class?* provide the best discussion of the course and consequences of Fish's move from his earlier to his later critical theory. For a critique of this move, see Steven Mailloux, "Stanley Fish's 'Interpreting the *Variorum*': Advance or Retreat?" *Critical Inquiry*, 3 (1976), 183–90; and for Fish's convincing response to this critique, see his "Interpreting 'Interpreting the *Variorum*,'" same issue, rpt. in *Is There a Text in This Class?*, pp. 174–80.

SUBJECTIVISM		PHENOMENOLOGY		STRUCTURALISM	
David Bleich's subjective criticism	Norman Holland's transactive criticism	Wolfgang Iser's phenomenological criticism	Stanley Fish's affective stylistics	Jonathan Culler's structuralist poetics	Stanley Fish's theory of interpretive strategies
primacy of subjectivity	transaction between reader and text within reader's identity theme	interaction between reader and text	text's manipulation of reader	reading conventions	authority of interpretive communities
PSYCHOLOGICAL MODEL		INTERSUBJECTIVE MODEL		SOCIAL MODEL	

ing and in which the individual reader and the constraining text lose their independent status). In his metacriticism, Fish has given up making descriptive claims for his earlier critical approach and abandoned its absolute priority over formalist criticism. He now views affective stylistics as only one of many possible interpretive strategies; it does not describe how all readers read but instead suggests one way they could read. Though Fish now holds it to be an act of persuasion rather than objective description, he continues to use his earlier approach when he does practical criticism. He therefore occupies two places on the schema of reader-response criticism shown in the chart.

This schema locates each critic on a continuum of reader-oriented approaches. A detailed examination of these approaches will reveal not only the interrelations among the critics placed here but also the problems within each of their reader-response theories. All five critics construct a theory consisting (in more or less detail) of an account of interpretation, a model for critical exchange, and a model of reading. These critics' theories of interpretation try to account for meaning-production in both reading and criticism. Their models of critical discussion specify the nature of critical procedures (observation, description, explication, and explanation) and the ways interpretations are exchanged in critical dialogue. These hermeneutic theories and critical models are based on models of reading, accounts of how readers actually interact with the text during the temporal reading process. Norman Holland's work provides a useful starting point for the following discussions of reader-response criticism because his writings carefully examine all three of these components making up a critical theory.[5]

---

5. I do not intend these three levels of the critical enterprise to be exhaustive. For example, I have deliberately excluded a component for literary evaluation, since most reader-response critics find hierarchies of literary values irrelevant to their descriptive projects. (But see Steven Mailloux, "Evaluation and Reader Response Criticism: Values Implicit in Affective Stylistics," *Style,* 10 [1976], 329–43.) My purpose here is not to provide a detailed discussion of these three components of critical theory but to use this tripartite division as a loose framework for the analyses that follow. Cf. Leroy Searle, "Tradition and Intelligibility: A Model for Critical Theory," *New Literary History,* 7 (1976), 402 and 415, n. 29.

Transactive Criticism

Holland's transactive criticism "takes as its subject-matter, not the text in supposed isolation, as the New Criticism claimed it did, nor the self in rhapsody, as the old impressionistic criticism did, but the *transaction* between a reader and a text."[6] The notion of an "identity theme" is central to Holland's approach: "we can be precise about individuality by conceiving of the individual as living out variations on an identity theme much as a musician might play out an infinity of variations on a single melody." A person brings this "unchanging inner core of continuity" to all transactions between Self and Other, including reading.[7]

Holland's model of reading proceeds from his more general theory of the relation between personality and perception. Perception is a "constructive act," not merely reflecting but forming reality: "the individual apprehends the resources of reality (including language, his own body, space, time, etc.) *as he relates to them* in such a way that they replicate his identity."[8] That is, perception is also interpretation, and "*interpretation is a function of identity*, specifically identity conceived as variations upon an identity theme." Holland particularizes this view of perception in his central thesis about reading: identity re-creates itself. "All of us, as we read, use the literary work to symbolize and finally to replicate ourselves. We work out through the text our own characteristic patterns of desire and adaptation."[9]

Within this principle of identity re-creation, Holland isolates four specific modalities, which he conveniently organizes under the acronym DEFT—defenses, expectations, fantasies, and transformations. "One can think of these four separate principles as emphases on one aspect or another of a single transaction: shaping an experience to fit one's identity and in doing so, (D) avoiding anxiety, (F) gratifying unconscious wishes, (E) absorbing the event as part of a sequence of events, and (T) shap-

---

6. Norman N. Holland, "Transactive Criticism: Re-Creation Through Identity," *Criticism*, 18 (1976), 334.

7. Holland, "Unity Identity Text Self," *PMLA*, 90 (1975), 814; "Transactive Criticism," p. 338.

8. Holland, "The New Paradigm: Subjective or Transactive?" *New Literary History*, 7 (1976), 343.

9. Holland, "Unity," p. 816.

ing it with that sequence into a meaningful totality."[10] The concept of a "meaningful totality" or unity is pivotal for Holland's reading model (and is equally important in his general theory of interpretation).[11] According to Holland, the reader makes sense of the text by creating a meaningful unity out of its elements. Unity is not in the text but in the mind of a reader. "By means of such adaptive structures as he has been able to match in the story, he will transform the fantasy content, which he has created from the materials of the story his defenses admitted, into some literary point or theme or interpretation."[12] For Holland, *meaning* is the result of this interpretive synthesis, the transformation of fantasy into a unity which the reader finds coherent and satisfying. As with all interpretation, "the unity we find in literary texts is impregnated with the identity that finds that unity." Each reader creates a unity for a text out of his own identity theme, and thus "each will have *different* ways of making the text into an experience with a coherence and significance that satisfies."[13] Therefore, Holland's model of reading accounts exceptionally well for varied responses.

On the other hand, Holland's present theory has trouble with the phenomenon of similar responses. Similarity was easily explained by his earlier model. In *The Dynamics of Literary Response* (1968), he spoke as if "fantasies and their transformations were embodied in the literary work, as though the work itself acted like a mind"; different readers could take in ("introject") the

---

10. Holland, "Transactive Criticism," p. 342. For other accounts of DEFT, see Holland, *Poems in Persons: An Introduction to the Psychoanalysis of Literature* (New York: Norton, 1973), pp. 76–78; 5 *Readers Reading* (New Haven: Yale University Press, 1975), pp. 113–28; "Unity," pp. 816-18; and "The New Paradigm," p. 338.

11. As Holland writes, "*Identity* is the *unity* I find in a *self* if I look at it as though it were a *text*" ("Unity," p. 815). He further explains that "*interpretation is a function of identity*, identity being defined operationally as what is found in a person by looking for a unity in him, in other words, by interpretation. We seem to be caught in a circular argument, but it is not the argument which is circular—it is the human condition in which we cannot extricate an 'objective' reality from our 'subjective' perception of it" ("Transactive Criticism," p. 340).

12. Holland, 5 *Readers Reading*, pp. 121-22; for a detailed description of this transformational process, see Holland, *The Dynamics of Literary Response* (New York: Oxford University Press, 1968), chs. i-vi.

13. Holland, "Unity," p. 816, emphasis added.

same text and "participate" in whatever psychological process was embodied there. Accounting for recurrent responses has become much more difficult in Holland's revised model, in which "processes like the transformation of fantasy materials through defenses and adaptations take place in people, not in texts."[14] No longer embodying psychological processes, autonomous texts no longer serve as a guarantee of recurrence in Holland's present model of reading. Instead, similar identity themes must somehow account for similar response.[15] This psychological explanation contrasts with Fish's "sociological" ones. In Fish's earlier theory, all informed readers had the same basic reading experience because they shared linguistic and literary competence; in his present theory, *communal* reading strategies account for similar interpretive responses. The comparison between Fish's and Holland's reading models becomes more complex when we examine the precise status of the text in their revised theories.[16]

Holland and Fish both claim that perception is a constructive act: we interpret as we perceive, or rather, perception *is* an interpretation. For Fish, interpretive strategies constitute the text; not even as words-on-the-page does the text have any autonomy. As soon as we read, we interpret; and thus our interpretive strategies create the text that we later discuss in critical exchange. Holland seems to hold a similar view: "A literary text, after all, in an objective sense consists only of a certain config-

14. Holland, *5 Readers Reading*, p. 19, and see Holland, "A Letter to Leonard," *Hartford Studies in Literature*, 5 (1973), 9–30.
15. Cf. Holland, "Unity," p. 815: "the same identity theme may describe several different people."
16. The difference between Fish's and Holland's present models of reading is not that one accounts for similarities and the other for differences. Both models claim to account for both kinds of response: shared interpretive strategies and similar identity themes explain recurrence, and different interpretive strategies and dissimilar identity themes account for variability. Rather, the relevant distinction here is the ability to account for unique, idiosyncratic responses. Holland's model allows the possibility of a unique personality and thus a unique interpretive response. Fish's present model denies the possibility of a unique interpretation because idiosyncratic interpretive strategies are impossible; strategies for making sense are always *shared* strategies, according to Fish—see *Is There a Text in This Class?*, pp. 14, 335, 338. For how Fish's earlier model of reading accounted for differences and similarities in response, see ibid., pp. 4–6, 15.

26

uration of specks of carbon black on dried wood pulp. When these marks become words, when those words become images or metaphors or characters or events, they do so because the reader plays the part of a prince to the sleeping beauty."[17] However, Holland runs into the same problem as Fish: if interpretation constitutes the text, what is the interpretation *of*? Fish throws up his hands: "I cannot answer that question, but neither, I would claim, can anyone else, although formalists try to answer it by pointing to patterns and claiming that they are available independently of (prior to) interpretation."[18] Holland tries to solve the paradox but in so doing necessarily equivocates. In one place he writes, "A reader reads something, certainly, but if one cannot separate his 'subjective' response from its 'objective' basis, there seems no way to find out what that 'something' is in any impersonal sense."[19] Throughout *Poems in Persons* (1973), however, Holland constantly refers to "raw materials" in the text, which are presumed to be separate from the reader, not created by his interpretation during the reading process. The reader "reaches into the poem and *takes materials from it* with which to achieve an experience within the characteristic pattern of ego choices he uses to minimize anxiety and cope with reality."[20] Holland often gives these "raw materials" a status inconsistent with his emphasis on the reader's total domination of the text's meaning. He mentions (but does not explain) "constraints" in the work[21] and speaks of doing "violence" to the text.[22] For example, he writes that "different builders can assemble the same stones into a building in many different ways, with more and less violence to the raw materials, just as different readers

17. Holland, *5 Readers Reading*, p. 12.
18. Fish, "Interpreting the *Variorum*," p. 165.
19. Holland, *5 Readers Reading*, p. 40.
20. Holland, *Poems in Persons*, pp. 115-16, emphasis added. See also pp. 77, 96, 99, 117, 145, and 147.
21. Ibid., pp. 96, 148. Cf. Holland, *5 Readers Reading*, p. 286: "To be sure, the promptuary [the structured language of the words-on-the-page] includes constraints on how one can put its contents together, but these constraints do not coerce anyone." The point to notice here is not that Holland claims constraints can be ignored (all critics admit this) but that he assumes constraints are in the text and need only be recognized (not created) by readers.
22. Holland, *Poems in Persons*, pp. 118, 146. Cf. Holland, *5 Readers Reading*, pp. 219-20.

can construct different experiences of a poem, with more and less contortion of the words and the plain sense."[23] These references to raw materials, plain sense, and constraints all suggest a preexistent text independent of a reader's interpretation and experience.

Holland's discussions of response in *5 Readers Reading* (1975) also assume some aspects of the text prior to interpretation; he often talks about *elements of a story* that are combined according to the reader's identity theme.[24] He does not focus on how these elements (language, dialogue, character, plot) are constituted (are they in the text as raw materials or are they also constructed in the transaction?). Holland's discussion of interpretation occurs at a higher level of reader activity. That is, the story (as a combination of preexistent elements) is re-created by the reader's identity through the modalities of DEFT, and interpretation ("the making sense") is a unity that the story takes on for the reader. Put another way, for Holland, meaning is the output of a psychological process; the input to that process is the story. Like Holland, Fish believes that meanings are "not extracted but made," but he claims further that the text is constituted (in all its aspects) by the interpretive process and is not prior to it.[25]

Concerning the nature of critical discussion, the form of Fish's and Holland's arguments is the same; both use the interpretive

23. Holland, *Poems in Persons*, pp. 116–17.
24. See, for example, Holland, *5 Readers Reading*, pp. 116–19. But perhaps a phrase such as "elements in the story" or "materials of the story" is merely what Holland calls a "useful fiction" (p. 19), for he writes in another place that the reader "will try to make *the language, events, or people he creates from the text* function in multiple directions to work out the compromise among the demands of inner and outer reality that is his own style" (p. 126, emphasis added). Still, he never qualifies such statements as: "The difference [in experiences] comes from the differences in character. The sameness comes from the sameness in the resources used to create the experience" (pp. 247–48).
25. Fish, "Interpreting the *Variorum*," p. 172. In more recent formulations of his model, Holland continues to deny that "the text limits response in any significant way" but still writes that "the literent [reader] builds a personal response by a personal use of the several elements of the text, a response that the text may or may not reinforce. In a transactive model, I am engaged in a feedback loop (or, to be less technical, a dialogue) with the text. I bring schemata to bear on the text, and the text either does or does not reward them." (These statements are from Holland's exchange with Iser in "Interview: Wolfgang Iser," ed. Rudolf E. Kuenzli, *Diacritics*, 10, No. 2 [1980], 58, 60.)

operations they describe for readers as explanations for the interpretive acts performed by critics. For Fish, critics interpret in their criticism in basically the same way they interpret as they read. Similarly, Holland views critics "as simply another group of readers operating under special stringencies"; in reading and criticism the process is the same: re-creation through identity.[26] For Holland, the critic's interpretation is merely an extension of the reader's interpretive synthesis. And since "all interpretations express the identity themes of the people making the interpretations," the interpretations by critics ("professional readers") are also manifestations of their identity themes.[27]

Since Fish and Holland agree that we do criticism in the same way that we read (that is, we use the same interpretive strategies in reading and criticism), their explanations of recurrent responses carry over to their discussions of critical consensus. Fish presents a sociological argument, Holland a psychological one. Fish moves from the community to its members, Holland from the individual to the group. Critics agree when they belong to the same interpretive community, says Fish; and interpretive communities "are made up of those who share interpretive strategies not for reading (in the conventional sense) but for writing texts, for constituting their properties and assigning their intentions."[28] Holland argues that critics agree when they can assimilate the others' identity re-creations into their own. He implies that this agreement can take place either because two critics have similar identity themes or because two critics with widely divergent identity themes are still able to utilize each other's interpretations in their own re-creations. People "distinguish different readings of a text or personality 'objectively' by how much and how directly they seem to us to bring the details of a text or a self into convergence around a centering theme. We also compare them as to whether they 'feel right' or 'make sense.' That is, do we feel we could use them to organize and make coherent our own experience of that text or person?"[29]

26. Holland, "A Letter to Leonard," p. 21.
27. Holland, "Unity," p. 816; *5 Readers Reading*, p. 246. Cf. Holland, *Poems in Persons*, p. 129.
28. Fish, "Interpreting the *Variorum*," p. 171.
29. Holland, "Unity," p. 816. Also see Holland, *Poems in Persons*, pp. 125-26.

However, Holland again goes against the grain of his theory by using "raw materials" in the text to help explain critical agreement. For example, in discussing a similar theme arrived at by three different readers, he argues that "this consensus does not come about simply because the poem 'caused' it, but because the three readers all took some of the same elements from the poem to make up their individual syntheses." And again: "We see consensus because different readers are using the same material."[30]

In terms of their overall critical projects, both Fish and Holland try to present compact conceptual frameworks. Their theories of interpretation provide explanatory centers (interpretive communities or identity themes) which account for the acts of reading, criticism, and critical exchange, though Holland's model of reading has difficulty in consistently explaining similar responses and critical agreement.

Subjective Criticism

On several occasions David Bleich and Norman Holland have exchanged views on each other's work.[31] Their conversation in print at times proves especially illuminating not only for what it shows about the contrast between their two approaches, but also for how it illustrates their shared differences from other reader-oriented critics. In *Readings and Feelings* (1975), Bleich's model of reading consists of perception, affect, and association. Like Holland, Bleich holds that "the perception of the poem is a subjective reconstruction rather than a simple recording of facts," and he sometimes discusses a reader's "style of perception," the forms of "individuated perception created by the particular biases of the reader." A reader's report of perception tells "what he sees in the poem or what he thinks the poet says," while reports of affective response describe "the actual affect [fear,

---

30. Holland, *Poems in Persons*, pp. 115–16.
31. See, for example, Holland, "A Letter to Leonard," pp. 21–28, "The New Paradigm," pp. 335–45, and *5 Readers Reading*, p. 407, n. 52; David Bleich, "Pedagogical Directions in Subjective Criticism," *College English*, 37 (1976), 462–63, and "The Subjective Paradigm in Science, Psychology, and Criticism," *New Literary History*, 2 (1976), 332; and Norman N. Holland and David Bleich, "Comment and Response," *College English*, 38 (1976), 298–301.

satisfaction, indignation, etc.] he felt while reading the poem."[32] Associative response embodies those aspects of the reader's previous experience that are stimulated by the affect derived from his reading experience.

Like most reader-response approaches, Bleich's subjective criticism places meaning in readers, not in texts. Bleich explicitly rejects the notion of an objective text completely independent of the reader, but he does not wrestle with the problematic relation of interpretation to text during the reading process. Instead, he refers primarily to *critical* interpretation, an activity subsequent to the reading experience: "For the reader, the interpretation is the response to his reading experience."[33]

Bleich's most recent book, *Subjective Criticism* (1978), presents the most detailed elaboration of his views on interpretation and reading, and here Bleich is more consistent than Holland in developing the absolute priority of individual selves as creators of texts.[34] However, this same rigorous consistency provides Bleich's theory with its own problems. For though *Subjective Criticism* is challenging in its pedagogical proposals and wide-ranging in its use of interdisciplinary resources, it is ultimately incomplete as a hermeneutic project. The book outlines a framework for literary engagement that begins with the individual reader as the center of critical concern. Bleich's model progresses from subjective response, to resymbolization, to negotiation resulting in validated knowledge. We need to examine each step in this model before considering the problems in Bleich's theory of interpretation.

On the level of reading: "Subjective response" refers to an individual reader's "first perceptual initiative toward a symbolic object" (p. 96). When there are no prior utilitarian motives constraining these initiatives, response will be an act of "evaluative symbolization"—a combination of perception and affect—which serves as the basis for all further discussions of the text (p. 98).

32. David Bleich, *Readings and Feelings: An Introduction to Subjective Criticism* (Urbana, Ill.: NCTE, 1975), pp. 27–33.

33. Bleich, "The Subjective Character of Critical Interpretation," *College English,* 36 (1975), 754.

34. Bleich, *Subjective Criticism* (Baltimore: Johns Hopkins University Press, 1978). All page citations in the text of this section refer to this book.

In fact, for Bleich the text as symbolic object does not exist prior to or independent of subjective initiative. It is only on the basis of such individual subjective creations that interpretation can proceed.

On the level of criticism: The second stage in Bleich's model, resymbolization, occurs when the first acts of perception and identification—the subjective response or symbolization—produce in the reader "a need, desire, or demand for explanation" (p. 39). Resymbolization "is the conceptualization of symbolized objects and processes in terms of subjective motives" (p. 88). In most cases, resymbolization is motivated and motivational explanation: it is motivated by the initial subjective response which requires an explanation, and it is motivational in that the explanation provided is in the form of psychological motives. This individual resymbolization "is commonly known as *interpretation*" (p. 67).

In the third and most problematic stage of Bleich's model, the level of critical exchange, individual interpretations are negotiated within communities and new knowledge is produced. Negotiations in Bleich's classes, for example, begin with an individual student's "response statement," which Bleich defines as "a symbolic presentation of self, a contribution to a pedagogical community, and an articulation of that part of our reading experience we think we can negotiate into knowledge" (p. 167). Response statements resymbolize individual reading experiences in terms of perceptions, affects, and associations (as described in *Readings and Feelings*), and these resymbolizations are then negotiated into knowledge about language and literature.

In discussing negotiation, Bleich writes that "the synthesizing of communal knowledge cannot begin without the substrate of individual subjective knowledge" (p. 151). This statement points to a problem area within Bleich's hermeneutic theory: the dynamics of moving from the individual to the communal. Given the primacy of the individual self as creator of texts, how can Bleich's model account for agreement in negotiation? More specifically, if, as Bleich argues, texts are functions of individual subjective initiatives, resymbolized on an individual basis, how can different subjectivities participate in a *negotiating* process? What is negotiated, and how? Since texts are individually constituted, readers might be able to share their resymbolizations in a kind of show-and-tell ritual,[35] but "negotiation" seems a rather misleading name for such a process because the term suggests some kind of interpretive trade-off. Furthermore, following Bleich's logic, response statements must have the same ontological status as literary works: as texts, both are constituted by subjective initiative. In negotiation, then, there could be a different version of each negotiator's response statement created by each of his or her fellow negotiators, just as all the response statements represent (constitute) various versions of the literary text (or reading experience). Each reader creates a different text, which when shared is constituted differently by different perceivers. If no text (either literary or critical) is prior to *individual* initiative, no negotiating process is comprehensible, let alone possible in practice.

The strongest attempt that Bleich makes to resolve this hidden impasse is his explanatory use of the concept of "motive." Within his theory, motives function as explanations of subjective response in resymbolization and of resymbolization itself. In both cases, motives serve as why's and not how's: "*a motive is a subjectively regulated cause* and is the name for causes originating in human initiative" (p. 44). Bleich also attempts to use motives to explain the dynamics of negotiating resymbolizations, and, as I have noted, here is where he runs into problems: how to move from individually motivated responses to negotiated consensus. He attempts to bridge the gap by positing a category of *shared* motives, such as a desire to reach consensus, a need for perceptual validation, or a goal of self-enhancement. However, this move explains why negotiation occurs but not how it works. Unlike Thomas Kuhn's "paradigms" or Fish's "interpretive strategies" (to which Bleich refers), "motives" cannot provide specific *constraints* for insuring the possibility of shared interpretations.

Bleich has, in fact, presented himself with an apparently impossible task: to account for interpretive agreement after having established the absolute primacy of the individual as interpreter. This theoretical impasse is buried by his attempt to associate his

35. See, for example, Bleich, *Subjective Criticism*, p. 98.

individualistic model of reading with interpretive theories that have agreement built into them from the start. Bleich points to what he sees as theoretical analogues to negotiated consensus, first in Kuhn's concept of paradigm[36] and then in Fish's notion of interpretive community. Unfortunately, Bleich appears to misunderstand the social foundation of the work by these theorists he takes to be his allies.

Bleich at first seems well aware of the social basis of Kuhn's notion of paradigm, which Bleich defines as "a shared mental structure, a set of beliefs about the nature of reality subscribed to by a group of thinkers large enough to exercise leadership for those similarly wishing to observe and understand human experience" (p. 10). Furthermore, he takes what I would call a "maximally constitutive" view of Kuhn's central concept: a dominant paradigm does not simply guide the perception and investigation of nature, it constitutes nature itself. This interpretation of Kuhn's theory makes it look very much like Bleich's. Just as for Bleich there is no text prior to subjective response, for a maximally constitutive paradigm theory, there is no reality independent of a paradigm. "The paradigmatic perception of reality at any moment in history *is* the reality at that time. The implication of this thought is that for all practical purposes, reality is invented and not observed or discovered by human beings" (p. 11). Bleich then proceeds to distort the social nature of Kuhn's paradigm theory in the following way.

When Bleich speaks of "the socially subjective character of knowledge" (p. 25), he means "consensually validated perception" (p. 11). For Bleich, "knowledge in general comes through synthesized interpretations" (p. 33), that is, negotiated consensus. The "common world of sense," then, is "determined by extended negotiation among perceivers" (p. 20). Bleich believes Kuhn's position is essentially in agreement with his own on these matters. I do not think this is the case at all. Bleich talks about *consensus reached after perception,* but Kuhn emphasizes *shared examplars prior to and constituting perception.* Bleich's consensus is achieved after negotiation; Kuhn's shared paradigms are what

36. Thomas S. Kuhn, *The Structure of Scientific Revolutions,* 2d ed. (Chicago: University of Chicago Press, 1970).

make negotiations possible. In fact, Kuhn's sociological theory directly contradicts Bleich's psychological model of individuated perception. For Kuhn, initial perceptions are communal, not individual, with paradigms being shared by scientists (in the same community) from the start.[37] If Bleich wants help explaining how individual subjective responses and resymbolizations become validated knowledge through negotiation, he will not find it in Kuhn's theory of paradigms.

Nor will Fish's account of interpretive communities provide the needed theoretical support. Bleich construes Fish's theory in a way Fish would not accept. Specifically, Bleich fails to realize that the communities he refers to are radically different from the interpretive communities Fish describes.[38] In his later theory, Fish agrees with Bleich that there is no text prior to interpretation. For Fish, however, interpretation is a communal affair from the outset, constrained by shared interpretive strategies. Texts are constituted by interpretive communities, which consist of interpreters who share ways of reading (and therefore constructing) texts. For Bleich, communities are groups where negotiations of resymbolizations take place; a community exists so that new knowledge can be synthesized in discussions. The interpretive communities Fish describes form the basis for such discussions; they provide the conditions necessary for the interpretive and persuasive acts that Bleich's negotiators perform.

A single community (in Bleich's sense) can consist of representatives from several interpretive communities (in Fish's sense). Fish's communities can include members not present (that is, interpreters who share strategies but are not members of

---

37. At least during periods of normal science—see Kuhn, pp. 23–51. In conversations that I have found very helpful, Bleich has suggested to me that his use of Kuhn focuses not on periods of normal science but on periods of paradigm revolutions, more exactly on the movement from paradigm uncertainty to new paradigm acceptance. Even here, however, I think Bleich and Kuhn are talking about two radically different processes. For Kuhn, a new paradigm becomes established not through Bleich's two-way negotiation but through *one-way* persuasion in which holders of the new paradigm (sometimes) convert holders of the old and no new-paradigm holders seem to be converted back to the old paradigm—see Kuhn, pp. 150–52.

38. Bleich discusses Fish's theory in *Subjective Criticism*, pp. 122–26.

Bleich's discussion group). Thus, interpretive communities cannot be viewed simply as physical groupings of individuals with similar concerns (p. 125); rather they are constitutive of the discussions taking place within those groupings. For Bleich, MLA meetings, classrooms, and journal forums are the communities in which individuals come to consensus (or fail to achieve it).[39] For Fish, such physical spaces have little to do with the set of members composing interpretive communities; membership in an interpretive community is not determined by proximity or similar concerns, but by shared ways of interpreting. Consensus can then be seen as the agreement articulated in critical discussion; shared interpretive strategies assure that agreement, providing the foundation for its recognition.

As with Kuhn's concept of paradigms, Bleich misses an essential point about Fish's notion of interpretive communities. Bleich cannot use either of these sociological theories to support his attempt to move from individual subjectivities to group consensus, because agreement is built into these theories from the start as it can never be in Bleich's psychological account. Negotiation as ongoing accomplishment and consensus as achieved goal remain unexplained in Bleich's interpretive theory.

I have discussed these two examples of misunderstanding at such length because I believe they are symptomatic of Bleich's central theoretical problem. His discussions of Kuhn and Fish unintentionally disguise a theoretical impasse which, if it continues unacknowledged and unresolved, will undermine the most important goal of *Subjective Criticism*. That goal is a bold one: to reinscribe the organized discussion of literature within a discourse that aggressively advocates the freedom of the individual self in a pedagogical community. Bleich's approach to teaching places the individual student and his subjective response at the center of literary study. "Subjective criticism assumes that each person's most urgent motivations are to understand himself," Bleich writes in his final paragraph. These pedagogical premises challenge teachers to reevaluate their notions of authority, to reexamine their attitudes toward their stu-

---

39. See Bleich, "Negotiated Knowledge of Language and Literature," *Studies in the Literary Imagination*, 12, No. 1 (1979), 73–92.

dents, and to redefine their rationales for teaching literature. Such challenges raise basic questions that deserve serious consideration. Unfortunately, such consideration may be withheld because a problematic theory of interpretation supports Bleich's pedagogical program. The problems in his account of negotiation need to be resolved before discussions of his challenging proposals for teaching can proceed.[40]

Bleich shares with Holland this pedagogical focus, which distinguishes both of their theories from those of Iser, Fish, and Culler.[41] However, Bleich and Holland have found many places to disagree over their respective theoretical projects. For example, Bleich views the subjective/objective distinction as absolute and therefore criticizes Holland's transactive paradigm, which denies that absoluteness. Holland claims that " 'objective reality' and 'pure experience' are themselves only useful fictions, vanishing points we approach but never reach. The problem, then, is not to sort out subjective from objective but to see how the two

40. Since the publication of *Subjective Criticism,* Bleich appears to have recognized some of the problems with the concept of negotiation but not the particular issues I have raised in this section; see Bleich, "Negotiated Knowledge," p. 75, n. 1. In conversation he has pointed out to me that he considers *Subjective Criticism* as a first attempt to establish an area of study and understand it, and he feels it already looks forward to further examinations of how the individual relates to the social, especially in terms of language, e.g., see *Subjective Criticism,* pp. 265 and 296.

41. See, for example, Holland, *5 Readers Reading,* pp. 108-18, and Holland and Murray Schwartz, "The Delphi Seminar," *College English,* 36 (1975), 789-800. Long before either Bleich or Holland began working on the problem, Louise Rosenblatt argued for the pedagogical relevance of the reader's individual experience of literature. See Louise M. Rosenblatt, *Literature as Exploration* (New York: Appleton-Century, 1938); the third edition (1976) is presently distributed by the Modern Language Association. In her most recent book, Rosenblatt is critical of "aggressively subjective approaches" to reading (presumably Bleich's and Holland's) and argues that her "transactional view, while insisting on the importance of the reader's contribution, does not discount the text and accepts a concern for validity of interpretation"—Louise M. Rosenblatt, *The Reader, the Text, the Poem: The Transactional Theory of the Literary Work* (Carbondale: Southern Illinois University Press, 1978), p. 151. Though it puts greater emphasis on the individuality of reading experiences, Rosenblatt's transactional theory more closely resembles Iser's phenomenology than Holland's and Bleich's psychological perspectives. Perhaps this is because Rosenblatt's work derives from that of William James, to whom Edmund Husserl expressed indebtedness (see Rosenblatt, *The Reader,* p. 111n.), and because Husserl's phenomenology is the ultimate source (by way of Ingarden) for Iser's theory. For Bleich's comments on Rosenblatt's work, see *Subjective Criticism,* pp. 108-10.

combine when we have experiences."[42] Bleich rejects this view and criticizes Holland's "assumptions and formulations" which "continue to try to appease the demands of objectivity."[43] For Bleich, Holland is simply not subjective enough.

Nonetheless, despite their differences, Holland and Bleich can be grouped together in that they define their critical paradigm (subjective or transactive) from a psychological perspective (not a sociological one). They emphasize the individual over the group; reading is a function of personality, not shared strategies. Furthermore, Bleich and Holland both study the reported responses of readers in developing their theories. As Holland remarks, "it is the close analysis of what readers actually say about what they read that differentiates" reader-response critics like himself and Bleich from those like Iser and Fish (and he could have included Culler as well).[44]

The kind of critical project that Holland and Bleich advocate runs counter to the dominant activities of American literary study. Practical criticism, for example, currently depends on intersubjective theories of literature which make possible critical consensus and validity in interpretation; while textual scholarship requires a communication model of reading which assumes the availability of authorial intention. As I have shown in this chapter, both Holland and Bleich have difficulties providing this intersubjective basis for reading and criticism: Holland lapses into assertions about a preexistent text that contradict the thrust of his theory, and Bleich, who is more consistent in assuming individual readers as creators of texts, cannot move convincingly from individual response to group consensus. Furthermore, both Holland and Bleich explicitly reject any communication model for reading. Holland argues that "interpretation is not decoding. Each reader constructs meaning as part of his own artistic experience. . . . He does not recover some preexisting intention latent in the work."[45] And Bleich's "logic of interpre-

---

42. Holland, *Poems in Persons*, p. 2.
43. Bleich, "The Subjective Paradigm," p. 332; and see Bleich, *Subjective Criticism*, pp. 111–22.
44. Holland, "Unity," p. 882, n.8.
45. Holland, *Poems in Persons*, p. 117; cf. p. 99: "The poet does not speak to

tation excludes consideration of whether and how the author is communicating anything to us."[46] Without an intersubjective foundation or a communication model, Holland and Bleich's psychological approach to reader-response criticism will have a very difficult time influencing the institutional study of literature.

---

the reader directly so much as give the reader materials from which to achieve the poem in his own style." See similar claims in Holland, 5 *Readers Reading*, pp. 218–19. Holland has presented some alternatives to traditional practical criticism in his self-conscious "transactions" of literary texts in "Hamlet—My Greatest Creation," *Journal of the American Academy of Psychoanalysis*, 3 (1975), 419–27; "Transacting My 'Good-Morrow' or, Bring Back the Vanished Critic," *Studies in the Literary Imagination*, 12, No. 1 (1979), 61–72; and "Re-Covering 'The Purloined Letter': Reading as a Personal Transaction," in *The Reader in the Text*, ed. Susan R. Suleiman and Inge Crosman (Princeton: Princeton University Press, 1980), pp. 350–70; and with others, Holland presents a collective transaction of a poem in "Poem Opening: An Invitation to Transactive Criticism," *College English*, 40 (1978), 2–16.

46. Bleich, *Subjective Criticism*, pp. 95–96; and see pp. 89, 93; also cf. pp. 259, 262–63 on "The Conception and Documentation of the Author."

CHAPTER TWO

Literary Theory and
Social Reading Models

> It has been said of Boehme that his books are like a picnic to
> which the author brings the words and the reader the
> meaning. The remark may have been intended as a sneer at
> Boehme, but it is an exact description of all works of literary
> art without exception.
> —Northrop Frye, *Fearful Symmetry*

> Writing is not the communication of a message which starts
> from the author and proceeds to the reader; it is specifically
> the voice of reading itself: *in the text, only the reader speaks.*
> —Roland Barthes, *S/Z*

Unlike psychological reader-response theories, social models of reading do provide both an intersubjective base
and an account of literary communication. I use "social" here in
the narrow sense of "tied to conditions specified by a society."[1]
Social accounts of reading employ models based on intersubjective categories and strategies shared by members of a group.
Of course, social reading models differ radically from psychological models in that the former build their explanations on
reading communities rather than individual readers. In the
previous chapter, I showed how Fish's "sociological" account
contrasted with Holland's and Bleich's psychological models,
and the present chapter will stress the social or intersubjective
aspects of Wolfgang Iser's and Jonathan Culler's reader-
oriented theories.

---

1. Stanley E. Fish, "How To Do Things with Austin and Searle: Speech Act
Theory and Literary Criticism," *MLN*, 91 (1976); rpt. in *Is There a Text in This
Class?* (Cambridge: Harvard University Press, 1980), p. 225.

It is perhaps misleading to call these reading theories "sociological," primarily because they each ignore elements traditionally included in sociological explanations. Indeed, the social reading models of Fish, Iser, and Culler have been specifically criticized for neglecting economic and political factors in their accounts.[2] Such critiques make a valid point, for reading certainly does not take place in a social vacuum independent of economic and political forces. For example, economic factors determine the availability of books and the material circumstances in which they are read; political structures condition motives for and effects of reading; and larger social forces (class, gender, and so on) influence audience interest and literary taste.[3] A complete sociological model of reading would have to take all these factors into account. However, such an observation does not negate the value of the more limited projects begun by Fish, Iser, and Culler. Their social or intersubjective models describe the reading process whose *exact details* are relatively unaffected by broader economic and political conditions *once the process is in motion.* That is, the institutional conventions governing reading may be grossly determined by economic, political, and larger social structures; but once the conventions are in place, those extrainstitutional forces do not affect the specific dynamics of interpretation in reading. Therefore, Fish, Iser, and Culler can safely focus on the intersubjective categories and shared conventions of reading literature while bracketing more general sociological considerations. In just this way, their socially oriented theories provide the intersubjective foundation and communication model required by American literary study but

2. This charge is specifically made against Iser in Terence Hawkes, "Taking It as Read," *Yale Review,* 69 (1980), 560; against Culler in Frank Lentricchia, *After the New Criticism* (Chicago: University of Chicago Press, 1980), p. 111; and in part against Fish in William E. Cain, "Constraints and Politics in the Literary Theory of Stanley Fish," *Bucknell Review,* 26, No. 1 (1981), 84–87.
3. See various studies in the sociology of literature, such as Robert Escarpit, *Sociology of Literature,* trans. Ernest Pick (1958; Painesville, O.: Lake Erie College Press, 1965), pp. 75–95; Lennox Grey, "Literary Audience," in *Contemporary Literary Scholarship: A Critical Review,* ed. Lewis Leary (New York: Appleton-Century-Crofts, 1958), pp. 403–61; and Jacques Leenhardt, "Toward a Sociology of Reading," in *The Reader in the Text: Essays on Audience and Interpretation,* ed. Susan R. Suleiman and Inge Crosman (Princeton: Princeton University Press, 1980), pp. 205–24.

not available in the psychological accounts of Bleich and Holland.

For instance, Jonathan Culler's structuralist poetics convincingly explains the communication between author and reader (and agreement among readers) by positing a shared system of reading conventions. He writes that to "intend a meaning is to postulate reactions of an imagined reader who has assimilated the relevant conventions." In his structuralist approach, intersubjectivity depends on a shared recognition of intertextuality: "A text can be a poem only because certain possibilities exist within the tradition; it is written in relation to other poems. A sentence of English can have meaning only by virtue of its relations to other sentences within the conventions of the language. The communicative intention presupposes listeners who know the language. And similarly, a poem presupposes conventions of reading which the author may work against, which he can transform, but which are the conditions of possibility of his discourse."[4] The author makes use of these conventions in his writing and his intended readers use them to understand his text.

Wolfgang Iser's phenomenological theory also presents a communication model of reading. For Iser, "a literary text contains intersubjectively verifiable instructions for meaning-production." His reading model emphasizes not a message extracted from a text, but a meaning assembled and experienced by a reader. The strategies in the text orient the reader's search for the intention underlying the author's selection and combination of conventions, and the "communicatory function" of literature ensures "that the reaction of text to world will trigger a matching response in the reader."[5] A close examination of Iser's theory will show exactly how this communicative process works.

---

4. Jonathan Culler, *Structuralist Poetics: Structuralism, Linguistics, and the Study of Literature* (Ithaca: Cornell University Press, 1975), p. 30; also see p. 116.

5. Wolfgang Iser, *The Act of Reading: A Theory of Aesthetic Response* (Baltimore: Johns Hopkins University Press, 1978), pp. 25, 61, 99. All page citations in the text of the following section refer to this book. In ch. 3 of his study, Iser employs the convention-based model of communication developed in the speech act theory of J. L. Austin and John Searle. However, Iser's adaptation of this social model is open to criticism (see below, Ch. 6, pp. 157–58) and actually adds little to his account of reading.

Phenomenological Criticism

Phenomenology forms the philosophical center of the reader-response schema in Chapter 1. Iser's phenomenological criticism emphasizes the epistemological assumption of all reader-oriented approaches: the object of knowledge can never be separated from the knower; the perceived object can never be separated from perception by a perceiver. For literary criticism, this means that discussion of the literary work must focus on the reader's response to that work. Bleich calls this response "subjective re-creation," while Holland talks of a "transaction" and Iser refers to the "interaction of text and reader." Fish's affective stylistics is "a method of analysis which takes the reader, as an actively mediating presence, fully into account."[6] Even Culler has underlined a phenomenological basis of his structuralist poetics: "Structural analysis must take place within phenomenology in that its goal must be that of explicating and formalizing what is phenomenally given in the subject's relation to his cultural objects."[7] Iser sums up his own approach in this way: "The phenomenological theory of art lays full stress on the idea that, in considering a literary work, one must take into account not only the actual text but also, and in equal measure, the actions involved in responding to that text."[8]

Though sharing a phenomenological assumption, reader-response critics diverge in following out its consequences. As we have seen, this divergence is particularly clear in the formulation of the text's status within their theories. Bleich makes everything subjective and therefore "solves" the problem of an intersubjective text by denying its existence as a problem. Fish's latest solution is that interpretive strategies constitute the text. Holland tends to agree with Fish, substituting individual identity themes for interpretive communities as the source of interpretive strategies. But in trying to answer the question that sometimes

6. Fish, "Literature in the Reader: Affective Stylistics," in *Is There a Text in This Class?*, p. 23.
7. Culler, "Phenomenology and Structuralism," *The Human Context*, 5 (1973), 37-38.
8. Iser, *The Implied Reader: Patterns of Communication in Prose Fiction from Bunyan to Beckett* (Baltimore: Johns Hopkins University Press, 1974), p. 274. See also *The Act of Reading*, pp. 20-21.

troubles Fish (what are interpretations interpretations *of?*), Holland inconsistently assumes some notion of a fixed text (raw materials, constraints, or elements of a story) that puts limits on response. Iser goes further than Holland: he explicitly posits a preexistent text which interacts with the reader and in that interaction restricts the reader's interpretations. Of the reader-response approaches considered in this book, Iser's theory is the closest to the traditional objectivist position that most reader-oriented criticism denies, and his shared assumptions with that position form the basis for his potential persuasiveness within American critical theory.

Though Iser does assume a stable text of some kind, his rhetoric emphasizes the creative role of the reader: "a text can only come to life when it is read, and if it is to be examined, it must therefore be studied through the eyes of the reader." Reading involves a hermeneutic process: "meanings in literary texts are mainly generated in the act of reading; they are the product of a rather difficult interaction between text and reader and not qualities hidden in the text."[9] In *The Act of Reading* (1978) Iser presents his fullest account of this difficult interaction. *The Act of Reading,* a theoretical companion to *The Implied Reader* (1974), offers contemporary American criticism a detailed model of aesthetic response by describing the reading process and the effects of that process. This account of reading begins with a functionalist model of the literary text, which focuses on two interrelated areas, the intersection between text and social reality and the interaction between text and reader.

Iser argues that "literature supplies those possibilities which have been excluded by the prevalent [thought] system" of the work's historical period (p. 73). Literature accomplishes this, however, not by formulating these possibilities in the text but by causing the *reader* to formulate them for himself. According to Iser, the author extracts social and historical norms (and references to past literature) from their original contexts and places them together to form the "repertoire of the text" (p. 69). In a

9. Iser, "Indeterminacy and the Reader's Response in Prose Fiction," in *Aspects of Narrative,* ed. J. Hillis Miller (New York: Columbia University Press, 1971), pp. 2–3, 4.

novel, these "depragmatized" norms are distributed among various textual "perspectives"—the narrator, the characters, the plot, and the fictitious reader—and the system of perspectives they form outlines the author's view without stating it and provides the potential structure for the reader to actualize. The connections among the various perspectives emerge during the reading process, "in the course of which the reader's role is to occupy shifting vantage points that are geared to a prestructured activity and to fit the diverse perspectives into a gradually evolving pattern" that forms the "configurative meaning" of the text.[10]

By presenting familiar norms in unfamiliar arrangements, the literary text points up the deficiencies of those norms and manipulates the reader into formulating a reaction to these deficiencies. Iser gives Fielding's *Tom Jones* as a partial example of this process: Fielding presents Allworthy as a representative of perfect Christian benevolence, but then he juxtaposes the Allworthy perspective to Blifil, whom the reader comes to see as the embodiment of hypocritical piety. But why does Allworthy trust Blifil? The reader soon draws the conclusion that Allworthy is naive and impractical in that his "perfection is simply incapable of conceiving a mere pretense of ideality." Fielding has forced the reader to this conclusion though he has not stated it in the text itself. The reader combines the various perspectives—Allworthy, Blifil, and the plot—into a "consistent gestalt" which resolves the tensions that resulted from the juxtaposition of the perspectives. But, again, "this gestalt is not explicit in the text—it emerges from a projection of the reader, which is guided in so far as it arises out of the identification of the connections between the signs" (p. 121).

In Iser's model of reading, interpretation becomes the reader's production of this gestalt or configurative meaning. Such consistency-building during the reading process can be further analyzed in terms of holistic and sequential interpretive acts performed by the reader. Holland emphasizes holistic interpretation in his model of reading: a reader interprets the text

---

10. Iser, *The Act of Reading,* pp. 35, 115. For more on "configurative meaning," see *The Implied Reader,* pp. 284 ff.

by finding a coherent and satisfying unity among its elements. Similarly, Iser's model describes how the reader groups "together all the different aspects of a text to form the consistency that the reader will always be in search of." As with Holland's "unity," Iser's "consistency" is created by individual readers: "This 'gestalt' must inevitably be colored by our own characteristic selection process. For it is not given by the text itself; it arises from the meeting between the written text and the individual mind of the reader with its own particular history of experience, its own consciousness, its own outlook."[11] However, *The Act of Reading* does not emphasize this individuality of response, its subjectivity; rather it focuses instead on the intersubjective nature of the time-flow of reading and the textual perspectives that guide the consistency-building and put restrictions on the range of configurative meanings.

Closely related to holistic consistency are sequential connections. Such sequential interpretations must precede or accompany holistic interpretation.[12] "In every text there is a potential time-sequence which the reader must inevitably realize, as it is impossible to absorb even a short text in a single moment." Reading, then, is a temporal process of anticipation and retrospection. Iser describes the content of that process: "We look forward, we look back, we decide, we change our decisions, we form expectations, we are shocked by their nonfulfillment, we question, we muse, we accept, we reject; this is the dynamic process of recreation."[13] Iser's description of the "time-flow" of the reading process (pp. 109–12) resembles Fish's "structure of the reader's experience." It is an emphasis on this temporal interaction of reader and text that charactizes Fish's practical criticism, "an analysis of the developing responses of the reader in relation to the words as they succeed one another in time. . . . The basis of the method is a consideration of the *temporal* flow of the

11. Iser, *The Implied Reader*, pp. 284. For Holland's analysis of what he calls "holistic method," see 5 *Readers Reading*, pp. 252–63. Iser's comments on Holland in *The Act of Reading*, pp. 39–45, are rather dated since they focus only on Holland's earlier account of reading in *The Dynamics of Literary Response*.

12. And sequential interpretations often consist of the reader's attempts to make holistic sense prematurely, i.e., before the entire text is read.

13. Iser, *The Implied Reader*, pp. 280, 288.

reading experience, and it is assumed that the reader responds in terms of that flow and not to the whole utterance."[14] Fish describes the content of the reading experience as a "succession of deliberative acts": "the making and revising of assumptions, the rendering and regretting of judgments, the coming to and abandoning of conclusions, the giving and withdrawing of approval, the specifying of causes, the asking of questions, the supplying of answers, the solving of puzzles."[15] Fish includes all these activities in his descriptions of the temporal reading process and thus gives value to responses usually neglected in traditional holistic explications.

Though similar in its focus on sequential interpretations and effects, Fish's practical criticism is much more microscopic than Iser's. Iser is primarily concerned with the larger units of the text marked by the perspectives, whereas Fish often describes sentence-by-sentence, clause-by-clause, even word-by-word reading experiences.[16] In his brief discussion of Fish in *The Act of Reading* (pp. 31–32), Iser focuses on the transformational linguistic model that sometimes underlies Fish's microscopic analyses. He argues that the problems Fish has with his concept of the informed reader are due to the inadequate linguistic model that is its base. This critique of the "informed reader" is only one of many such attacks on Fish's early theory, attacks that ultimately led Fish to give up the descriptive claims of his affective stylistics. Though he does not discuss Fish's revised position, Iser obviously would not agree with it. Fish now denies the priority of the independent text and has rejected the descriptive function of the informed reader; while for Iser the independent text maintains its priority as the "artistic pole" of the literary work and the "implied reader" continues to function for him in a way similar to Fish's now obsolete "informed reader." For example,

14. Fish, "Literature in the Reader," p. 27; and see Fish, "Facts and Fictions: A Reply to Ralph Rader," *Critical Inquiry*, 1 (1975), rpt. in *Is There a Text in This Class?*, pp. 136–46.

15. Fish, "Facts and Fictions," p. 142, and "Interpreting the *Variorum*," in *Is There a Text in This Class?*, pp. 158–59.

16. For a more detailed discussion of the strategies used by Fish and Iser in their practical criticism, see Steven Mailloux, "Learning to Read: Interpretation and Reader-Response Criticism," *Studies in the Literary Imagination*, 12, No. 1 (1979), 93–108.

affective stylistics claimed to describe the reading experience of the informed reader, that person most capable of having the experience the text provides; similarly, Iser's practical criticism analyzes the text's "implied reader," a term that "incorporates both the prestructuring of the potential meaning by the text, and the reader's actualization of this potential through the reading process."[17] Fish no longer claims to describe *the* reading process; but this descriptive focus continues to be the goal of Iser's phenomenology.

Iser incorporates the short- and long-term effects of reading literature into his descriptive model. For Iser, reading is not a one-way process in which the passive reader merely internalizes the structures in the text; rather, it is a "dynamic interaction" in which the active reader is constantly responding to the meanings he produces in this interaction. Consistency-building and image-making are continual reading activities guided by the text; the configurative meaning must be assembled by the reader, who is then, in turn, affected by what he has assembled. The result of this literary effect involves a restructuring of the reader's experience, a phenomenon which occurs most forcibly in the reading of those texts that incorporate the norms the reader already holds. Here the deficiencies that the text forces the reader to locate and resolve are deficiencies in the reader's own structuring of experience. A reader open to the text and its effects will have to reformulate his system of norms in order to accommodate the meaning the text has led him to assemble. Thus, the act of reading literature provides "an experience which entails the reader constituting himself by constituting a reality hitherto unfamiliar" (p. 151). It is in this way that literature significantly changes its readers.

Like others before him, Iser makes a distinction between *meaning* and *significance*.[18] "Meaning is the referential totality

---

17. Iser, *The Implied Reader*, p. xii; cf. *The Act of Reading*, p. 34: the implied reader "embodies all those predispositions necessary for a literary work to exercise its effect—predispositions laid down, not by an empirical outside reality, but by the text itself." See "Interview: Wolfgang Iser," ed. Rudolf E. Kuenzli, *Diacritics*, 10, No. 2 (1980), 72–73, for comments by Iser that support my claims about his probable view of Fish's revised theory.

18. Most familiar to American critics is E. D. Hirsch's discussion of the distinc-

which is implied by the aspects contained in the text and which must be assembled in the course of reading. Significance is the reader's absorption of the meaning into his own existence" (p. 151). Iser accounts for differing interpretations (meanings) of the same text and for different applications (significances) of the meanings assembled. But his phenomenology of reading is concerned primarily with describing the general structure of response and not the specific, historical actualizations of that structure. Thus, Iser correctly distinguishes his theory of response (with its account of the implied reader) from a related aesthetics and history of reception (which deals with actual readers and their documented responses). Similarly, he is more interested in the structure of potential applications than in the actual ways literary meanings have been applied in the experiences of historical readers or groups of readers. Because of these emphases in *The Act of Reading*, there are, by design, few examples of conflicting interpretations of the same text and few specific examples of significant changes produced in actual readers by literature. I find this exclusion disappointing because, by constantly refusing to discuss conflicting responses and actual examples of change, Iser talks about potential, prestructured effects on readers in a way that at times closely resembles very traditional discussions of texts in isolation. As we will see in a moment, this disguised talk of texts becomes an aspect of his persuasiveness within American critical discourse.

Nevertheless, Iser's account of the reading process and literary effects does offer much of real value to contemporary critical theory and its emerging concern with the reader's response to literature. This is one reason *The Act of Reading* has been welcomed by several American critics and theorists. In fact, among the theoretical models of reading now being promoted in this country, Iser's may have a good chance at persuading the most people to adopt its specifications. Such a prediction owes less to the present interest in readers than to the critical tradition that now manifests this interest. Put simply, Iser's book will persuade

---

tion in his *Validity in Interpretation* (New Haven: Yale University Press, 1967), passim. Also see Hirsch, *The Aims of Interpretation* (Chicago: University of Chicago Press, 1976), ch. 1.

not only because of what it says about readers but even more decisively because of what it does (and doesn't) say about texts.

The Act of Reading and the American critical tradition share some basic assumptions about literary texts, and these common assumptions constitute the main source of Iser's persuasive power for American criticism. However, these shared premises are often concealed by Iser's rhetoric of reading and his critique of influential forces in recent American theory. A close look at his direct attack on American New Criticism reveals much about Iser's hidden agreement with aspects of the hegemonic position he is attacking.

Iser's critique of New Criticism occurs within his more general attack on the "classical norm of interpretation," which he characterizes as an outdated mode of referential analysis searching for an extractable meaning in the text (instead of a meaning experienced by the reader). This extractable meaning is at the service of a mimetic truth and manifests itself in the text as a harmonized totality of balance, order, and completeness. Iser writes that New Criticism marked "a turning-point in literary interpretation" to the extent that it rejected "the vital elements of the classical norm, namely, that the work is an object containing the hidden meaning of a prevailing truth." In place of the search for the hidden message and representational meaning, New Criticism was concerned with "the elements of the work and their interaction," with the *functions* operating within the text. But Iser points out that despite this important revision in the critical tradition, New Criticism still preserved the classical norm of harmony, which took on "a value of its own, whereas in the past it was subservient to the appearance of truth." This harmonizing of textual elements with its discovery and eventual removal of ambiguities was "the unacknowledged debt of New Criticism to the classical norm of interpretation," and it was here that New Criticism set and reached its limits. New Critics attempted to define the functions of the literary text through the same interpretive norm—harmony—used to uncover representational meaning. But "a function is not a meaning—it brings about an effect, and this effect cannot be measured by the same criteria as are used in evaluating the appearance of truth" (pp. 15–16). Iser's functionalist model of the text and his phenomenology of reading attempt to move beyond New Critical limitations. His theory's relationship to New Criticism, however, is similar to the complicitous relation he describes between New Criticism and the classical norm of interpretation: New Critics rejected the classical norm while preserving its value of harmony; Iser rejects New Criticism while preserving its assumption of a prior and independent text. Iser's continued valorization of the text affects his theory just as crucially as the preservation of harmony limited the New Criticism.

It is not simply the general valorization of the text that signals a disguised continuity between Iser's functionalist theory and the critical tradition that New Criticism represents. A more surprising link is the role played by Polish philosopher Roman Ingarden and his phenomenology of the literary work. René Wellek and Austin Warren's 1949 study, *Theory of Literature,* crystallized the American movement toward intrinsic criticism, a movement dominated by New Criticism. Wellek made acknowledged use of Ingarden in his central chapter, "The Analysis of the Literary Work of Art," in which he defined a poem as a "system of norms" consisting of "several strata, each implying its own subordinate group"; Ingarden had outlined these strata in section 8 of *The Literary Work of Art.*[19] Ingarden's stratified view of the literary work thus formed the foundation of Wellek and Warren's theory of intrinsic criticism, and *Theory of Literature,* in turn, became one of the most influential theoretical statements of the dominant force in American criticism.

Iser's theory of reading has a twofold relation to Ingarden's phenomenology and to Wellek and Warren's *Theory of Literature.* Though he too borrows many of Ingarden's concepts, Iser's initial use of Ingarden differs from Wellek's: Iser emphasizes the model of reading given fullest treatment in Ingarden's *The Cog-*

19. For Wellek's discussion, see Wellek and Warren, *Theory of Literature* (New York: Harcourt, Brace, 1949), pp. 151–57. In the Preface, Wellek takes primary responsibility for this chapter; he published an earlier version in *Southern Review,* 7 (1942), 735–54. Wellek used the German version of Ingarden's book, *Das literarische Kunstwerk* (Halle: Max Niemeyer, 1931). The third German edition (1965) has been translated into English as *The Literary Work of Art,* trans. George G. Grabowicz (Evanston: Northwestern University Press, 1973); on pp. lxxix–lxxx, Ingarden criticizes Wellek's presentation of the stratum concept in the *Theory of Literature,* but his critique is irrelevant to the point I am making.

nition of the Literary Work of Art,[20] while Wellek used only the model of the work presented in Ingarden's earlier book, *The Literary Work of Art.* Furthermore, Iser criticizes Ingarden's account and considerably revises it. For example, he praises Ingarden for proposing the idea of concretization but rejects its development in Ingarden's theory, where "concretization was just the actualization of the potential elements of the work—it was not an interaction between text and reader; this is why [Ingarden's] 'places of indeterminacy' lead only to an undynamic completion, as opposed to a dynamic process" in which the reader is made to switch textual perspectives and establish connections between them (p. 178).

But Iser's second criticism of Ingarden signals a more subtle relation to the latter's theory (and ultimately a closer connection to the critical tradition Wellek and Warren represent). Iser lists as one of the major drawbacks of Ingarden's account the fact that Ingarden cannot " accept the possibility that a work may be concretized in different, equally valid, ways" (p. 178). Wellek's use of Ingarden was motivated by the very characteristic that Iser *seems* to be rejecting here. Wellek wrote that "we can distinguish between right and wrong readings of a poem, or between a recognition or a distortion of the norms implicit in a work of art, by acts of comparison, by a study of different false or incomplete realizations.... A hierarchy of viewpoints, a criticism of the grasp of norms, is implied in the concept of the adequacy of interpretation."[21] Adequacy, or validity, in interpretation represents an overriding concern for the American critical tradition. This concern has grown in recent years because of the challenge from reader-response and post-structuralist theories. In a 1978 essay in *Critical Inquiry,* Wellek responded to these new onslaughts against interpretive adequacy, characterizing them as "the new anarchy which allows a complete liberty of interpreta-

20. Trans. Ruth Ann Crowley and Kenneth R. Olson (Evanston: Northwestern University Press, 1973). The original appeared in Polish as *O poznawaniu dziela literackiego* (Lvov: Ossolineum, 1937), but the English version is based on the revised and enlarged German edition, *Vom Erkennen des literarischen Kunstwerks* (Tübingen: Max Niemeyer, 1968).
21. Wellek and Warren, *Theory of Literature,* pp. 143-44.

tion."[22] In a recent issue of *The Sewanee Review,* Cleanth Brooks, another respected advocate of intrinsic criticism, has more colorfully communicated the continuing fear of "what can happen when there is a lack of theoretical restraints": "Literary interpretation becomes a game of tennis played without a net and on a court with no backlines."[23]

But does Iser's critique of Ingarden indicate a rejection of validity in interpretation? This does not seem to be the case. Iser is rejecting only the notion that each text offers just one valid concretization, one correct meaning. For Iser, there is a pre-structured *range* of meanings that the reader can validly assemble from the same text: "the structure of the text *allows* for different ways of fulfillment" (p. 37). Iser's stand is simply a reader-oriented version of the critical pluralism quite respectable within traditional American literary theory (as most recently demonstrated by Wayne Booth's *Critical Understanding*).[24]

But what is not acceptable in this tradition is a critical pluralism without limits—note Booth's subtitle, *The Powers and Limits of Pluralism,* and the extended discussion in *Critical Inquiry* among Booth, M. H. Abrams, J. Hillis Miller, and others over "The Limits of Pluralism."[25] In American theory, validity in interpretation has been guaranteed most often by constraints in the literary text that limit the range of permissible meanings to

22. Wellek, "The New Criticism: Pro and Contra," *Critical Inquiry,* 4 (1978), 623.

23. Cleanth Brooks, "The New Criticism," *Sewanee Review,* 87 (1979), 604.

24. Wayne C. Booth, *Critical Understanding: The Powers and Limits of Pluralism* (Chicago: University of Chicago Press, 1979). For other recent accounts of pluralism within the tradition, see Norman Friedman, *Form and Meaning in Fiction* (Athens: University of Georgia Press, 1975), and Walter A. Davis, *The Act of Interpretation: A Critique of Literary Reason* (Chicago: University of Chicago Press, 1978). Iser's pluralism differs from these others in that he bases his on different valid concretizations by readers, whereas Booth, Friedman, and Davis base their pluralism on the availability of different valid approaches *by critics.* Still, all these pluralisms, including Iser's, assume that it is the *text* (its multiple structures, potential meanings, etc.) that makes pluralism possible.

25. The limits Booth proposes are quite complex, but they do include the "demands" of the text, which he admits can (and sometimes should) be violated after they have been recognized—see Booth, *Critical Understanding,* pp. 238–59. For "The Limits of Pluralism" debate, see *Critical Inquiry,* 3 (1977), 405–47, and the "Critical Response" sections of subsequent issues.

be derived from that text. Iser's account of reading supplies just the kind of textual constraints that make most critics comfortable. These constraints are the manipulative devices for ensuring that the reader is directed appropriately: "Although the reader must participate in the assembly of meaning by realizing the structure inherent in the text, it must not be forgotten that he stands outside the text. His position must therefore be manipulated by the text if his viewpoint is to be properly guided" (p. 152).

For Iser, the text's arrangement of perspectives guides the reader as he attempts to project a consistent pattern resolving the tensions among the various norms distributed among the perspectives. "The interaction fails if . . . the reader's projections superimpose themselves unimpeded upon the text" (p. 167). How exactly does the arrangement of perspectives guide the reader's activities and impede his projections? Between and within the textual perspectives, there are *blanks*, which are vacancies in the overall system of the text. "They indicate that the different segments of the text *are* to be connected, even though the text itself does not say so. They are the unseen joints of the text, and as they mark off schemata and textual perspectives from one another, they simultaneously trigger acts of ideation [image-building] on the reader's part" (pp. 182–83). The blanks "function virtually as instructions" (p. 212) in the "theme-and-horizon structure" of the reading process. As the reader moves through the text, he constantly shifts from one perspective to another. The perspective he assumes at any one moment becomes the "theme" that is read against the "horizon" of the previous perspectives in which he had been situated (p. 97); in the *Tom Jones* example given above, the Allworthy perspective is first a theme, then part of the horizon for judging the Blifil perspective, and then a theme again but this time one that is interpreted against the changed horizon that now contains the perspective of Blifil. The reader fills the blanks between perspectives according to the theme-and-horizon structure, which guides him to negate or modify each thematic perspective in light of the accumulated horizon of previous perspectives. The perspectives, blanks, and theme-and-horizon structure constitute the constraints that Iser's account places on the reader's interpretation of the whole text.

It might in the end seem a bit odd to say that Iser promotes the notion of an independent text, even in the complex way I have described. After all, his is a phenomenological theory of reading, and he continually emphasizes how the subject-object division is destroyed during the reading process. But these claims must be examined closely. For in Iser's account, it is the literary work and not the text that is dependent on the reader for its existence: "the literary work has two poles, which we might call the artistic and the aesthetic: the artistic pole is the author's text and the aesthetic is the realization accomplished by the reader. In view of this polarity, it is clear that the work itself cannot be identical with the text or with the concretization, but must be situated somewhere between the two" (p. 21). The text remains independent and prior to the reader's activities as it initiates, guides, and corrects the reader's concretization of the literary work. I would argue, then, that despite his critiques of New Criticism and Ingarden, Iser ultimately demonstrates that he shares with Wellek, Brooks, and Booth a belief in interpretive validity guaranteed by constraints in a prior and independent text; and these shared assumptions make Iser's detailed account of reading extremely attractive to traditional literary theorists in America.[26]

Unfortunately, by presenting a reading model that is easily adapted to the American critical tradition, Iser is in danger of undercutting one of his purposes for writing *The Act of Reading:* in his preface he suggests that the "anthropological side of literary criticism" deserves more attention, and he hopes that some hints in his book might encourage concern for the "actual function of literature in the overall make-up of man" (p. xi). Within today's critical discourse, these are admirable goals, and indeed many of Iser's discussions do direct our attention to how literature functions in this humanistic way. His account of literary effect, of how literature changes its readers, certainly moves in

26. See, for example, the review of Iser's *Act of Reading* by one author of the prohibition against the Affective Fallacy. He writes that among reader-response theorists, "Iser is notable for the phenomenological subtlety of his account of what goes on in the reader's mind and for his sensitivity to the implicit demands by which the text exercises supervision over those goings-on"—Monroe Beardsley, "Reader Meets Text," *Sewanee Review,* 87 (1979), 645.

this direction. But this fine attempt may be erased because of the text-centered theory of reading that is its foundation. The emphasis on textual constraints and the prestructuring of effect, combined with the lack of examples of differing interpretations and significant changes in readers, will make it quite easy for Iser's theory to be grafted onto the American critical tradition without really affecting the text-centered, often a-rhetorical criticism and theory that tradition fosters.

Thus, while it actually contains the seeds of a radically social and rhetorical approach, *The Act of Reading* is persuasive because it appears to be safe: it gives the American critic just enough of the reader but not too much. More exactly, it provides an acceptable model of the text partially disguised as an innovative account of reading. Very economically, then, it fulfills both needs of current American theory: it incorporates the reader into a theory of literature while it maintains the traditional American valorization of the autonomous text. Iser allows American theorists to have their text and reader too.

Structuralist Poetics

The reading model proposed by Jonathan Culler fills an important gap in reader-response theory. It provides the consistent intersubjective base missing from Bleich's and Holland's psychological models, while it refuses to be easily incorporated into the a-rhetorical critical tradition the way Iser's model might be.[27] Culler argues that "the task of literary theory or poetics . . . is to make explicit the procedures and conventions of reading, to offer a comprehensive theory of the ways in which we go

27. In his review of Iser's *Implied Reader,* Culler notes that the book "continually hovers on the borders of elementary and traditional interpretation" and he finds Iser's theory "much more interesting than his practice" ("The Frontier of Criticism," *Yale Review,* 64 [1975], 610–12). Frank Lentricchia argues that Culler's *Structuralist Poetics* is a conservative appropriation of Continental structuralism for the American critical tradition (Lentricchia, pp. 103–11). But however much Culler has domesticated structuralism for American critics, he has also derived from it a theory of reading conventions that pushes those critics in a new direction by focusing on the reading process instead of the autonomous text and by replacing practical criticism with descriptions of the institution of literature.

about making sense of various kinds of texts."[28] In *Structuralist Poetics* (1975), Culler uses structuralism as a heuristic to generate a description of "literary competence," implicit knowledge of reading conventions.[29] Culler's reading conventions resemble Fish's interpretive strategies in that both make interpretation possible, and the two reading models suggest that a "poem be thought of as an utterance that has meaning only with respect to a system of conventions which the reader has assimilated."[30] Furthermore, in contrast to Holland and Bleich, Fish would agree with Culler's statement that "meaning is not an individual creation but the result of applying to the text operations and conventions which constitute the institution of literature."[31] In reference to the schema of reader-response criticism in Chapter 1, we have, then, a continuum that moves from Holland's and Bleich's psychological reading models that emphasize unique responses, through Iser's phenomenological model that includes subjective and intersubjective readings, to the social models that stress shared responses (Fish's early informed reader, Culler's reading conventions, and Fish's later interpretive communities).[32]

28. Culler, "Stanley Fish & the Righting of the Reader" *Diacritics*, 5, No. 1 (1975); slightly revised in Culler, *The Pursuit of Signs: Semiotics, Literature, Deconstruction* (Ithaca: Cornell University Press, 1981), p. 125.

29. Though structuralist in its character, Culler's theory of reading conventions is not completely restricted to structuralist insights or emphases; for example, see *Structuralist Poetics*, pp. 160 and 242, for Culler's distancing of his theory from many structuralist enterprises.

30. Ibid., p. 116.

31. Culler, "Stanley Fish," p. 127; see also *Structuralist Poetics*, pp. 28-30, 258. Not surprisingly, Culler's comments on Holland's work attack his psychological model's emphasis on differences in reading responses—see Culler, rev. of Holland's 5 *Readers Reading, JEGP*, 75 (1976), 461-62, and "Prolegomena to a Theory of Reading," in Suleiman and Crosman, pp. 46-66.

32. The most influential reader-oriented approaches not discussed here are the semiotic theories of such critics as Umberto Eco, Michael Riffaterre, and Gerald Prince. However, Culler's structuralism exemplifies the semiotic emphasis of these approaches, and his theory is more reader-centered than Eco's semiotics of the text, less stylistic than Riffaterre's research using the "superreader," and more concerned with the reading process than Prince's work on "narratees" in fiction. For examples and references to the work of these semioticians, see the collections by Tompkins and by Suleiman and Crosman cited in my Bibliographical Note; see also Culler, "Riffaterre and the Semiotics of Poetry," in *The Pursuit of Signs*, pp. 80-99. One approach that I have excluded here but

In Culler's model, "reading poetry is a rule-governed process of producing meanings; the poem offers a structure which must be filled up and one therefore attempts to invent something, guided by a series of formal rules derived from one's experience of reading poetry, which both make possible invention and impose limits on it."[33] The limits come not from the text but from the reader's literary competence; indeed, the structure of the text is a creation by the reader.[34] Culler views reading as a structuring activity, essentially a process of *naturalization:* "to naturalize a text is to bring it into relation with a type of discourse or model which is already, in some sense, natural and legible." That is, "to assimilate or interpret something is to bring it within the modes of order which culture makes available."[35] Such naturalization can be understood as a type of holistic interpretation, something like Holland's "transformation toward a unity" and Iser's "consistency-building," but with a structuralist difference. Holland's and Iser's interpreters relate the various textual elements intrinsically to an overall unity or configurative meaning; whereas Culler's interpreter relates the elements

---

which is sometimes called "reader-oriented" is deconstructive criticism, especially in its American version. I recognize that deconstructionists do talk about readers reading—see, for example, J. Hillis Miller, "Tradition and Difference," *Diacritics,* 2, No. 4 (1972), 12, and "Stevens' Rock and Criticism as Cure," *Georgia Review,* 30 (1976), 11. But such talk is subordinate to deconstruction's concern with language and the play of signification. Deconstruction as an interpretive strategy (especially in Miller's domesticated version) does imply a mode of reading, but so did American New Criticism; Miller's deconstructive criticism suggests that readers struggle unsuccessfully with the text's contradictory meanings, while New Criticism implied that readers constantly discovered irony, ambiguity, and finally unity. To call deconstruction "reader-oriented" would blur as many useful distinctions as calling New Criticism "reader-oriented." If I included deconstruction as a reader-oriented approach, my attempt to establish and disseminate reader-response criticism would be unnecessarily encumbered and the point of this study somewhat blunted. (Also, see below, n. 39.)

33. Culler, *Structuralist Poetics,* p. 126.

34. Cf. Culler's discussion of how various interpreters of Blake's "London" all follow "the same convention of unity, performing interpretive operations to fill, in their different ways, a structure they have all posited. . . . [A] limited number of formal interpretive operations give them the structures that they flesh out with their own referential and ethical discourse"—"Semiotics as a Theory of Reading," in *The Pursuit of Signs,* pp. 72, 76.

35. Culler, *Structuralist Poetics,* pp. 138, 137, and, for the different levels of naturalization, see pp. 140–59.

extrinsically—intertextually—to established codes or cultural forms. Thus, in explaining how a reader naturalizes three apparently unrelated lines of poetry, Culler cites a reading convention that uses available structural models to organize the text. "The most basic models would seem to be the binary opposition, the dialectical resolution of a binary opposition, the displacement of an unresolved opposition by a third term, the four-term homology, the series united by a common denominator, and the series with a transcendent or summarizing final term."[36] Such structuralist descriptions distinguish Culler's account of holistic interpretation from those of Holland and Iser. Another difference is also crucial: Holland emphasizes and Iser acknowledges that holistic interpretation can be individual and therefore idiosyncratic, whereas Culler claims it is communal, determined by shared reading conventions. And, finally, while Iser bases the intersubjectivity of reading primarily on the textual perspectives, Culler locates it in the socially given literary competence of readers.

On the level of critical exchange, Culler's theory resembles Fish's later account in that his social model for reading also serves to explain criticism. For Culler, "the possibility of critical argument depends on shared notions of the acceptable and the unacceptable, a common ground which is nothing other than the procedures of reading." Like Fish, Culler ties critical consensus to reading conventions, which limit acceptable interpretations: "The claim is not that competent readers would agree on an interpretation but only that certain expectations about poetry and ways of reading guide the interpretive process and impose severe limitations on the set of acceptable or plausible readings."[37] Both Fish and Culler agree that the reading conventions which constitute the "set of acceptable or plausible readings" are always evolving.[38] And Culler has recently ex-

36. Ibid., p. 174.
37. Ibid., pp. 124, 127. Frank Kermode discusses the constraining force of an "institutionalized competence," which he compares to Culler's notion of "literary competence"; see his "Can We Say Absolutely Anything We Like?" in *Art, Politics, and Will: Essays in Honor of Lionel Trilling,* ed. Quentin Anderson, Stephen Donadio, and Steven Marcus (New York: Basic Books, 1977), p. 162.
38. See Fish, "Interpreting the *Variorum,*" pp. 171–72, and "What Makes In-

plained that his theory of literary competence does allow for the presence of different interpretive communities existing simultaneously (that is, contemporaneous groups with literary competencies embodying radically different notions of interpretive acceptability).[39]

---

terpretation Acceptable?" in *Is There a Text in This Class?*, pp. 342–49; and Culler, *Structuralist Poetics*, pp. 130, 249–54, "Reading and Misreading," *Yale Review*, 65 (1975), 88–89, and "Semiotics," in *Princeton Encyclopedia of Poetry and Poetics*, 2d ed., ed. Alex Preminger (Princeton: Princeton University Press, 1974), p. 982.

39. See Culler, "Semiotics as a Theory of Reading," pp. 51, 73, 77. These recent clarifications begin to answer the objection that Culler had misleadingly portrayed "literary competence" as monolithic—see Paul Bové, "The Poetics of Coercion: An Interpretation of Literary Competence," *boundary 2*, 5 (1976), 277. In attacking Culler's competence model as too "inflexible," Bové (p. 283, n. 16) cites Paul de Man's treatment of all reading as misreading. Indeed, de Man's recent *Allegories of Reading: Figural Language in Rousseau, Nietzsche, Rilke, and Proust* (New Haven: Yale University Press, 1979) appears to be the most serious challenge not only to Culler's theory but to all social reading models (including the one I will propose). However, a closer examination of de Man's argument indicates it is actually a counterproposal that either is incommensurate with reader-response theories or that subsumes their social reading models. First of all, *Allegories of Reading* is not about how readers read; it is about how certain texts "represent" how readers read. That is, de Man does not describe the reading process, he *thematizes* it. This thematization is then elaborated through deconstructive readings that focus on the play of figuration *in the text*. Such a focus makes reading into an unreadable trope: a narrative like Proust's or Rousseau's is an allegory of reading, and "reading is the metaphor of writing" (de Man, p. 68). Like the texts he deconstructs, de Man's rhetorization of reading (reading as trope) is initially readable; but again like those texts, this readability, when questioned, turns out to be a disguise for a more radical indeterminacy. For example, the statement that "reading is the metaphor of writing" can at first be understood as a substitute for the following claim: "the moment that marks the passage from 'life' to writing corresponds to an act of reading that separates from the undifferentiated mass of facts and events, the distinctive elements susceptible of entering into the composition of a text" (p. 57). Most reader-response critics could accept this descriptive claim (which de Man attributes to Georges Poulet). But de Man's deconstructive project does not allow such claims to remain unproblematic: to say reading is like writing is actually to contaminate reading with all the indeterminacy de Man reveals in written discourse—rhetorical reversals, figural play, incompatible meanings, etc. De Man's *Allegories of Reading* therefore appears to be incommensurable with reader-response criticism in three ways: (1) it is not a description of reading but a thematization of it; (2) it focuses on the play of figures in a text rather than on readers reading; and (3) any of its suggestions about reading are made so problematic that they cannot be placed on all fours with reader-response models. There is, however, another way to characterize the relation of *Allegories of Reading* to reader-response criticism. From this perspective, de Man's deconstructive project *assumes* a social reading

In terms of his interpretive theory, Culler stops short of Fish's present position. Both agree that the "real world" is the "socially given text" (Culler) or the "standard story" (Fish).[40] This position would seem to commit both theorists to Fish's claim that "no use of language matches reality but that all uses of language are interpretations of reality."[41] For Fish, "the rules and conventions under which speakers and hearers 'normally' operate don't demand that language be faithful to the facts; rather, they specify the shape of that fidelity . . . creating it, rather than enforcing it." Fish writes further: "I am not denying that what will and will not be accepted as true is determined by the standard story. I am only pointing out that its being (or telling; it amounts to the same thing) the truth is not a matter of a special relationship it bears to the world (the world does not impose it on us), but of a special relationship it bears to its users."[42] Culler seems to back off from conclusions similar to these (though his exact position is unclear). In one place he describes the first type of *vraisemblance* (naturalization) as relating a text to "a discourse which requires no justification because it seems to derive directly from the structure of the world." He then quickly adds: "Recognition of this first level of *vraisemblance* need not depend on the claim that reality is a convention produced by language. Indeed, the danger of that position is that it may be interpreted in too sweeping a fashion. Thus, Julia Kristeva argues that anything expressed in a grammatical sentence becomes *vraisemblable* since language is constitutive of the world."[43] Culler would likely accuse Fish of a similar distortion of the relation between language and reality. Ultimately, the difference between their hermeneutic theories is that Culler refuses to give up the descriptive claims

---

model in order to produce the intersubjective, totalizing interpretations de Man then dismantles. His rhetorical readings demonstrate how the reader's production of sense or unity for a text must always be a misreading because it ignores the figural play that undermines the coherent meaning the reader produces. Thus de Man does not so much reject reader-response models as move beyond them to reveal the disruptive play of figures they necessarily neglect or minimize.

40. Culler, *Structuralist Poetics*, p. 140; Fish, "How To Do Things with Austin and Searle," p. 239.

41. Fish, "How To Do Things with Austin and Searle," p. 243.

42. Ibid., pp. 238, 241.

43. Culler, *Structuralist Poetics*, pp. 140–41.

Fish now rejects. Culler believes it is possible to describe and explain the specific facts of reading; Fish believes that all such accounts produce the facts they claim to describe.[44]

Still, Fish's present theory of interpretation has closer affinities to Culler's than to that of any other reader-response critic we have examined. Fish is no longer guilty of the deficiency Culler noted in his review of *Self-Consuming Artifacts*: "here Fish's theoretical enterprise quite abruptly vanishes; to the question, how does the reader create meaning, he has no general reply to make."[45] Fish's social concept of interpretive strategies now fills this explanatory void. Though Culler's theory is descriptive and Fish's creative, both would agree that any change in interpretive strategies "can proceed only step by step, relying on the procedures which readers actually use."[46] It is Culler's goal to describe the procedures readers actually use, while Fish has given up this exclusively descriptive focus: "Rather than restoring or recovering texts, I am in the business of making texts and of teaching others to make them by adding to their repertoire of strategies."[47]

For rather different reasons, neither Fish nor Culler supplies an important part of a reader-response critical theory: the needed link between a social model of reading and a practical criticism based on that model. Fish still uses his affective stylistics in his literary analyses, but his revised theory of interpretation is only indirectly connected with it. Just as he began to elaborate an account of the informed reader's literary competence to justify his practical criticism, Fish jettisoned the whole concept of the informed reader and the descriptive claims of his affective stylis-

---

44. Culler's most recent comments on deconstruction indicate that he still maintains the possibility of describing and explaining determinate facts, though he now admits limitations on the consistency of descriptive theories and on the stability of the described object. See Culler, "In Pursuit of Signs," *Daedalus*, 106, No. 4 (1977), revised in *The Pursuit of Signs*, pp. 39–43; and "Structuralism and Grammatology," *boundary 2*, 8, No. 1 (1979), 75–85.

45. Culler, "Stanley Fish," p. 125; also see Culler, "Beyond Interpretation: The Prospects of Contemporary Criticism," *Comparative Literature*, 28 (1976), 252.

46. Culler, *Structuralist Poetics*, p. 253.

47. Fish, "Interpreting 'Interpreting the *Variorum*,'" in *Is There a Text in This Class?*, p. 180.

tics. This is a bold move to be sure, but a move that leaves his temporal reading model and his reader-response criticism with no theoretical foundation. In fact, by denying that any approach captures or reflects its descriptive object, Fish has rejected the possibility of justifying any critical procedures. According to him, all practical criticism—formalist or reader-response— constitutes what it claims to describe, and therefore no metacritical theory can establish the priority of a critical methodology by claiming it captures what is really there in the text or reading experience. For Fish, "what is really there" is always produced by the procedures used to describe it.[48] This theory of interpretation is both revolutionary and inconsequential. It is revolutionary because it completely changes the way we understand the activities of literary study. But it is inconsequential in that it actually changes nothing in critical practice: critics will continue to use their habitual interpretive strategies in practical criticism (as Fish himself has done) and will continue to erect metacritical justifications for their criticism. As Fish recognizes, his revised hermeneutics simply accounts (in a new way) for how literary criticism functions and does not prescribe how it should function. His present theory does not argue for any one way to describe literature or reading experiences (in fact, on principle it cannot do so); and therefore it no longer provides a justification for a specifically reader-oriented approach to practical criticism.

A further complication makes Fish's present hermeneutic theory even less useful as a rationale for criticism. His rejection of descriptive claims also means that his theoretical account of interpretive strategies (in reading and criticism) is itself an interpretation masquerading as neutral description. To be consistent, Fish has to say that his *theoretical* discourse produces the "facts" of criticism in the same way that his *critical* discourse (affective stylistics) produced the "facts" of reading. Thus, if on hermeneutic principle Fish's criticism cannot neutrally reflect a preexistent reading experience, then his literary theory cannot reflect the preexistent situation of criticism.[49] In any case,

48. Cf. Fish, "Interpreting the *Variorum*," p. 167.
49. Fish begins to address this issue at the end of *Is There a Text in This Class?*, pp. 368–70.

whether Fish's hermeneutics denies the traditional descriptive capacity of criticism or of criticism *and* theory, it certainly provides no metacritical foundation for a specific reader-response approach to literary study.

Culler's structuralist poetics also excludes a connection between his theory and a specific approach to doing criticism, but for reasons very different from Fish's. As a general principle, Culler rejects the explication of individual texts as the central activity of literary study. He argues that "the most important and insidious legacy of the New Criticism is the widespread and unquestioning acceptance of the notion that the critic's job is to interpret literary works." Culler prefers a poetics of literature to explications of texts. "To engage in the study of literature is not to produce yet another interpretation of *King Lear* but to advance one's understanding of the conventions and operations of an institution, a mode of discourse."[50] Culler's argument justifies the writing of *Structuralist Poetics,* but, like Fish's revised theory, it offers no rationale for employing a reader-response approach in practical criticism.

I can now refocus this survey and critique of current reader-response criticism by asking: What version of reader-oriented theory has the most to offer the institutional study of American fiction? All of the reading theories have their deficiencies in light of this purpose. Holland's and Bleich's psychological models of reading and criticism are too difficult to adapt in any form to the traditional study of literature, primarily because they lack the intersubjective base assumed by the discipline and necessary for the kind of practical criticism that dominates American literary study. Iser's phenomenological model provides the intersubjective foundation—perspectives in the text—but is perhaps too easily incorporated into the American text-centered, a-rhetorical tradition of criticism and theory. Fish's early affective stylistics presents a more useful approach, especially in its emphasis on

---

50. Culler, "Beyond Interpretation," p. 246. See also Culler, "The Critical Assumption," *SCE Reports,* No. 6 (1979), pp. 77–84; and the revised version of "Beyond Interpretation" in *The Pursuit of Signs,* pp. 18–43. Cf. *Structuralist Poetics,* pp. 128, 258–59.

the temporal dimension of reading (a dimension that is also included, though less centrally, in Iser's model). However, Fish's later theory of interpretation explains only how practical criticism works and does not provide a metacritical justification for what approach to use. Culler's theory of conventions is more specific about the details of how readers read, and it proposes a convincing social reading model that not only provides an intersubjective foundation for criticism but also presents a theory that is neither too hard nor too easy to incorporate into American literary study. Still, Culler does not make a connection between his theory of reading conventions and the needs of practical criticism; in fact, he rejects practical criticism as a desirable activity within literary study.

What we have left, then, is a useful reader-centered program for practical criticism in Fish's and Iser's work without an adequate theoretical base; Fish moved on to his present theory of interpretive communities before he provided such a base, and Iser's theoretical proposals do not present a viable alternative to the objectivist tradition in literary theory. And we have Culler's theory of reading conventions, which does provide a strong theoretical base for a reader-response approach; but Culler refuses to connect this base to practical criticism. What we need, therefore, is an intersubjective model of reading and criticism that takes the best from the work of Fish, Iser, and Culler and supplies what is missing: *a social model of reading that supports a reader-response approach to literary criticism.* In the chapters that follow, I will supply this missing account by proposing a temporal and convention-based reading model for the study of American fiction.

CHAPTER THREE

Practical Criticism:
The Reader in American Fiction

> In every novel the work is divided between the writer and
> the reader; but the writer makes the reader very much as he
> makes his characters.
> —Henry James, "The Novels of George Eliot"

> The author creates ... an image of himself and another
> image of his reader; he makes his reader, as he makes his
> second self, and the most successful reading is one in which
> the created selves, author and reader, can find complete
> agreement.
> —Wayne Booth, *The Rhetoric of Fiction*

The existence of literature depends as much on
readers reading as it does on authors writing. This obvious fact
has had little influence on the American critical tradition in the
twentieth century. Dominating that tradition, formalist analysis
and intrinsic criticism have not only ignored the reader but have
actively discouraged talk about him by positing the "Affective
Fallacy."[1] Though primarily directed against using psychological
effects as evaluative criteria, the proscription against the Affective Fallacy also implied a strong rejection of using the reader in
interpretation. American New Criticism, the most influential intrinsic approach, simply assumed that the text contained all relevant meanings and forms and that an interpretive emphasis on
the reader was not only unnecessary but dangerous. During the
hegemony of intrinsic criticism, only a few literary theorists like
Louise Rosenblatt and Kenneth Burke ventured outside the text

---

1. Monroe C. Beardsley and W. K. Wimsatt, Jr., "The Affective Fallacy,"
Sewanee Review, 57 (1949), 31-55.

to discuss the reader.[2] Later, Wayne Booth helped begin the project of reestablishing talk about readers through his influential *Rhetoric of Fiction,* which contained discussions of the novel's effects on its audience.[3]

Most American criticism, however, continued to ignore the reader as it devalued the reading process itself. The New Critical focus on "close reading" was always more pedagogical prescription than critical description; that is, it advocated *doing* close reading but not *describing* the reading process. And New Criticism equated "close reading" with detailed explications of a literary work. For example, in their influential textbooks Cleanth Brooks and Robert Penn Warren argued for a "close analytical and interpretive reading" that was concerned with how the parts of the story or poem "cohere into a total meaningful pattern."[4] This kind of criticism tried to *produce readings* rather than *describe reading,* and the readings it produced focused on the text's "total structure," its "set of organic relationships."[5]

2. See especially "Psychology and Form" and "Lexicon Rhetoricae" in Burke, *Counter-Statement* (1931; 2d ed. 1953; rpt. Berkeley: University of California Press, 1968); and on Rosenblatt's work, see above, Ch. 1, n. 41. For discussions of some other early talk of readers, see reader-response critics on I. A. Richards: David Bleich, *Subjective Criticism* (Baltimore: Johns Hopkins University Press, 1978), pp. 34, 153; Stanley Fish, "Literature in the Reader: Affective Stylistics," in *Is There a Text in This Class?,* pp. 52–57; Norman N. Holland, *5 Readers Reading* (New Haven: Yale University Press, 1975), pp. 6–8; and Wolfgang Iser, *The Act of Reading* (Baltimore: Johns Hopkins University Press, 1978), pp. 44–48.

3. Wayne C. Booth, *The Rhetoric of Fiction* (Chicago: University of Chicago Press, 1961), e.g., chs. 4 and 5. In a review of Iser's *Implied Reader,* Frank Kermode called Booth "the rejected father" of reader-response criticism (Kermode, "The Reader's Share," *Times Literary Supplement,* 11 July 1975, p. 751.) Actually, Iser makes limited but respectful use of Booth's work in *The Implied Reader* and *The Act of Reading,* and most other reader-response critics seem to ignore Booth's theories rather than reject them. These later critics do, however, put less emphasis on the author than Booth does in *The Rhetoric of Fiction* and *A Rhetoric of Irony* (Chicago: University of Chicago Press, 1974). Cf. Wayne Booth, Wolfgang Iser, et al. "In Defense of Authors and Readers," ed. Edward Bloom, *Novel,* 11 (1977), 5–25; and also the Booth-Iser exchange in "Interview: Wolfgang Iser," ed. Rudolf E. Kuenzli, *Diacritics,* 10, No. 2 (1980), 66–72.

4. Cleanth Brooks and Robert Penn Warren, *Understanding Fiction,* 2d ed. (New York: Appleton-Century-Crofts, 1959), pp. xiii, 173.

5. Ibid., p. xiii. Cf. Brooks and Warren, *Understanding Poetry,* 2d ed. (New York: Henry Holt, 1950), pp. 694–95: "The unity of a poem, like that of any work of art, is a unity of final meaning." Also, see Reuben A. Brower and

Such New Critical exegesis typifies the American tradition of holistic interpretation, which neglects the nature of reading as a temporal process. Most old and new critical approaches specify meanings that are spatial or holistic, whether they look for unities or myths, symbolic systems or allegorical messages, whether they find ethical, psychological, and political themes or generic, structural, and imagistic patterns.[6] All such meanings and forms are retrospective configurations that a reader might construct *after* his temporal reading experience. To focus only on this final holistic synthesis completely ignores the sequential process leading up to it. Indeed, traditional critical approaches are unnecessarily hampered by an "ideology of totality."[7] In such approaches, as Fish argues, "the reader's activities are at once ignored and devalued. They are ignored because the text is taken to be self-sufficient—everything is *in* it—and they are devalued because when they are thought of at all, they are thought of as the disposable machinery" for extracting holistic meanings and unified structures.[8]

To recover these reader activities and the process they constitute, a practical critic must adopt a temporal reading model that consists of sequential interpretations and effects. In *Counter-Statement* Kenneth Burke proposed a model for what he called

---

Richard Poirier's statement that the essays in their collection, *In Defense of Reading: A Reader's Approach to Literary Criticism* (New York: Dutton, 1962), have as their "final purpose . . . to interpret the work as a *total* expression" ("Preface," p. vii).

6. There have been a few modern attempts to incorporate literature's temporal dimension into critical analyses, e.g., certain discussions of sequential plot structures. But such attempts have usually been text-centered, not reader-oriented, focusing on the work's presentation of actions rather than on the reader's sequential activities in responding to that presentation. But cf. R. S. Crane, "The Concept of Plot and the Plot of *Tom Jones*," in *Critics and Criticism*, ed. R. S. Crane (Chicago: University of Chicago Press, 1952), pp. 616–48; Meir Sternberg, *Expositional Modes and Temporal Ordering in Fiction* (Baltimore: Johns Hopkins University Press, 1978); and Menakhem Perry, "Literary Dynamics: How the Order of a Text Creates its Meanings," *Poetics Today*, 1 (1979), 35–64, 311–61.

7. Roland Barthes, *S/Z*, trans. Richard Miller (New York: Hill and Wang, 1974), p. 15.

8. Fish, "Interpreting the *Variorum*," in *Is There a Text in This Class?*, p. 158. Cf. Michael Riffaterre, "The Self-Sufficient Text," *Diacritics*, 3, No. 3 (1973), 39–45.

the "psychology of the audience," arguing that literary discourse produces needs in its readers so that it can then satisfy them. For example, when *Hamlet* announces the appearance of a ghost, it creates in the audience an expectation and a desire to see the apparition; the ghost then appears and the audience is (for the moment) satisfied. Burke calls this expectation-fulfillment structure in the reader's experience the "form" of the literary work: "A work has form in so far as one part of it leads a reader to anticipate another part, to be gratified by the sequence."[9] More recently, Roland Barthes has proposed a similar reader-oriented view of literary form, most specifically in his description of the "hermeneutic code," one of five codes that a text can employ. Under the hermeneutic code, Barthes lists "the various (formal) terms by which an enigma can be distinguished, suggested, formulated, held in suspense, and finally disclosed." These formal terms (thematization, formulation, snare, equivocation, partial answer, disclosure, and the like) elaborate the code in the discourse and "structure the enigma according to the expectation and desire for its solution" in the reader.[10]

The mystery-solution model of Barthes's hermeneutic code is a particular instance of the expectation-fulfillment structure proposed by Burke. However, one aspect of Barthes's model— the continual, frustrating postponement of the enigma's solution—suggests another structure for a temporal reading model.[11] This expectation-*disappointment* structure can often be found in the models assumed by reader-response critics such as Stephen Booth, Stanley Fish, and Wolfgang Iser. In an essay on *Hamlet,* Booth incorporates the same example Burke uses into a more complex structure of response, as Booth demonstrates how the first scene of the play "frustrates and fulfills expectations simultaneously." The audience has been wondering why the play begins with sentinels and then discovers the reason has something to do with an apparition. As one sentinel finally be-

9. Burke, *Counter-Statement,* pp. 29–31, 124.
10. Barthes, *S/Z,* pp. 19, 75.
11. Though he does not emphasize this characteristic of the expectation-fulfillment structure, Burke also mentions that the satisfaction of the need created by the text "at times involves a temporary set of frustrations" (*Counter-Statement,* p. 31).

gins to explain exactly what is going on, the ghost appears. Its arrival, according to Booth, "both fulfills and frustrates our expectations: it is what we expect and desire, an action to account for our attention to sentinels; it is unexpected and unwanted, an interruption in . . . the exposition that was on its way to fulfilling the same function."[12] Fish and Iser exhibit a similar expectation-disappointment structure in the temporal reading model they assume for their practical criticism. In his analysis of *Paradise Lost,* for instance, Fish describes how Milton encourages expectations in his reader so that he can later disappoint them and use that disappointment to educate the reader's perceptions. And Iser demonstrates how Fielding shatters "false expectations" in *Joseph Andrews* to help the reader "sharpen his sense of discernment."[13]

As important as these expectation-(non)fulfillment structures are, they only serve as frameworks for the sequence of reader activities described by a criticism based on a temporal reading model. Instead of making these activities extraneous to holistic meaning (and therefore negligible), a reader-response approach based on a temporal model makes them central to its critical analyses. Such a criticism gives significance not only to the final holistic interpretation by the reader, but also to the series of interpretations and effects leading up to that final synthesis. As Fish points out, a temporal reader-response approach agrees with traditional criticism that "we hypothesize comprehensive intentions, get through tangles of references, eliminate ambiguities, exclude or rule out partial and incomplete meanings"; but where traditional holistic analysis implies "that we do these things only once or that only one of the times we do them counts," reader-response criticism believes "that we do them again and again . . . and that each instance of our doing of them (not merely the last) has value."[14] A temporal model of reading

12. Stephen Booth, "On the Value of *Hamlet*," in *Reinterpretations of Elizabethan Drama,* ed. Norman Rabkin (New York: Columbia University Press, 1969), pp. 139, 142.

13. Stanley E. Fish, *Surprised by Sin: The Reader in* Paradise Lost, 2nd ed. (Berkeley: University of California Press, 1971), ch. 1; and Wolfgang Iser, *The Implied Reader* (Baltimore: Johns Hopkins University Press, 1974), p. 39.

14. Stanley E. Fish, "Facts and Fictions: A Reply to Ralph Rader," in *Is There a Text in This Class?*, p. 145.

makes available for description a wide range of reader activities, which include making and revising judgments, solving mysteries and puzzles, experiencing attitudes, taking on and rejecting perspectives, discovering sequential structures of similarity and contrast, formulating questions and answers, making and correcting mistakes.

By neglecting these activities, the temporal reading process, and the reader himself, traditional holistic criticism not only distorts the actual effects literature produces; it also omits an important part of the author's intention and artistic technique. Ultimately, holistic interpretation can only describe the author's attempt to communicate a thematic message or to provide an aesthetic experience of the artistic whole. What such formalist approaches overlook are the discourse strategies the author uses to control the reader's temporal interaction with the text. In addition, as Richard Strier has argued, a holistic "demonstration of the relations of each part of a literary work to the whole does not and cannot serve to establish the relation of part to part."[15] Only a temporal analysis of the reader's response can fully explain how each part of an author's text relates to those parts before and after it.

The fiction of Nathaniel Hawthorne can serve as a case in point. Here is an author whom critics have long considered a master of American literature, an author whose work has always had a secure place near the center of the privileged canon. Modern critics generally agree that within the (sometimes narrow) space of his thematic concerns, Hawthorne's artistic technique is unrivaled in the tradition.[16] These critics have devoted pages and pages of analysis to dissecting Hawthorne's fictional strategies, yet they have always fallen short of an adequate description because formalist and holistic assumptions have unnecessarily limited the scope of their analyses.

15. Richard Strier, "The Poetics of Surrender: An Exposition and Critique of New Critical Poetics," *Critical Inquiry*, 2 (1975), 188.

16. The well-known attacks on Hawthorne's artistry by W. C. Brownell, Yvor Winters, and Martin Green assume this agreement even as they challenge it. On the history of Hawthorne's reputation, see J. Donald Crowley, Introduction to his *Hawthorne: The Critical Heritage* (New York: Barnes & Noble, 1970), 31–36; and Jay B. Hubbell, *Who Are the Major American Writers?* (Durham: Duke University Press, 1972), esp. pp. 39–42.

Four types of criticism, all holistic, dominate explications of Hawthorne's fiction: allegorical, symbolic, ethical, and psychological. Of these, the ethical interpretation constitutes the center of critical concern, with each of the other three modes either building upon it or reacting against it. Allegorical criticism usually extracts a moral message from Hawthorne's discourse, while symbolic explications demonstrate how the author's ethics are more complex, more ambiguous than allegorical, one-to-one readings indicate. Taking a different tack, psychological criticism argues that moral messages (simple or complex) are not the point of Hawthorne's fiction at all; rather, morality serves only as the starting point, the subject matter, for Hawthorne's intense psychological investigations.[17] Despite these disagreements over the exact content and function of Hawthorne's ethics, all the critical approaches treat ethical interpretations as in some way central, either as a position to elaborate or as one to transcend.

17. These four holistic approaches are by no means mutually exclusive; and to be useful even as an informal classification of Hawthorne criticism, the category of ethical approaches must include religious and theological interpretations and the symbolic approach must include studies of image patterns and mythic structures. (For a good alternative categorization of holistic approaches to Hawthorne's fiction, see Kenneth Dauber, *Rediscovering Hawthorne* [Princeton: Princeton University Press, 1977], pp. 12–13.) Modern allegorical and symbolic readings of Hawthorne's work refer most often to the basic discussions in F. O. Matthiessen, *American Renaissance* (Oxford: Oxford University Press, 1941), and Charles Feidelson, Jr., *Symbolism and American Literature* (Chicago: University of Chicago Press, 1953). The major Hawthorne studies of the 1950s established the ethical-religious approach as dominant in Hawthorne criticism, combining that approach with studies of image patterns and symbolic structures: see Richard Harter Fogle, *Hawthorne's Fiction: The Light and the Dark* (Norman: University of Oklahoma Press, 1952); Hyatt H. Waggoner, *Hawthorne: A Critical Study* (Cambridge: Harvard University Press, 1955); and Roy R. Male, *Hawthorne's Tragic Vision* (Austin: University of Texas Press, 1957). In the 1960s Frederick Crews's controversial psychoanalytic interpretation rejected the earlier moralistic readings of Hawthorne's fiction—see *The Sins of the Fathers: Hawthorne's Psychological Themes* (New York: Oxford University Press, 1966). Nina Baym also proposed a secular interpretation to replace traditional theological readings in *The Shape of Hawthorne's Career* (Ithaca: Cornell University Press, 1976), a book that often employs a non-Freudian psychological approach. Edgar A. Dryden's recent phenomenological readings do not fit neatly into any of my four categories of Hawthorne criticism, but his *Nathaniel Hawthorne: The Poetics of Enchantment* (Ithaca: Cornell University Press, 1977) continues the tradition of holistic interpretation by arranging Hawthorne's writings around "a thematic self, a self that may be defined simply as the organizing principle or conceptual center of his work" (p. 11).

72

Most of these traditional approaches note how "the Unpardonable Sin" in Hawthorne's fiction serves as an index of the author's ethics, primarily his preoccupation with man's moral responsibility for his actions toward others.[18] However, traditional holistic criticism has never effectively demonstrated how Hawthorne develops an ethical concern in his fiction. Usually overlooked are Hawthorne's techniques for involving readers in the discovery *and experience* of his ethical position.[19] In contrast, a reader-response criticism, based on a temporal model, can easily make this rhetoric apparent by describing the series of activities forced on the reader by Hawthorne's discourse.

How Swift develops an ethical concern in his Fiction [handwritten annotation]

A Rhetoric of Entanglement

"Rappaccini's Daughter," one of Hawthorne's most thoroughly explicated tales, provides a good, compact example of the author's techniques of reader involvement. All of the major holistic approaches have been applied rigorously to the tale, yet no explication has successfully described Hawthorne's strategies of entanglement.[20] These strategies result in a series of

18. Actually, the term "Unpardonable Sin" marks the ethical approach of Hawthorne's *critics* as much as it reflects Hawthorne's own moral concerns. (For the notebook definition cited so often by critics, see Nathaniel Hawthorne, *The American Notebooks,* ed. Claude M. Simpson [Columbus: Ohio State University Press, 1972], p. 251.)

19. Cf. the enlightening discussions of Hawthorne and his contemporary audience in Baym, *The Shape of Hawthorne's Career,* passim; and the thematization of reading in Dryden, *Nathaniel Hawthorne,* pp. 111-42. Also, see Frank Kermode's comments: "in Hawthorne the reader's share is always a great one.... [Hawthorne's] texts, with all their varying, fading voices, their controlled lapses into possible inauthenticity, are meant as invitations to co-production on the part of the reader"—*The Classic: Literary Images of Permanence and Change* (New York: Viking, 1975), pp. 105, 113. Even more useful for my present purposes is a comment by Hawthorne himself, taken from one of his book reviews: "To be the prophet of Art requires almost as high a gift as to be a fulfiller of the prophecy. Mr. Simms has not this gift; he possesses nothing of the magic touch that should cause new intellectual and moral shapes to spring up in the reader's mind, peopling with varied life what had hitherto been a barren waste"—rev. of *Views and Reviews,* by W. G. Simms, *The Salem Advertiser,* 2 May 1846; rpt. in Randall Stewart, "Hawthorne's Contributions to *The Salem Advertiser,*" *American Literature,* 5 (1933-34), 332.

20. Holistic interpretations of "Rappaccini's Daughter" have been many, with the allegorical approach dominating. But, as J. Donald Crowley has recently

overlapping structures of response for the reader. Put most simply, the discourse begins with the presentation of an enigma that is slowly resolved while the text introduces two related plot conflicts; Hawthorne works out the conflicts as he simultaneously puts the reader through a test of his moral judgment.[21]

The reader encounters the first enigma of Hawthorne's text in its title: Who (and soon what) is Rappaccini's daughter?[22] The discourse introduces a mysterious garden into the narrative and specifically formulates a second enigma for the reader: What is the garden? (To whom does it belong?).[23] The reader soon re-

---

written, "There is clearly no evidence of an emerging consensus yet regarding the meaning of 'Rappaccini's Daughter'" ("Hawthorne," in *American Literary Scholarship: An Annual/1978,* ed. J. Albert Robbins [Durham: Duke University Press, 1980], p. 26). Nina Baym claims that the tale "is susceptible of a number of partial explanations but seems to evade any single wholly satisfactory reading. It offers itself as an allegory of faith, an allegory of science, and an allegory of sex all at once" (*The Shape of Hawthorne's Career,* p. 107). The two reading scenarios I propose below do not *necessarily* displace these allegorical explanations nor any other holistic interpretations that have been proposed for the tale. Rather, a description of the temporal response structure underlies (and the described reading experience precedes) all these past critical syntheses—especially allegorical ones, for the symbolic meanings given the characters are often based on the judgments made of those characters in the time-flow of reading. Of course, some of the previous holistic interpretations do provide evidence that supports certain claims about the experience of reading "Rappaccini's Daughter," and I will cite much of this evidence in the notes that follow.

21. "Rappaccini's Daughter" was originally published in the *United States Magazine and Democratic Review,* 15 (December 1844), 545–60, with a humorous introduction to the writings of "M. de l'Aubépine." The witty preface was left off when the tale was collected in *Mosses from an Old Manse* (New York: Wiley and Putnam, 1846), and then restored, with Hawthorne's permission, in the second edition of *Mosses* (Boston: Ticknor and Fields, 1854). All page citations given parenthetically in the text of this chapter refer to *Mosses from an Old Manse,* vol. X of the Centenary Edition of the Works of Nathaniel Hawthorne, ed. Fredson Bowers and J. Donald Crowley (Columbus: Ohio State University Press, 1974).

22. Giovanni later formulates this first enigma when he asks, "What is this being?—beautiful, shall I call her?—or inexpressibly terrible?" (p. 103). Various critics have focused on this enigma: for example, Jac Tharpe, *Nathaniel Hawthorne: Identity and Knowledge* (Carbondale: Southern Illinois University Press, 1967) entitled his chapter on the tale "Who is Beatrice?" (p. 81); Bernard McCabe noted that Beatrice is "a question of skillfully delayed revelation" ("Narrative Technique in 'Rappaccini's Daughter,'" *MLN,* 74 [1959], 214); and Morton L. Ross pointed out that "the narrator has induced the reader's initial participation in the mystery" of Beatrice ("What Happens in 'Rappaccini's Daughter,'" *American Literature,* 43 [1971], 343).

23. "Rappaccini's Daughter," p. 94. In the 1963 revised edition of his *Haw-*

ceives partial answers to these questions: the landlady tells Giovanni that the garden belongs to Rappaccini, whose daughter works as his helper. The landlady's further description of the garden functions as an equivocation (a misleading truth)[24]: the garden's plants are distilled "into medicines that are as potent as a charm" (p. 94); but these plants are not merely curative, the reader later discovers. Thus the discourse has given the reader a truth (the garden is used to produce medicinal herbs), but it has also misled him into thinking that the plants' strangeness consists only of their being magically therapeutic rather than at times fatally poisonous.

But the reader soon finds that Rappaccini treated the garden's most magnificent plant "as if all this beauty did but conceal a deadlier malice" (p. 96). This early, partial disclosure of the second enigma—What is the garden?—introduces a preoccupation the reader experiences throughout Hawthorne's tale: the problematic relation between appearance and reality. Early on, this preoccupation takes the form of worrying over enigmas—apparent mysteries with delayed but real solutions—but later it becomes first a psychological and then an ethical matter: actions disguise motives, motives reveal morality. Before these later concerns become the reader's, however, the enigmas must run their course.

A third enigma, combining the first two, is suggested in Giovanni's comparison of the garden's flowers to Rappaccini's daughter (p. 97): What exactly is the relation between the garden and Beatrice?[25] Following the analogy is the first in a succession of snares set by the discourse for the as yet innocent

---

thorne, Waggoner called attention to this second enigma when he asked, "What strange sort of garden is it that merits so much emphasis?" (p. 112).

24. An equivocation is a "double understanding" that both reveals a truth and misleads the reader simultaneously (Barthes, *S/Z,* p. 145).

25. In his review of *Mosses,* Henry F. Chorley provided the earliest recognition of Hawthorne's slow unfolding of this enigma: "Mr. Hawthorne leads us by imperceptible degrees into the fearful garden, full of its sumptuous blossoms—then insinuates the dark sympathy between the nature of the lady and her sisters, the death-flowers"—*Athenaeum,* 8 August 1846; rpt. in Seymour L. Gross, "Hawthorne and the London *Athenaeum,* 1834–1864," *Nathaniel Hawthorne Journal,* 3 (1973), 47.

reader.[26] The narrator claims that the comparison between the suspicious garden and the beautiful Beatrice must be a result of Giovanni's fancy "grown morbid" (p. 97). The narrator's claim and Giovanni's analogy initiate a structure of response that often recurs throughout the first half of the narrative: the discourse presents the reader with an observation (about Beatrice and the garden) and this observation is introduced or followed by a statement that seems to call it into question.[27] Something has to give here; either the reader learns to distrust the character's perceptions or he comes to suspect the narrator's undercutting statements.

Just before Giovanni observes that a drop of moisture from a garden flower kills a lizard, the narrator remarks, "But now, unless Giovanni's draught of wine had bewildered his senses, a singular incident occurred." And the character's observation is less conditionally called into question two sentences later, where the reader finds: "It appeared to Giovanni—but, at the distance from which he gazed, he could scarcely have seen anything so minute" as a drop falling upon a lizard (pp. 102–3). The reader encounters the same equivocating discourse again and again. "Here it could not be but that Giovanni Guasconti's eyes deceived him" when he "fancied" that he saw Beatrice's breath kill a winged insect (p. 103). And again: "it seemed to Giovanni . . . that his beautiful bouquet was already beginning to wither in her grasp." Followed immediately by: "It was an idle thought; there could be no possibility of distinguishing a faded flower from a fresh one at so great a distance" (p. 104). Which part of the discourse is the reader to believe?[28]

26. Barthes defines a snare as "a kind of deliberate evasion of the truth" (*S/Z*, p. 75). An equivocation, then, consists of a snare and a revelation.
27. As several critics have noted, this discourse strategy is a particular instance of Hawthorne's "device of multiple choice" (Matthiessen, p. 276) or "formula of alternative possibilities" (Yvor Winters, *Maule's Curse* [Norfolk, Conn.: New Directions, 1938], p. 18). However, to make this general observation does not really tell us much about how the use of this formula or device varies in each individual text; for it functions quite differently in the experiences of reading "The Birth-mark," "Young Goodman Brown," and *The Scarlet Letter.* In what follows I will try to pinpoint its exact effect in the response structure of "Rappaccini's Daughter."
28. If the reader's version of the text begins with the preface (see n. 21, above) he will find the facetious remark that "the ensuing tale is a translation of [M. de

The reader enters into this series of equivocations after having read the landlady's remark about "the strange flowers that grow in the garden" (p. 94), and he gathers along the way independent evidence that what *appears* to happen does indeed take place in the fictional world. Though Giovanni might be mistaken about a small lizard or tiny insect, it is less likely that he mistakes the gestures of Beatrice, who crosses herself immediately after the death of each creature, or of Rappaccini, who carefully avoids touching the plants. The structure of the reader's response, then, is not quite one of ambivalence between two equally weighted poles, character's observation and narrator's undercutting. More and more the reader comes to believe the observations, to trust what appears to happen. But this lesson is one the reader must work at, because the narrator seems so reliable in all other ways. Eventually, the reader tries to ignore the snares and to concentrate on the truth revealed by the character's observations. The solution to the enigmas, though delayed by equivocations, snares, and partial answers, slowly emerges for the reader.

Certainly, the *method* for reaching the solution becomes clear: read the observations closely and trust appearances. Beatrice articulates this method when she says to Giovanni, "Believe nothing of me save what you see with your own eyes" (p. 111). Though she makes this statement only in reply to the "idle rumors" about her skill in medicine, Giovanni (and the reader) turn the remark into a commentary upon all that has gone before. When Giovanni places Beatrice's statement in this context— "And must I believe all that I have seen with my own eyes?"—her

l'Aubépine's] '*Beatrice; ou la Belle Empoisonneuse,*' recently published in '*La Revue Anti-Aristocratique*'" (p. 93). The inclusion of this fake French title in the preface does not short-circuit the reading experience I am describing. Though the title does appear to be a premature (though still partial) disclosure of the enigmas, its significance is evident only in retrospect. For the reader coming to the story for the first time, the information in the French title still needs to be interpreted; its meaning cannot be understood immediately. In the beginning the reader does not yet know who Beatrice is or what her exact relation to the garden could be; nor does he know whether "empoisonneuse" should be taken literally ("one who poisons") or figuratively ("one who corrupts morals"). Furthermore, even after Giovanni's problematic observations, the remembered French title could still be interpreted ironically as referring to a "fancied," not a real phenomenon.

next response seems to be a misleading snare: "Forget whatever you may have fancied in regard to me" (p. 112). Here, the discourse again asks the reader to disregard Giovanni's "fancied" observations about Beatrice and the garden. Beatrice then generalizes the earlier statement about beauty of appearance disguising real malice: "If true to the outward senses, still it may be false in its essence." This remark is equivocating for the reader because it would be a *snare* if Beatrice is referring to outward evidence of poison, since she would then be misleading Giovanni by suggesting that, though it may seem that she is poisonous, she is really not; and it would be the *truth* if she is referring to the outward reality of her being poisonous, since she would then be saying that, though she is physically poisonous, she is not inwardly "poisonous" or evil.

To recapitulate: The opposition between appearance and reality is not simply a theme that hovers over the narrative giving it holistic coherence;[29] rather it is an ambivalence that is elaborated in the reader's experience, through a temporal structure of response provided by the text. This structure consists of the reader's entanglement in an enigma whose solution is delayed through a series of equivocating interpretations that finally result in a partial disclosure. The reader learns to avoid the snares (the narrator's undercutting of true observations) and to trust in appearances, what the character sees. Beatrice's equivocating statement about essential truth marks the last time the enigmas retain all of their previous force as mysteries.

The discourse resolves the first enigmas when Beatrice stops Giovanni from touching the plant in the garden: "'Touch it not!' exclaimed she, in a voice of agony. 'Not for thy life! It is fatal!'" (p. 114). No matter how the reader interpreted her ambiguous remark about essence and outward appearance (as a lie, an

29. For the theme of appearance vs. reality treated holistically in Hawthorne criticism, see Herman Melville, "Hawthorne and His Mosses," *Literary World,* 17 and 24 August 1850, rpt. in Harrison Hayford and Hershel Parker, ed., *Moby-Dick* (New York: Norton, 1967), pp. 535–551; also see Matthiessen, p. 258; Fogle, p. 11; and Menno M. Friesen, "The Mask in Nathaniel Hawthorne's Fiction," Ph.D. diss., University of Denver, 1964. Cf. Dryden, p. 126: "the emphasis in the prefaces on the relation between the hidden and the revealed in Hawthorne's work creates a suspicious, probing reader" who attempts to separate the essential from the inessential.

equivocation, or something entirely different), Beatrice's action provides the evidence the reader requires: the garden must be poisonous, and since Beatrice can tend the plants with no danger to her person, she must have immunity. Some readers may suspect that this too is only a partial disclosure of the enigmas. And the next paragraph confirms these suspicions when it makes a full disclosure. Giovanni notices the "burning and tingling" prints of four fingers on the hand Beatrice had grasped to prevent him from touching the plant. Both the garden *and* Beatrice must be poisonous. Giovanni does not make the connection— and in effect sets a snare for himself when he wonders "what evil thing had stung him." He ignores the resolution of the enigmas, while the reader fully grasps it for the first time.[30] Later, Baglioni confirms this revelation by telling Giovanni and the reader that Rappaccini has intentionally raised his daughter to be as poisonous as his garden.

For two thirds of the story, the reader has participated in the hermeneutic code. The tale begins with the reader's recognition of a mystery and his desire for its solution; the discourse poses a question and the reader expects and eventually finds the answer. With the enigmas solved, desire fulfilled, the reader's participation in the hermeneutic code ends. A proairetic code dominates the rest of the narrative: in traditional terms, the tale sets up a conventional conflict and the actions in the narrative move toward resolving it.[31] The reader recognizes two conflicts that

30. Commentators have ignored the implicit criticism of Giovanni's self-deception here, an oversight caused by the critics' exclusive focus on when the *character* learns the truth, not when the *reader* does.

31. The proairetic code is the code of actions arranged in a sequence and named. The usual paradigm for these actions "is something like *begin/end, continue/stop*" (Barthes, *S/Z*, p. 51). I extend these action sequences into the conventional plot conflicts I will name. The hermeneutic and proairetic codes are the only two of Barthes's formal codes that reflect the temporal dimension of literature. Unlike the other three codes he discusses (symbolic, referential, thematic), the hermeneutic and proairetic impose their terms (enigma/solution, conflict/resolution) in "an irreversible order" within the constraints of time (*S/Z*, p. 30). The two codes are simultaneously internal and external to the text, with the reader actively participating in both codes: in the hermeneutic he must search out the delayed answer to the enigma, and in the proairetic he must recognize ("name") the text's sequence of actions as a specific plot conflict in order for the resolution to have significance (as Barthes writes, "the proairetic

overlap with the question-delay-answer sequence of the enigmas: the thwarted affair of the young lovers and the rivalry
between the old doctors, Rappaccini and Baglioni.[32] These conflicts are intertwined since the two men of science are intensely
concerned over the outcome of the love affair between Rappaccini's daughter, Beatrice, and Giovanni, the son of Baglioni's old
friend. Baglioni gives Giovanni a vial to cure Beatrice of her
physical poison and to thwart Rappaccini's plan to have
Giovanni join Beatrice by making him poisonous. But the cure
turns out to be worse than the disease, and Beatrice dies. Both
conflicts are resolved in the final line of the discourse. Beatrice's
death signals the end of the love relation and a personal triumph
for Baglioni over Rappaccini. A simple conflict and resolution
structure. Or so it seems. But the discourse has sometimes
cautioned against such obvious truths: "There is something
truer and more real, than what we can see with the eyes, and
touch with the finger" (p. 120). The reader's involvement with
appearance and reality in the discourse is indeed more complex
than what I have so far described.

The Reader's Trial

The hermeneutic and proairetic codes constitute the text of
enigma and conflict, and the reader's participation in these
codes is one layer of response to the tale. But the text of enigma
and conflict also initiates and disguises a second text, which challenges the reader's judgment. The two texts and the experiences
they provide are not completely independent of each other in
the discourse. The first text initiates the second by testing the

---

sequence is never more than the result of an artifice of reading" and "the sequence exists when and because it can be given a name" [*S/Z,* p. 19]). My description of the "location" of these two codes in and out of the text can be contrasted
with the analysis in Ruth V. Gross, "Rich Text/Poor Text: A Kafkan Confusion,"
PMLA, 95 (1980), 168. On Barthes's concept of plot in reading, see Jonathan
Culler, "Defining Narrative Units," in *Style and Structure in Literature,* ed. Roger
Fowler (Ithaca: Cornell University Press, 1975), pp. 134–38.

32. Cf. one of many stories Kenneth Dauber (p. 33) identifies in "Rappaccini's
Daughter": it is "a star-crossed lovers' tale" in which "a positive Giovanni and a
positive Beatrice are kept apart by the rivalries of their respective negative el-
ders."

reader's judgment of narrative facts, and then it distracts the reader—a distraction that becomes part of the reader's trial—as the discourse delays the resolution of the enigmas and conflicts. In fact, the first text sets a trap for the reader: by suggesting that he trust appearances in solving the enigmas, it encourages him to adopt an interpretive habit that is inappropriate for the text of judgment, a text in which the reader must constantly go beyond appearances to pass its trial of his discernment.

The reader's participation in the conventional hermeneutic and proairetic codes *could* proceed with no realization that his judgment is being tested, resulting in his failure of that test. This reading scenario begins with solving enigmas and then moves to tracing the traditional plots of doomed lovers and competing professionals, plots that are resolved by the death of Beatrice.[33] Baglioni's final accusation marks the climax of the conflict plots and ends the story with an attribution of responsibility for Beatrice's death: "'Rappaccini! Rappaccini! And is *this* the upshot of your experiment?'" The reader's experience of the conflict plots concludes with his simply noting this narrow assignment of guilt.[34] This final sentence in the discourse, however, also triggers the climax of another "plot," the test of the reader's moral judgment: Who is really responsible for Beatrice's death?

33. The Public Broadcasting Service's film adaptation of "Rappaccini's Daughter" (in its 1980 American Short Stories Series) was an interpretation that re-presented this first reading scenario. It excluded almost all of the trial of the reader's judgment and thus did not encourage the viewer to evaluate either Giovanni or Baglioni. Significantly, the PBS version even left out Baglioni's accusation against Rappaccini in the original conclusion. Instead, Beatrice's final words to Giovanni end the film: "Oh, was there not, from the first, more poison in thy nature than in mine?" This vestige of the reader's trial takes on a different meaning in its new context as it tends to emphasize Beatrice's innocence rather than Giovanni's culpability.

34. Before the 1950s, most readers who gave evidence of their responses in their criticism seem to have agreed with Baglioni's judgment. The earliest recorded judgment was that by Charles Wilkins Webber, who referred to Rappaccini's "cold, intellectual diabolicism"—in "Hawthorne," *American Whig Review*, 4 (September 1846), rpt. Crowley, *Hawthorne: The Critical Heritage*, p. 134. Typical of the judgments during the next hundred years was Randall Stewart's statement that Rappaccini is "a heartless monster who ... sacrifices his daughter in an experiment to determine the effect of poisonous plants on the human body"— *Nathaniel Hawthorne: A Biography* (New Haven: Yale University Press, 1948), pp. 248–49.

Hawthorne has carefully prepared the reader to answer this question through a second layer of response provided by the discourse.[35]

In this second reading scenario, the reader begins by judging the physical facts and the narrator's reliability regarding those facts. This early test of judgment involves the enigmas and their delayed resolution, as described above. The function of the narrator's misleading comments in this second layer of response will now help to restore his reliability, called into question in the first reading scenario. The narrator's snares question, rather than contradict, the character's observations. The narrator's "under-cutting" remarks do not in fact say that the observed events did not or could not happen, though the remarks' *effect* on the reader does pressure him toward making that judgment for himself, thus providing a snare that he must learn to avoid in order to solve the enigmas. This misleading effect delays the answers to the opening enigmas. The first function of the narrator's undercutting comments, then, is to prolong the narrative; and this produces an open space for the test of the reader's judgmental powers. The second function is to begin filling that space by forcing the reader to judge which of the sources of

35. These two reading scenarios assume a distinction among readers comparable to one Melville made between the "superficial skimmer of pages" and the "eagle-eyed reader" (see Melville, "Hawthorne and His Mosses," p. 549). For example, Melville began *Pierre* in the hope that he could provide two different reading experiences: a sensationalist gothic romance for the popular audience and a profound psychological and philosophical drama for the eagle-eyed reader. The two planned reading scenarios were almost completely independent of each other in their main features. See Hershel Parker, "Herman Melville," in *The Norton Anthology of American Literature,* ed. Ronald Gottesman et al. (New York: Norton, 1979), I, 2039, and Leon Howard, "Historical Note," in *Pierre,* ed. Harrison Hayford, Hershel Parker, and G. Thomas Tanselle (Evanston and Chicago: Northwestern University Press and The Newberry Library, 1971), p. 372. A similar independent status is true for the reading scenarios Frank Kermode describes based on his distinction between a general public interested only in sequence and message and a professional group of readers who find secrets advertised and concealed by the text—"Secrets and Narrative Sequence," *Critical Inquiry,* 7 (1980), 83–101. In contrast, the two reading scenarios I am describing are not independent of each other. They interpenetrate, as the participation in the hermeneutic code during the first scenario becomes the judgment of external facts in the second. The first scenario could take place without the second occurring, but the second depends on part of the first to get started. Thus, the two scenarios do not so much clash as overlap.

information to trust. That is, by making the communication of even simple external facts problematic, the narrator's misleading remarks cause the reader to be wary of the discourse and its story, putting him on notice that he must exercise his powers of judgment from the beginning. The issue of judgment is actually inscribed in the text quite early, though in disguised form (during one of the narrator's snares for the reader): "But there is an influence in the light of morning that tends to rectify whatever errors of fancy, *or even of judgment,* we may have incurred during the sun's decline" (p. 98, emphasis added).

Even before the enigmas are finally solved and the reader's attention shifts from the hermeneutic to the proairetic code, a more important shift should begin—the reader should move from a judgment of external facts to a discernment of internal motivation. Why are the characters doing what they are doing? Why, for example, does Baglioni really condemn Rappaccini's science? Again, the discourse encourages the reader's judgment by inscribing it explicitly in the text: regarding Baglioni's vested interests, the narrator mentions the "professional warfare" between the two doctors, which "if the reader be inclined to judge for himself, we refer him to certain black-letter tracts on both sides, preserved in the medical department of the University of Padua" (p. 100). To judge for oneself—this self-reliance is the ultimate goal in the test of the reader's discernment.[36]

At this moment in the structure of response, the discourse encourages the reader to examine the motivation of actions toward others. Baglioni constantly points out Rappaccini's motives and designs, while the narrator continually emphasizes Giovanni's "depth" of love and Beatrice's innocence as motives for their acts. From the judgment of external facts and internal motivation, the discourse pressures the reader to move toward a judgment of moral responsibility. The points at which the discourse

---

36. This judging "for oneself" must not be misunderstood as an individual reader's decision to make any choice he wants. Rather the "self-reliance" referred to here is that of a self formed by the discourse. This self is an implied reader whose role is to make judgments, judgments that the text prepares the reader to make before it gives him the opportunity to make them. Failing the test at the end of "Rappaccini's Daughter" is a failure to take on the role of the tale's implied reader—a point to be discussed shortly.

applies this pressure provide moments in the response structure that prepare the reader to answer the question suggested by the final line: Who is really responsible for Beatrice's death?

The narrator warns the reader in the first paragraph that Giovanni has "the tendency to heart-break natural to a young man for the first time out of his native sphere." The discourse amplifies this hint of shallowness a bit later in the story, when the narrator describes Giovanni's infatuation with Beatrice: "Guasconti had not a deep heart—or at all events, its depths were not sounded now—but he had a quick fancy, and an ardent southern temperament, which rose every instant to a higher fever-pitch" (p. 105). Soon the reader discovers that Giovanni questions his own motivation along these same lines (though only for a moment): "there came across him a sudden doubt, whether this intense interest on his part were not delusory . . . whether it were not merely the fantasy of a young man's brain, only slightly, or not at all, connected with his heart!" (p. 109). The narrator later suggests that Giovanni possesses "that cunning *semblance* of love which flourishes in the imagination, but strikes no depth of root into the heart" (p. 115, emphasis added). In this and the following judgment of Giovanni's motives, we again find that play on the appearance/reality opposition that characterizes the whole discourse: "By all appreciable signs, they loved" (p. 115). The reader, prepared by the cumulative effect of the questions about Giovanni's motives, automatically translates this sentence into another suggestion that Giovanni only *appears* to love but is really incapable of such depth of feeling.

All that seems good in the relationship is actually a measure of Beatrice's nature, not Giovanni's. The narrator tells the reader that Giovanni's confidence in Beatrice results from "the necessary force of her high attributes" rather than "any deep and generous faith, on his part" (p. 120). Here the focus of the discourse begins shifting from a neutral description of motives to a moral judgment of character. The tale quickly provides the reader with a more damaging evaluation of Giovanni. About to test for himself whether Beatrice is poisonous, "Giovanni failed not to look at his figure in the mirror; a vanity to be expected in a beautiful young man, yet, as displaying itself at that troubled and feverish moment, the token of a certain shallowness of feeling and insincerity of character" (p. 121). Then, after becoming convinced of her poisonous physical nature, Giovanni shows no trust in Beatrice and forgets all the evidence of her innocent and pure spiritual nature. The narrator gives the reader a clear condemnation of Giovanni in one more variation on the appearance/reality opposition: Giovanni has "recollections which, had Giovanni known how to estimate them, would have assured him that all this ugly mystery was but an earthly illusion, and that, whatever mist of evil might seem to have gathered over her, the real Beatrice was a heavenly angel." But Giovanni was "incapable ... of such high faith" (p. 122). Beatrice bestows the final judgment (before the reader's) when she says to Giovanni: "Oh, was there not, from the first, more poison in thy nature than in mine?" (p. 127).

The discourse provides this build-up of judgments in order to prepare the reader for the concluding sentence. By this final moment in the structure of response, the reader has learned that Giovanni believes and doubts, acts and does not act, for all the wrong reasons. He is blind to Beatrice's physical poison because of his delusory infatuation, and later the shallowness of these same feelings makes him blind to her true spiritual goodness. Shallowness, vanity, insensitivity, selfishness—these characteristics of Giovanni have been brought out in the text of judgment. When the reader responds to the question posed by the last sentence of the discourse—who is really responsible for Beatrice's death?—he should include Giovanni Guasconti in his answer.[37]

Stung by Giovanni's lack of trust, Beatrice drinks the "antidote," not caring about the consequences. But the vial originates with Baglioni, and the discourse encourages the reader to examine the doctor's role in Beatrice's death just as it has Giovanni's.

---

37. In "Hawthorne's 'Rappaccini's Daughter,'" *Nineteenth-Century Fiction*, 7 (1952), 217–19, Frederick L. Gwynn appears to be the first to note the negative judgments of Giovanni. In "The Heart, the Head, and 'Rappaccini's Daughter,'" *New England Quarterly*, 27 (1954), Sherwood R. Price claimed that "Giovanni must share with Rappaccini the responsibility for the tragedy" of Beatrice's death (p. 402); Price acknowledged that some readers entirely miss the build-up of judgments against Giovanni when he noted that Beatrice's final words about Giovanni's more "poisonous" nature "come as something of a shock" to "a reader who has perhaps sympathized with Giovanni" (p. 400).

Again the response structure consists of a series of negative judgments concerning the character's motives. This series of negations is much less complex (and interesting) than the build-up of judgments against Giovanni, so I will point out only two moments in the time-flow of reading that are typical of the reader's prestructured reaction to Baglioni.

In Giovanni's first encounter with Baglioni, the old doctor demonstrates a thoughtful concern for the student, and the reader finds the doctor amiable enough. But after reading Baglioni's condemnation of Rappaccini as one who "cares infinitely more for science than for mankind" (p. 99), the reader moves through a passage that begins the reversal in his opinion of Baglioni. Giovanni admits that Rappaccini's coldness toward mankind is indeed awful, but he asks, "'And yet, worshipful Professor, is it not a noble spirit? Are there many men capable of so spiritual a love of science?'" Baglioni responds, "'God forbid,'" confirming the reader's positive opinion of the speaker. But after an interruption that gives the reader a moment to rest in this positive judgment—"answered the Professor, somewhat testily"—Baglioni continues, "'at least, unless they take sounder views of the healing art than those adopted by Rappaccini. It is his theory, that all medicinal virtues are comprised within those substances which we term vegetable poisons'" (p. 100). In this passage, Baglioni qualifies his judgment of Rappaccini's morality with a more *self-revealing* judgment of Rappaccini's science. By the end of the monologue the reader discovers that Baglioni's objections to Rappaccini are based less on a concerned feeling for mankind than on a cold intellectual disagreement and professional jealousy. In the course of a few lines, the discourse has moved the reader from a positive judgment, in which he was allowed or even encouraged to rest, to a negative judgment of Baglioni. Soon the reader discovers more emphatic evidence of Baglioni's self-centeredness and pride, of which this reversal passage is but a symptom.[38] The conclusion of the story evokes the reader's most damning judgments of Rappaccini's rival. As he watches Beatrice's death, a death he helped cause, Baglioni is jealous and insensitive enough to speak the final line "*in a tone of*

38. See, for example, "Rappaccini's Daughter," pp. 101 and 108.

86

triumph mixed with horror" (p. 128, emphasis added). Here and at the very end, the discourse allows the reader to pass judgment by holding back its own.[39]

The end of the discourse, then, serves as the final test of the reader's discernment, a test the reader passes if he rejects Baglioni's narrow attribution of guilt to Rappaccini alone and replaces it with a judgment that all three male characters are morally responsible for the death of an innocent: the cause of Beatrice's death was not only Rappaccini's "unpardonable sin" but also Baglioni's prideful jealousy and Giovanni's shallow lack of trust.[40] This judgment is more than a pious lesson the reader can take away from the text; it is the *experience* of an ethical position. There is no moral "done up neatly, and condensed into the final sentence," only a judgment withheld by the text and required of the reader.[41]

39. Charles E. Eisinger was one of the first readers to record a negative judgment of Baglioni, but he failed to condemn the doctor's actions: "Hawthorne does not admire Baglioni's mean spirit and factitious joviality, but he gives the triumph to this man in the end because Baglioni recognizes human limitations" unlike Rappaccini ("Hawthorne as Champion of the Middle Way," *New England Quarterly*, 27 [1954], 49). Cf. Sydney P. Moss's claim that "if there is a diabolic character in the story, it is Baglioni" ("A Reading of 'Rappaccini's Daughter,'" *Studies in Short Fiction*, 2 [1965], 150). Some readers have reacted so strongly against Baglioni that they claim the doctor intentionally tries to murder Beatrice; see Robert L. Gale, "Rappaccini's Baglioni," *Studi Americani*, 9 (1963), 83–87.

40. Readers whose critical analyses indicate that they judged all three male characters to be responsible for Beatrice's death include: William Rossky, "Rappaccini's Garden or the Murder of Innocence," *ESQ*, No. 19 (1960), pp. 98–100; Norman A. Anderson, "'Rappaccini's Daughter': A Keatsian Analogue?" *PMLA*, 83 (1968), 271–83; M. D. Uroff, "The Doctors in 'Rappaccini's Daughter,'" *Nineteenth-Century Fiction*, 27 (1972), 70; and Hershel Parker, "Introduction" to his edition of *Shorter Works of Hawthorne and Melville* (Columbus, O.: Charles E. Merrill, 1972), p. 3.

41. The quoted phrase is from Hawthorne's "Wakefield"; see *Twice-told Tales*, vol. IX of the Centenary Edition of the Works of Nathaniel Hawthorne, ed. Fredson Bowers and J. Donald Crowley (Columbus: Ohio State University Press, 1974), p. 131. I believe that Richard Fogle is partially correct when he argues that Hawthorne does make moral judgments in his fiction, "but he permits the reader a choice." My description of the reader's experience shows exactly how influenced that "choice" is at the end of reading "Rappaccini's Daughter." See Fogle, "Nathaniel Hawthorne: Introduction," in *Eight American Writers: An Anthology of American Literature*, ed. Norman Foerster and Robert P. Falk (New York: Norton, 1963), p. 591. And cf. James G. Janssen, "Impaled Butterflies and the Misleading Moral in Hawthorne's Short Works," *Nathaniel Hawthorne Journal*, 6 (1976), 269–75.

The text of judgment makes demands of the reader in this concluding passage, and the text's cumulative effect *forms* him as well. That is, the discourse requires a reader sensitive to various kinds of moral issues, and it encourages this sensitivity through the series of judgments it calls upon the reader to make. Ultimately, the implied reader of "Rappaccini's Daughter" is an ethical reader, one who must be concerned about moral responsibility, one capable of making the judgment at the conclusion of the narrative. But the reader arrives at this point only by passing through a succession of different concerns pressed on him by the discourse. From a worrying over external facts, the discourse moves the reader to judge first internal motivation and then moral responsibility.

The discourse marks this movement by the three references to appearance and reality I have already quoted. Distributed throughout the text, these very similar statements take on different shapes for the reader depending on where they are encountered in the structure of response. Again, the relation of appearance to reality is not a theme functioning holistically to give the text meaning; rather it is a meaning experienced sequentially in the time-flow of reading. "As if all this beauty did but conceal a deadlier malice" (p. 96) is a partial disclosure for the reader involved in a search for external facts, the solution to the enigma "What is the garden?" The second formulation, Beatrice's remark, "If true to the outward senses, still it may be false in its essence" (p. 112), occurs when the reader's attention begins to shift from the need to discover external facts to the desire to discern internal motives and morals. What appeared as an equivocation in the hermeneutic code can now be seen as straightforward advice to a reader concerned with psychology and ethics. It is advice that is reiterated by antithesis through the example of Giovanni, who totally disregards it: for Giovanni, evidence of poison in Beatrice would always serve as proof "of a frightful peculiarity in her physical and moral system" (p. 114). The reader finds the third formulation, "there is something truer and more real, than what we can see with the eyes, and touch with the finger" (p. 120), when the discourse is about to require the final judgment of moral responsibility. Again Giovanni serves as a contrasting example for the reader:

Giovanni believes that if Beatrice does have "those dreadful peculiarities in her physical nature," they "could not be supposed
to exist without some corresponding monstrosity of soul" (p.
120).

The implied reader finds his mirror image in Giovanni. Both
"read" Rappaccini's daughter; one reads the whole discourse,
the other misreads a character within that discourse. Giovanni
never learns the reader's hard-earned lesson: appearances *betray*
the truth, both in the sense of revealing, giving it away, and in
the sense of distorting, keeping it disguised. The reader must
judge how appearances function in any particular situation. It is
these judgmental powers that Giovanni lacks and that the discourse has attempted to bring out in its reader again and again.
Giovanni stands as the antithesis of the discerning, ethical reader
that Hawthorne has gone great lengths to create.[42]

42. Throughout this book I follow the traditional convention of using the
masculine pronoun to refer to all readers. Of course, as feminist criticism has
shown, this convention is not politically innocent. But, at least in this chapter, its
use turns out to be quite accurate. For in examining the reader's experience of
"Rappaccini's Daughter," I have actually been talking only about the judgments
made by male readers and by female readers who have assumed the male
perspective. It is true that any reader with literary competence can understand
Hawthorne's intention to elicit negative judgments toward the male characters in
the way I have described. But it is *not* true that all readers must agree with
Hawthorne's judgments once they are understood. In fact, a feminist reader
("the resisting reader," to use Judith Fetterley's term) could just as easily condemn
Beatrice for allowing herself to be a victim. A more likely move by the resisting
reader would be to hold Hawthorne himself responsible, for it is the author who
perpetuates through his fiction the patriarchal system in which women are often
victims. He does this by presenting Beatrice as passive and by forcing his readers
(male and female) to *accept* her passivity as they condemn the male characters.
From this perspective, Hawthorne has deviously concealed the *fact* of female
passivity by directing the reader's attention to the external causes of her victim-
age. Ironically, then, what appears to be profeminist about my reader-response
interpretation (condemnation of the males) is actually antifeminist in that it
assumes (and thus encourages) acceptance of a passive female role which makes
the male characters' actions and the male readers' judgments possible. Not surprisingly, I cannot accept this characterization of my analysis. I would suggest
instead that the reading experience I describe underlies feminist readings in the
same way it precedes traditional holistic interpretations. That is, every feminist
and nonfeminist approach must posit some kind of reading experience upon
which to base its interpretation. Only after a reader-response description is completed or assumed can a feminist critique begin. The (explicit or assumed) *description* cannot be antifeminist; only the further use (or nonuse) of it can be.
Actually, a reader-response approach lends itself especially well to the kind of

This analysis of "Rappaccini's Daughter" exemplifies a reader-response criticism based on a temporal reading model. Similar reader-oriented analyses should be attempted with other American texts to correct the imbalance produced by spatial, holistic explications which devalue the author's strategies of temporal reader engagement.[43] Criticism based on a temporal model interprets American fiction by bringing to the foreground the author's rhetoric of entanglement, a rhetoric resulting in sequential responses from the reader. Again, this kind of criticism does not reject traditional holistic interpretation; it simply takes the final interpretive synthesis as a part of a response structure that gives value to temporal intentions and effects. Holistic criticism includes only this final synthesis, while reader-response criticism includes this synthesis and all the discourse strategies and reading activities leading up to it. Reader-response criticism thus presents a more comprehensive picture of both the author's techniques and the reader's experience.

A reading model is incomplete, however, if it includes only a description of the sequential activities of reading. It must also provide an account of what constrains these activities. The question is deceptively simple: At any moment in the temporal structure of response, what ensures that the reader will have the reactions intended by the author? The temporal aspect of reading suggests the first answer to this question: the cumulative effects of the text put pressure on the reader to react to later

---

project feminist critics are engaged in—see Judith Fetterly, *The Resisting Reader: A Feminist Approach to American Fiction* (Bloomington: Indiana University Press, 1978), and the special feminist criticism issue of *Reader*, No. 8 (1980). For Hawthorne's treatment of women in his fiction, see Nina Baym, "Hawthorne's Women: The Tyranny of Social Myths," *Centennial Review*, 15 (1971), 250–72.

43. Some initial steps in the right reader-oriented direction can be found in Liane Norman, "Bartleby and the Reader," *New England Quarterly*, 44 (1971), 22–39; Iser, *The Implied Reader*, pp. 136–52, on Faulkner's *Sound and the Fury;* Warwick Wadlington, "Godly Gamesomeness: Self-taste in *Moby-Dick*," in his *The Confidence Game in American Literature* (Princeton: Princeton University Press, 1975), pp. 73–103; Steven Mailloux, "Learning to Read: Interpretation and Reader-Response Criticism," *Studies in the Literary Imagination*, 12, No. 1 (1979), 96–99, on *Moby-Dick;* Perry, "Literary Dynamics," pp. 62–64, 311–54, on Faulkner's "A Rose for Emily"; and George L. Dillon, *Language Processing and the Reading of Literature* (Bloomington: Indiana University Press, 1978), pp. 129–81, passim, on the effects of Faulkner's and James's sentence structures.

passages in particular ways. For instance, at the end of "Rappaccini's Daughter," Hawthorne encourages the reader to condemn
the male characters through the cumulative effect of the judgments preparing the reader for this final test. But how does the
reader recognize the earlier judgments? Again, still earlier passages set the reader up to make discernments (searching for
solutions to enigmas and considering characters' motives). This
regress of preparatory effects leads, however, to an apparent
dead end at the story's beginning; in fact, there are many interpretations required of the reader that have no preparation
earlier in the discourse. Obviously, the reader must come to the
text with some basic reading abilities and must use them
throughout his reading experience. As many recent commentators have pointed out, the reader cannot be the virtual tabula
rasa that objectivist criticism sometimes assumed. Rather, he
comes to the text with a complex literary competence, what Culler describes as a set of shared reading conventions. The author
employs these conventions, linguistic and literary, to "control"
the reader's response; and the reader uses these conventions to
make the sequential interpretations required by the discourse.

What we have, then, are two dimensions of reading that interact to constrain response at any particular moment in the time-
flow of reading. There is a diachronic dimension that includes
the temporal structure of response; this diachronic aspect focuses critical attention on the sequence of reading activities and
on their cumulative effects on the reader. A second dimension
is synchronic, atemporal; it freezes the diachronic process and
focuses attention on the communicative constraints at any one
moment of that process. These constraints are the reading conventions used by the author to affect his reader. In this chapter I
have emphasized the diachronic dimension of reading in my
analysis of "Rappaccini's Daughter"; in the rest of this study, I
will focus primarily on the synchronic dimension. But in reading
and criticism these two dimensions cannot be separated. Both
are necessary for understanding the reading process and must
be employed in a reader-response approach to literature.

The convention-based (synchronic) aspect of reading is a
rather complex affair. We can best come at this dimension of the
reader's response from the other end, authorial intention. In

order to focus on the intention-convention network in which the temporal reading process is embedded, I will now turn from the role of the reader in literary criticism to his role in textual scholarship.

CHAPTER FOUR

Textual Scholarship and "Author's Final Intention"

To revise is to see, or to look over, again—which means in the case of a written thing neither more nor less than to re-read it.

—Henry James, Preface to the New York Edition of *The Golden Bowl*

Textual editing does not give us the book to read; rather, reading gives us the book to edit.

—Guy Nishida

Authorial intention has taken a beating in modern literary criticism. First, American New Critics condemned the Intentional Fallacy, with W. K. Wimsatt and Monroe Beardsley mounting the most influential attack: "The design or intention of the author is neither available nor desirable as a standard for judging either the meaning or the value of a work of literary art."[1] More recently, structuralists have proclaimed "the death of the author," arguing that "it is language which speaks, not the author."[2] Alongside such attacks, there also appeared defenses of authorial intent. In literary theory, E. D. Hirsch made the most notable argument for the interpretive role of intention,

1. See W. K. Wimsatt, Jr. and M. C. Beardsley, "The Intentional Fallacy," *Sewanee Review*, 54 (1946), 468-88. The quotation here is taken from W. K. Wimsatt, "Genesis: A Fallacy Revisited," in *The Disciplines of Criticism*, ed. Peter Demetz, Thomas Greene, and Lowry Nelson, Jr. (New Haven: Yale University Press, 1968), p. 222.

2. Roland Barthes, "The Death of the Author," in his *Image/Music/Text*, ed. and trans. Stephen Heath (New York: Hill and Wang, 1977), p. 143. See also Michel Foucault, "What Is an Author?" in *Language, Counter-Memory, Practice*, ed. Donald F. Bouchard, trans. Donald F. Bouchard and Sherry Simon (Ithaca: Cornell University Press, 1977), pp. 113-38.

and in practical analyses even intrinsic critics often referred to intended meaning.[3] Today, the debate continues over the relevance of authorial intention to literary interpretation.[4] To discuss the interrelations among intention, response, and convention, I therefore propose to shift the focus from literary criticism to textual scholarship, where in its American practice the centrality of intention is considerably more secure.[5]

This chapter will temporarily submerge the issue of reader response only so that I can bring it back in a context including a developed notion of authorial intention. I will first discuss the different kinds of intention relevant to editing and then demonstrate how reader-response criticism and theory can contribute to the development of editing's central concept, "author's final intention." In the course of this discussion, I will present a preliminary account of communicative conventions and their relationship to authorial intention and reader response.

Inferred Intention

In a survey of American literary scholarship at mid-century, René Wellek observed that the bibliographical methods developed in England by W. W. Greg had not caught on widely in America.[6] Fifteen years later, however, Greg's copy-text theory formed the basis of the editorial principles of the Center for Editions of American Authors, principles that soon became the dominant force in American textual editing.[7] The goal of Greg's

3. For Hirsch's counterattacks on anti-intentionalist criticism and theory, see his *Validity in Interpretation* (New Haven: Yale University Press, 1967) and *The Aims of Interpretation* (Chicago: University of Chicago Press, 1976).

4. See, for example, David Newton-De Molina, ed., *On Literary Intention* (Edinburgh: Edinburgh University Press, 1976); K. K. Ruthven, *Critical Assumptions* (Cambridge: Cambridge University Press, 1979), pp. 135–48; and P. D. Juhl, *Interpretation: An Essay in the Philosophy of Literary Criticism* (Princeton: Princeton University Press, 1980).

5. Though even here the role of intention has been questioned—see Morse Peckham, "Reflections on the Foundations of Modern Editing," *Proof*, 1 (1971), 122–55, esp. n. 18.

6. René Wellek, "Literary Scholarship," in *American Scholarship in the Twentieth Century*, ed. Merle Curti (Cambridge: Harvard University Press, 1953), p. 128.

7. The CEAA was founded in 1963 to promote the production of new,

theory is to establish the text intended by the author. The notion of an author's *final* intention was implicit in certain sections of Greg's classic article, "The Rationale of Copy-Text." At one point Greg says that if an editor determines that a "later reading is one that the author can reasonably be supposed to have substituted for the former" then the editor should accept this later reading into the text.[8] Fredson Bowers championed Greg's theory in America (especially within the CEAA), and he expanded on some of its basic principles. Bowers saw the editor's basic task as providing a text that would "represent the nearest approximation in every respect of the author's final intentions." Later, Bowers referred to "final intention texts arrived at by eclectic methods" and viewed "final intentions as the basis for critical conclusions."[9] He and others gave wise currency to the term "author's final intentions," and editors now often use the phrase to mean an author's last known wishes or the latest authorial revisions.[10]

The central notion of "author's final intention," then, was implicit in Greg, amplified by Bowers, and used by textual editors during the last thirty years, most prominently in the period of the CEAA (1963–1976). Yet it is only within the last few years

---

authoritative editions of nineteenth-century American authors. It gained much of its influence from its affiliation with the American Literature Group of the Modern Language Association and from its power to disperse funds obtained from the National Endowment for the Humanities. The CEAA supported and evaluated critical editions produced by textual centers across the country, until it was replaced by the Center for Scholarly Editions in 1976. See the *Statement of Editorial Principles: A Working Manual for Editing Nineteenth-Century American Texts* (New York: MLA, 1967; rev. ed. 1972); *Professional Standards and American Editions: A Response to Edmund Wilson* (New York: MLA, 1969); Hershel Parker with Bruce Bebb, "The CEAA: An Interim Assessment," *Papers of the Bibliographical Society of America*, 68 (1974), 129–48; and Peter L. Shillingsburg, "Critical Editing and the Center for Scholarly Editions," *Scholarly Publishing*, 9 (1977), 31–40.

8. W. W. Greg, "The Rationale of Copy-Text," *Studies in Bibliography*, 3 (1950–51), 32.

9. Fredson Bowers, "Some Principles for Scholarly Editions of Nineteenth-Century American Authors," *Studies in Bibliography*, 17 (1964), 227, and "Remarks on Eclectic Texts," *Proof*, 4 (1975), 58, 60. See also his "Textual Criticism," in *The Aims and Methods of Scholarship in Modern Languages and Literatures*, 2d ed., ed. James Thorpe (New York: MLA, 1970), p. 31.

10. See, for example, Hershel Parker, "Melville and the Concept of 'Author's Final Intentions,'" *Proof*, 1 (1971), 157; and G. Thomas Tanselle, "The Editorial Problem of Final Authorial Intention," *Studies in Bibliography*, 29 (1976), 169–70.

that a textual theorist has come to grips with the problems inherent in this central concept and its application. Though Hershel Parker provided a useful examination of typical problems in his "Melville and the Concept of 'Author's Final Intentions'" (1971), G. Thomas Tanselle was the first to present a comprehensive theoretical and practical discussion in "The Editorial Problem of Final Authorial Intention" (1976). Tanselle's article is a milestone in editorial theory. I make this point now because the following discussion spends more time correcting or supplementing Tanselle's essay than praising it. As the most authoritative treatment of "author's final intention," Tanselle's discussion does more than merely represent the position of current textual scholarship. A critique of his proposals is a critique of American editorial theory at its best.

In attempting to isolate the kind of intention most relevant to editing, Tanselle depends on the helpful distinctions made by Michael Hancher in "Three Kinds of Intention." Tanselle adopts Hancher's definition of "active intention" without any qualifications: "Active intentions characterize the actions that the author, at the time he finishes his text, understands himself to be performing in that text."[11] Tanselle does not realize that this formulation is inadequate for editorial practice because it implies that relevant intention exists only after a work is finished. An example such as Melville's *Pierre* presents Hancher's definition with a problem. Melville wrote the first half of that book with one intention and then wrote most of the last half with a greatly differing intention and never reconciled the two. Melville does not seem to have had a coherent active intention when he completed the novel; it would make more sense to speak of his intention as he was writing each section.[12]

11. Michael Hancher, "Three Kinds of Intention," *MLN*, 87 (1972), 830; for Tanselle's acceptance of Hancher's definition, see "Final Authorial Intention," p. 175.
12. See Hershel Parker, "Why *Pierre* Went Wrong," *Studies in the Novel*, 8 (1976), 7–23; and Brian Higgins and Hershel Parker, "The Flawed Grandeur of Melville's *Pierre*," in *New Perspectives on Melville*, ed. Faith Pullin (Edinburgh: Edinburgh University Press, 1978), pp. 162–96. Though he does emphasize "the culminating act of *meaning-something-by-the-finished-text*," Hancher shows that he is not unaware of the problem I am raising here; see the insightful footnote 10 (ignored by Tanselle) in "Three Kinds of Intention," p. 831.

There is a more subtle objection to the phrase "at the time he finishes his text" in Hancher's definition. How are we to judge a work to be "finished"? Hancher implies that a work is finished when it is published.[13] But then what about the textual situation of Crane's *Red Badge of Courage,* a work that seems to have been "finished" long *before* it was published in an expurgated form.[14] The question about when a work was finished is a question about an author's *final* intentions. Hancher's formulation requires the textualist to face this issue before he has a clear notion of intention (in general) on which to build. By starting out with a definition that includes a solution to the problem he has set out to investigate, Tanselle is begging the question.

For these two reasons I propose the following redefinition:

(a) Active intentions characterize the actions that the author, *as he writes the text,* understands himself to be performing in that text.

Such a redefinition provides a process view of intention that will prove more useful to the textual scholar than Hancher's definition, primarily because it does not prematurely introduce the problem of when a work is finished. This formulation does not replace Hancher's static view but actually contains it; the moment of completion is merely one of many moments in a process view.

Hancher also defines "active intention" as the author's "intention to be (understood as) acting in a certain way."[15] A problem arises immediately for the editor using this version of Hancher's

13. Hancher, "Three Kinds of Intention," p. 831, n. 10. Cf. James Thorpe, *Principles of Textual Criticism* (San Marino, Cal.: Huntington Library, 1972), p. 38: "The work can have only such integrity, or completeness, as the author chooses to give it, and our only reasonable test of when the work has achieved integrity is his willingness to release it to his usual public. His judgment may not always be good, and he may release it too soon or too late or when (we think) he never should have; but it is his judgment not ours, his intention not ours, his work of art which he makes ours." In this passage and the discussion that follows it, Thorpe ignores the crucial factor of external pressure which might force the author to publish a text different from the version he prefers. Below I will discuss this factor and propose an alternative "reasonable test" different from the publication date Thorpe insists on using to establish the work's "integrity."

14. See Henry Binder, "The *Red Badge of Courage* Nobody Knows," *Studies in the Novel,* 10 (1978), 9-47; and my discussion of *Red Badge* in Ch. 7.

15. Hancher, "Three Kinds of Intention," p. 835.

definition, a problem that involves Hancher's distinction between active and ultimate intentions.[16] He states the difference as a distinction between meaning and effect, what is intended to be understood and what effect is intended. Tanselle adopts Hancher's distinction, but makes the mistake of viewing only meaning or active intention as relevant to editing. In practice, however, the editor is just as concerned with how a passage affects the reader as he is with what that passage means. A section from *The Red Badge of Courage* can serve as an illustration. In Crane's final chapter, Henry Fleming and his friend Wilson relax after a battle in which they both fought heroically, and Henry begins to examine his accomplishments. Then occurs a passage in the final manuscript that was deleted in the first published edition. Henry and Wilson hear about the death of a fellow soldier, Jimmie Rogers. Reacting to the news:

> His friend [Wilson] swore.
> But the youth [Henry], regarding his procession of memory, felt gleeful and unregretting, for, in it, his public deeds were paraded in great and shining prominence.[17]

By juxtaposing the two reactions with no authorial comment, Crane intends his reader to respond with a negative judgment of Henry. This intended effect is part of Crane's design to encourage the reader's recognition that Henry is still as egocentric and insensitive as he has been throughout the story while Wilson, previously "the loud soldier," has clearly grown from his war experiences.[18] In deciding whether to restore this deleted pas-

16. Hancher actually calls this latter kind of intention "final" intention. However, to avoid confusion with the editorial concept of "author's final intention," I have chosen to use the term "ultimate intention" which Hancher equates with his notion of "final intention" (ibid., p. 835, n. 16).

17. See the version of *The Red Badge of Courage* edited by Henry Binder based on Crane's final manuscript—in *The Norton Anthology of American Literature*, ed. Ronald Gottesman et al. (New York: Norton, 1979), II, 904.

18. In two earlier scenes, Crane used Wilson's reactions to Jimmie Rogers as a way of indicating how Wilson has changed from an argumentative and loud youth to a more mature and compassionate friend. In ch. 15 a previously combative Wilson prevents a fight involving Rogers and two other soldiers, because he hates "t'see th' boys fightin' 'mong themselves" (Crane, p. 869). Then in ch. 19, Wilson volunteers to get water for the badly wounded Rogers, while the other

sage, an editor must consider not only its meaning but its intended effect of eliciting the reader's negative judgment. To include such relevant immediate effects in a notion of authorial intention most useful to editors, I propose the following definition:

    (b) Operative intentions characterize the actions that the author, as he writes the text, understands himself to be performing in the text and the immediate effects he understands these actions will achieve in his projected reader.

This definition of operative intentions encompasses active intentions and the kind of ultimate intentions that involve *immediate* effects on the reader during the reading process (as opposed to after-effects, for instance, being moved to action).

Like Hancher's original definition of active intention, my definitions provide a description of intention from the author's point of view. For the critic and editor, an author's operative intention is an ideal construct, something in the author's mind, not capable of being directly apprehended. Therefore, what is needed to supplement a concept of operative intention is a notion of *inferred* intention that provides a perspective most directly applicable to the activity of editing:

    (c) Inferred intentions characterize the critic's description of the convention-based responses that the author, as he is writing, understands he will achieve as a result (at least in part) of his projected reader's recognition of his intention.[19]

---

soldiers are more concerned with getting their own canteens filled and Henry simply thinks about cooling himself off in the cold water (pp. 880–81). See the discussion of Crane's designs and the deleted passage in Binder, "The *Red Badge* Nobody Knows," pp. 27–28.

19. By the use of the term "*inferred* intention," I do not mean to imply that when an editor talks about active and operative intentions, his descriptions are somehow not inferences. My point is exactly the opposite: the positing of an intention for an author is *always* an inference. By using "inferred" in (c), I am trying to emphasize the inferential process an editor uses to posit a specific authorial intention. A distinction between operative and inferred intentions allows me, for example, to talk about the operative intention an author claimed he had and a perhaps differing inferred intention an editor arrives at after evaluating all the relevant evidence. Furthermore, a definition of "inferred intention" enables me to describe everything from the reader-critic-editor's side of the literary communication, an advantage that will prove useful in discussing "author's final intention" below.

This final definition requires several explanatory comments. Its main assertion is that inferred intention should be defined in terms of convention-based reading responses.[20] This claim raises three interrelated issues:

(1) Conventions shared between an author and his readers account exhaustively for inference of intention. As Quentin Skinner argues, any intention capable of being understood "must always be a socially conventional intention—must fall, that is, within a given and established range of acts which can be conventionally grasped as being cases of that intention."[21] Conventions can be changed, but any modifications must begin with employment of the old conventions. Recent speech act theory describes the most basic and stable kinds of communicative conventions which allow a hearer or reader to understand the intention of a speaker or writer.[22] To achieve understanding, the hearer invokes speech act conventions to infer intended mean-

20. I am using "convention-based" and "conventional" interchangeably to refer to responses performed because of, in accordance with, or following established conventions. I am decidedly not using "conventional" in the pejorative sense of "stock responses," as in I. A. Richards, *Practical Criticism* (New York: Harcourt, Brace, & World, 1929), ch. 5.

21. Quentin Skinner, "Conventions and the Understanding of Speech Acts," *Philosophical Quarterly*, 20 (1970), 133. My claim here for the absolute interdependence of inferring intention and invoking conventions gains support from most communication-intention accounts of meaning. Besides Skinner, see J. L. Austin, *How to Do Things with Words*, ed. J. O. Urmson (Cambridge: Harvard University Press, 1962), pp. 105, 115, 118, 127; John R. Searle, "What Is a Speech Act?" in *Philosophy in America*, ed. Max Black (London: Allen & Unwin, 1965), p. 230, and *Speech Acts: An Essay in the Philosophy of Language* (London: Cambridge University Press, 1969), e.g., pp. 37–45; and P. F. Strawson, "Meaning, Truth and Communication," in *Linguistics at Large*, ed. Noel Minnis (New York: Viking, 1971), p. 93. (I will postpone any consideration of those communication-intention accounts that *deny* the wholly conventional nature of inferring speaker's intention until Ch. 6, n. 23.) Also see E. D. Hirsch's discussion of how conventions and "the principle of sharability" make possible the reproducibility of intention in interpretation: *Validity in Interpretation*, pp. 31, 44, 66–67. In *The Structure of Literary Understanding* (Cambridge: Cambridge University Press, 1978), Stein Haugom Olsen also argues for the connection between convention and intention (p. 118), but his notion of the relevant conventions is too restrictive—see below, Ch. 5, n. 25. Cf. George L. Dillon, *Language Processing and the Reading of Literature* (Bloomington: Indiana University Press, 1978), p. xx.

22. For listings of the recent work in speech act theory, see Marcia Eaton, "Speech Acts: A Bibliography," *Centrum*, 2 (1974), 57–72; and Robert B. Meyers and Karen Hopkins, "A Speech-Act Theory Bibliography," *Centrum*, 5 (1977), 73–108.

ing (sense and reference) and illocutionary force (how an utterance is to be taken, as a promise, assertion, warning, greeting, order, or whatever).[23] For example, to interpret the utterance, "I'll definitely jog with you tomorrow," as a promise, the hearer must not only know the linguistic conventions governing the sense and reference of the words; he must also know the conventional rules for promising: the speaker intends to do an act; the hearer prefers the speaker doing it to his not doing it; the speaker intends his utterance to place him under an obligation to do the act; it is not obvious to both the speaker and hearer that the speaker will do the act in the normal course of events; etc.[24] A hearer understands the promise when he can invoke these speech act conventions that he shares with the speaker.

In literary acts and the natural narratives of everyday conversations, the interpretive situation is more complex. To understand such acts, a hearer or reader must recognize that speech acts can be "embedded" one within the other.[25] For instance, readers interpret the speech acts of fictional characters by using the conventions always in force in "ordinary" conversation. When Tom Buchanan asks Nick Carraway, "Have you read 'The Rise of the Colored Empires' by this man Goddard?" in *The Great Gatsby,* the reader invokes the appropriate conventions to interpret the utterance as a *question.*[26] This speech act is em-

23. Austin (p. 99) distinguishes between these two dimensions of a single speech act: the *locutionary* act which is the "performance of an act *of* saying something" and the *illocutionary* act which is the "performance of an act *in* saying something." More exactly, the locutionary act includes "the utterance of certain noises, the utterance of certain words in a certain construction, and the utterance of them with a certain 'meaning' in the favourite philosophical sense of that word, i.e., with a certain sense and with a certain reference" (p. 94), while the illocutionary act determines *how* the locution is used—to ask a question, make a promise, give an order, etc. Thus, the same utterance could have different illocutionary forces depending on how it is used (pp. 99–100). For example, "I'll be right back" could be a promise, an assertion, or a warning, according to the illocutionary force intended and the conventions invoked. Also see below, n. 35 of the present chapter.

24. See Searle's analysis of promising in *Speech Acts,* pp. 57–61.

25. Cf. Robert L. Brown's discussion of an author's intended "hierarchical layering of language acts within language acts"—in "Intentions and the Contexts of Poetry," *Centrum,* 2 (1974), 62–64.

26. F. Scott Fitzgerald, *The Great Gatsby* (New York: Scribner, 1925), p. 16. On the interpretation of fictional speakers' linguistic acts, see Marcia M. Eaton's

bedded in the larger act of Nick's *assertions,* as narrator, about past experiences. And the narrator's assertions are, in turn, embedded in the *literary act* of the implied and actual author.[27] Fitzgerald's literary speech act of "telling a story" or "displaying an experience" creates the framework in which the reader employs literary reading conventions to interpret the author's comprehensive intentions. Reading conventions, as we have seen, enable the reader to make sense of a text as literature, and include, for example, the strategies of creating a unity for the fiction and relating the text to genre conventions of past literary works.

Literary reading conventions are not just something added onto the reader's prior use of speech act conventions, for the two kinds of conventions are not independent. Rather, they continually interact at all levels to constitute the reader's interpretation of a literary text. For instance, when a reader interprets a character's speech act as praise for a country by virtue of the speech act conditions in force in the (real and fictional) world, the reader will simultaneously use a narrative reading convention recognizing a reliable narrator and thus gain assurance that indeed the fictional speaker did perform such an utterance; but at the same time an ironic reading convention associated with the implied author could undercut that praise and make it count as jingoistic propaganda or even a condemnation of the country praised.[28] My chief claim here is that the best positive evidence

---

discussion of "translocutionary acts" in "Art, Artifacts, and Intentions," *American Philosophical Quarterly,* 6 (1969), 165–69, and "Liars, Ranters, and Dramatic Speakers," in *Language and Aesthetics,* ed. Benjamin R. Tilghman (Lawrence: University Press of Kansas, 1973), pp. 43–63. Also see Ellen Schauber and Ellen Spolsky, "The Consolation of Alison: The Speech Acts of the Wife of Bath," *Centrum,* 5 (1977), 2–34, and "Readers, Language, and Character," *Bucknell Review,* 26, No. 1 (1980), 33–51. Cf. Michael Hancher, "Understanding Poetic Speech Acts," *College English,* 36 (1975), 632–39.

27. For a useful analysis of the general speech act of literature and natural ("nonliterary") narratives, see Mary Louise Pratt. *Toward a Speech Act Theory of Literary Discourse* (Bloomington: Indiana University Press, 1977), e.g., pp. 69, 136, 142–43. For a critique of some misguided applications of speech act theory to literature, see Stanley E. Fish, "How To Do Things with Austin and Searle: Speech Act Theory and Literary Criticism," in *Is There a Text in This Class?,* pp. 200–245.

28. Critics have only recently begun to investigate in detail the complex inter-

on which to base an inference about authorial intention is that
provided by these intersecting speech act and literary reading
conventions.[29]

(2) These shared conventions of literary communication determine the range of intended reader response in that they enable the author to predict what his projected reader will infer
about his intentions. "To intend a meaning is to postulate reactions of an imagined reader who has assimilated the relevant
conventions."[30] Furthermore, an author not only intends that
his readers recognize the conventions he is using but that they
recognize *his intention* to use precisely those conventions. Con-
versely, such reflexive intentions require that readers not simply
invoke certain conventions but that they recognize the author's
intention that they invoke those conventions.[31] What John
Searle says of speaking holds for writing as well: "In speaking I
attempt to communicate certain things to my hearer by getting

---

relations of these communicative conventions and the various speakers associated with literary texts. See Pratt, *Toward a Speech Act Theory*, pp. 173–210.

29. This model of literary communication excludes unconscious "intentions,"
but this exclusion does not imply that such so-called "intentions" are not relevant
to interpretive projects based on other models of literature. Cf. John Reichert's
suggestion that we "stop pretending that unconscious intentions are a kind of
intention," in his *Making Sense of Literature* (Chicago: University of Chicago Press,
1977), p. 76.

30. Jonathan Culler, *Structuralist Poetics* (Ithaca: Cornell University Press,
1975), p. 30. Reichert criticizes Culler's theory of reading conventions because he
feels it excludes an appropriate notion of authorial intention—see Reichert, p.
71 and cf. Gerald Graff, *Literature against Itself* (Chicago: University of Chicago
Press, 1979), p. 197. The following proposal to adapt Grice's account of intention
should help to answer Reichert's and Graff's objections.

31. This analysis incorporates Grice's account of "reflexive intention" into my
definition of inferred intention. In its earliest form this account specified: "'*A*
meant$_{NN}$ something by *x*' is (roughly) equivalent to '*A* intended the utterance of *x*
to produce some effect in an audience by means of the recognition of this
intention'" (where "meant$_{NN}$" is an abbreviation for "meant nonnaturally" as
contrasted to "meant naturally" in the sense that spots' naturally mean
measles)—see H. P. Grice, "Meaning," *Philosophical Review*, 66 (1957), 385. This
formulation has been widely discussed in the philosophy of language, and Grice
has provided further refinements of the concept in "Utterer's Meaning and
Intentions," *Philosophical Review*, 78 (1969), 147–77. P. F. Strawson introduced
Grice's account of meaning into the discussion of Austin's concept of speech acts,
and he conveniently uses the term "response" to describe intended effect—see
Strawson, "Intention and Convention in Speech Acts," *Philosophical Review*, 73
(1964), 439–60.

him to recognize my intention to communicate just those things.
... He understands what I am saying as soon as he recognizes
my intention in uttering what I utter as an intention to say that
thing."[32] From the writer's side, the author can depend on a
reader's inference of his reflexive intention when he knows that
they share a set of communicative conventions. From the
reader's side, understanding is constituted by his inference of
the author's reflexive intention to invoke certain speech act and
literary reading conventions.[33]

(3) The "reader responses" involved in inferred intention include all reading activities relevant to authorial intent; such overlapping terms as "cognitive," "attitudinal," and "emotive" suggest
the range of responses that an author intends to elicit by conventional means.[34] Thus response includes both understanding
(what J. L. Austin called "uptake" of meaning and illocutionary
force) and immediate effects (part of what Austin called the
"perlocutionary effects" of securing uptake, for example, belief,
surprise, humiliation, action).[35] The perlocutionary effects that
are relevant to *intended* reader response must be carefully restricted. They refer primarily to immediate intended effects
during reading and not to after-effects like becoming a bull-
fighter as a result of reading *The Sun Also Rises*. They include
cognitive and attitudinal responses, such as those described in my
reader-oriented analysis of "Rappaccini's Daughter." And they
include emotional reactions, but not physical sensations nor pri-
vate associations. Though the place of emotions in literary interpretation has always been problematic, I agree with John

32. Searle, *Speech Acts*, p. 43.
33. Inferred intention, then, focuses on the critic's description of the following complex situation: an author can be said to intend something when that
author understands himself to be performing acts (active intention) which will
produce a certain response in a reader (operative intention) by virtue at least in
part of the reader's recognition of the author's intention to invoke certain conventions (reflexive intention).
34. Cf. Reichert's discussion (pp. 78–89) of responses relevant to criticism.
35. Austin (p. 120) distinguishes three aspects of the speech act: "the locutionary act ... which has *meaning;* the illocutionary act which has a certain *force* in
saying something; the perlocutionary act which is the *achieving of* certain effects
by saying something." *Arguing, informing, warning,* and *urging* name illocutionary
acts, while *persuading, convincing, scaring,* and *inspiring* name perlocutionary acts;
see Searle, *Speech Acts*, p. 25.

Reichert that "there is a necessary connection between a reader's understanding of a situation and the emotions and attitudes he will feel toward it."[36] This is certainly the case in my example from *The Great Gatsby*, where Tom says, "Have you read 'The Rise of the Colored Empires' by this man Goddard? . . . Well, it's a fine book, and everybody ought to read it. The idea is if we don't look out the white race will be—will be utterly submerged. It's all scientific stuff; it's been proved." The reader is amused and repelled after he understands this foolish racist statement. At least Fitzgerald appears to intend this connection between the reader's understanding and emotional reaction since he reinforces the connection through the immediate reactions of the other characters and through the narrator's comment a few pages later, "Something was making him [Tom] nibble at the edge of stale ideas."[37]

Note that all of these intended reading responses—cognitive, attitudinal, and emotive—depend on the reader's *prior* interpretation. For example, a reader cannot react to a character's bigotry or foolishness until he has interpreted the text as portraying the character as bigoted or foolish. And the reader makes this interpretation by invoking the communicative conventions he assumes the author to be using in the text. For this reason, the effects relevant to inferred intention are not only restricted by their immediacy (during the reading process) but also by the possible communicative conventions available to the author.

By combining illocutionary effect (securing uptake of meaning and force) and certain perlocutionary effects (immediate reactions during reading) under the category "intended conventional response," I do not mean to deny the distinction usually made between illocutionary and perlocutionary acts: the success of illocutionary acts is conventional while the success of perlocutionary acts is contingent.[38] When a hearer recognizes a speaker's intention to invoke the conventions of greeting (an

36. Reichert, p. 88. On the difficult question of emotions in literary reading experiences, see Norman N. Holland, *5 Readers Reading* (New Haven: Yale University Press, 1975), p. 292.
37. Fitzgerald, pp. 16, 25.
38. See Austin, pp. 118–21.

illocutionary act), greeting has taken place; whereas when a hearer recognizes a speaker's intention to persuade (a perlocutionary act), persuasion may or may not then happen. Whether a text actually convinces, saddens, amuses, or worries a reader depends on a variety of contingent circumstances, from how skillful the author is to how much attention the reader pays to the text. Sometimes the author achieves effects without any reader recognition of his perlocutionary intent; for example, readers do not become sad reading a tragic love story *because* they recognize the author's intention that they become sad; and sometimes certain perlocutionary effects result *in spite of* the readers' recognition that another is intended, as when readers laugh at the clumsy bathos of a melodramatic farewell scene. There are times, however, when writers do achieve a perlocutionary effect through recognition of intent to achieve that effect, for example, when readers believe a statement totally on the basis of their recognition of a trusted author's attempt to persuade them of its truth. In such cases, conventions govern a reader's understanding of perlocutionary intent. This is true in at least two ways. First, recognition of perlocutionary intent to persuade depends on the prior recognition of illocutionary intent to assert, advise, request, warn, and perform other illocutionary acts involved in persuading; and uptake of such illocutionary forces is always convention-governed.[39] Second, the strategies of persuasion are conventional, as suggested by the long history of rhetorical taxonomies; and these conventional strategies can be recognized and the intent to persuade inferred from this recognition. In sum: a reader's understanding of authorial intention always depends on shared communicative conventions, but the success of the intention to achieve certain perlocutionary effects is not guaranteed by those conventions, only made possible by them.

A final point: though the reader's response is not necessarily dependent on the recognition of perlocutionary intent, the editor-critic's interpretation is. What the editor and intentionalist critic attempt to do is identify the intended conventional response. They do this when they recognize (like the reader) the

39. See the works cited in n. 21 of this chapter.

author's reflexive intention to invoke certain conventions of meaning and illocutionary force *and* when they recognize (sometimes unlike the reader) the author's intention to achieve certain immediate effects during the reading process. Moreover, every time the author forces his reader to evaluate his own reading response,[40] the reader becomes an intentionalist critic who interprets intended meaning *and* effects. The reader's self-conscious interpretation of perlocutionary intent will then cause him to confirm or revise his previous response.

In the past, editorial theory has chosen between two models of literary authorship: the originating view of an isolated figure freely expressing his uniquely individual and privileged intention and the collaborative view of the writer as merely one among many text-producers (author, scribe, house editor, publisher, and so on), none of whose intentions is absolutely privileged or retrievable.[41] My convention-based account of intention suggests a third alternative: literary authorship is socially constituted; it is a convention-governed role that individuals can take on.[42] Biographical circumstances can interfere with a writer successfully taking on this role and employing its conventions. In such cases the contingent impinges on the conventional. This view of literary authorship thus consists of three interrelated points: authorial intention is a function of the social role writers adopt; this role can be described in terms of the speech act and

40. As happens quite often in the reading experiences described by Stanley Fish; see his *Surprised by Sin: The Reader in Paradise Lost,* 2d ed. (Berkeley: University of California Press, 1971).

41. The originating view is, of course, the dominant model of authorship in current textual editing. For a discussion of both models that favors a collaborative view, see Peckham, pp. 136–54. Related to this collaborative view is the anti-intentionalist position of the new German editing theory presented by Hans Zeller, "A New Approach to the Critical Constitution of Literary Texts," *Studies in Bibliography,* 28 (1975), 231–64. Tanselle presents an originating view of authorship in his critique of Peckham's essay—see G. Thomas Tanselle, "Greg's Theory of Copy-Text and the Editing of American Literature," *Studies in Bibliography,* 28 (1975), 217–18.

42. An especially helpful formulation of this view can be found in Mary Louise Pratt, "The Ideology of Speech-Act Theory," *Centrum,* N.S. 1 (1980), 10: "'authorship' is a certain, socially constituted position occupied by a speaking subject and endowed with certain characteristics and certain relationships to other dimensions of that subject."

literary reading conventions I have outlined; and the successful individual performance of this social role can be influenced by, for example, pressure from a publisher. The advantage of this perspective is that it preserves scholarly editing's traditional emphasis on the "author's intention," while it allows the development of a more useful version of that concept—inferred intention defined in terms of convention-based reading responses.

The full definition of inferred intention in (c) solves all of the problems raised earlier. It makes authorial intention concurrent with the writing process; it does not make a false distinction between relevant meaning and irrelevant effect; and it presents a view of intention from the perspective of the editor and intentionalist critic. Not only does (c), as a definition of inferred intention, offer a more exact formulation of the kind of intention with which the editor-critic is most directly involved; but, unlike Tanselle's use of Hancher, it also provides a logical connection with a critical framework for editing; that is, implicit in "inferred intention" is a specific rationale for critical interpretation.

The Editing Process and Critical Interpretation

On what basis can an editor reconstruct the author's intended text? We can begin to answer this question by examining Figure 1, in which I have schematized the inferential process in scholarly editing.[43] Establishing the intended text is a historical reconstruction based on an editor's critical interpretation of the work and his examination of relevant historical, biographical, bibliographical, and linguistic evidence.[44] Critical interpretation

43. Of course there are other kinds of editing different from the scholarly editing that attempts a historical reconstruction of the author's intended text, e.g., a creative editing that aims to establish the "best" text and ignores what the author intended. But editing as historical reconstruction dominates American textual scholarship and is therefore my only concern in this chapter.

44. See Tanselle, "Final Authorial Intention," pp. 167–68, 179–83; and his "Textual Study and Literary Judgment," *Papers of the Bibliographical Society of America*, 65 (1971), 109–22. The critical and historical components in Figure 1 do not quite correspond to what has traditionally been called intrinsic and extrinsic criticism, since the communicative conventions relevant to interpreting authorial intention might be seen as "extrinsic" to the text. Actually, the simplistic

of textual versions is an inference about authorial intention based on positive and negative evidence: negative evidence excludes intentions that were historically impossible for the author to have had, while the reading of documents to be edited establishes the positive evidence. In contrast to the products of critical interpretation, biographical and historical evidence includes, for example, statements of authorial intention made by the author and friends in letters, essays, and other documents different from the text to be edited. Other kinds of historical or bibliographical evidence might indicate that portions of a text are nonauthorial or that external pressure caused authorial revisions. From positive and negative critical evidence, an editor can infer authorial intention, which combines with historical, bibliographical, and other evidence to determine an editor's historical reconstruction of the author's intended text.

Figure 1 and its explanation indicate the central role of in-

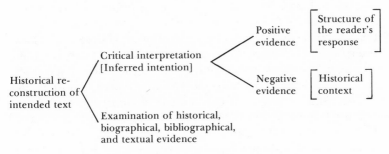

Figure 1. The inferential process of editing

ferred intention in the editorial process.[45] "Inferred intention,"

intrinsic/extrinsic distinction breaks down in a convention-based communication model of literature: communicative conventions are both inside and outside the text.

45. The concept of inferred intention is not alien to Tanselle's essay on intention; in one place he writes that "to explain the intention of a work . . . constitutes an inference about an event which took place in the past" ("Final Authorial Intention," p. 178).

defined in terms of intended conventional response, establishes a framework for critical interpretation, a framework missing from Tanselle's discussion of intention. That is, Tanselle defines the relevant intention for editing as "active intention" and then argues that an editor must make critical interpretations; however, he does not connect his definition with any approach to interpretation. Instead, in his critical analyses of textual examples, he relies on such notoriously vague formalist and expressive phrases as: "purpose, direction, or character of a work," "spirit of the original version," "representation of the author's vision," "conception of an organic whole," and "general tone and spirit of the whole."[46]

This is the major failing of Tanselle's important article. By separating his analysis of intention from a useful framework for critical interpretation, Tanselle ultimately cuts off his discussion from the most important criterion for establishing the author's final intention. For "author's final intention" should be defined not chronologically but *aesthetically*. Editors should reject chronology, the traditional determinant of an author's final intention, in favor of an aesthetic criterion established by critical interpretation.[47] This proposal is not a return to the creative editing of the nineteenth century or a rationale for an irresponsible eclecticism. The goal is still the conservative reconstruction of the author's intended text. This point must be emphasized because I do not want my proposal confused with the position of F. W. Bateson, who claims that an editor in deciding between variant passages should choose "whatever after due consideration he (the editor) believes the best authorial version to be,

46. Ibid., pp. 192–99. In terms of Figure 1, Tanselle is weakest on defining the nature of the positive evidence in critical interpretation. For example, he writes that "the only direct evidence one has for what was in the author's mind is not what he says was there but what one finds in his work" (p. 210). This might be a useful general heuristic to begin with, but a more detailed framework is needed for the critical interpretation of positive evidence.

47. In "Textual Study and Literary Judgment," Tanselle writes that "decisions about an author's final intention are more often matters of judgment than matters of fact" (p. 122). However, he is not questioning the chronological definition of author's final intention here. Rather, he is simply pointing out that *within the traditional view* of establishing final intentions, critical judgment plays a crucial role when the knowledge of bibliographical facts is inconclusive. The guiding principle remains the *chronologically* final intentions of the author.

whether it happens to be early, middle-period, or last."[48] I agree, instead, with Tanselle when he points out that Bateson's claim confuses two distinct approaches to editing: creative editing, which tries to produce the "best" text according to the editor's taste, and scholarly editing, which is historical reconstruction based on the editor's interpretation of authorial intention.[49] My attempt here is simply to provide an aesthetic criterion (for author's final intention) that will best guide editors in making these historical reconstructions.

In trying to achieve the goal of historical reconstruction, editors often overlook the fact that chronological criteria for final intention can work against their attempts to establish the text the author most wanted his audience to read. Instead of asking what was last, an editor should ask what was *most complete.* What was last is usually most complete, but this is not always the case. Certainly the majority of textual cases should not be allowed to blind editors to the significant minority of instances when what was last and authorial is not most complete and authoritative.

An obvious terminological problem now arises: Given this revised view of the concept, should the phrase "author's final intention" be retained as the term describing the guiding principle of scholarly editing? Or should editors adopt a new term (like an author's "most complete" or "fullest" intention)? Tanselle adopts the practical course of preserving the traditional term and its centrality but qualifying its application in textual situations involving, for example, external pressure on the author to revise his text. I will follow a similar course here. Even though I am reconceptualizing what "final intention" means, I still preserve the idea that the editor should incorporate into his critical edition all of the author's revisions up to the moment the author finished his text. But where most editors believe that the author has not really finished his text until he has completed his last revisions, I am arguing that the "finished" text is not a function

48. F. W. Bateson, "The Application of Thought to an Eighteenth-Century Text: *The School for Scandal,*" in *Evidence in Literary Scholarship,* ed. René Wellek and Alvaro Ribeiro (Oxford: Oxford University Press, 1979), p. 324.
49. G. Thomas Tanselle, "Recent Editorial Discussion and the Critical Questions of Editing," *Studies in Bibliography,* 34 (1981), 57.

of such revisions and can only be discovered through an editor's historical and critical examination of each known step in the author's composing process. In my view, discovering the author's last revisions does not then determine the moment of the text's completion; rather the interpreted "moment" of completion determines the relevant final revisions. Thus, it is possible to reject some authorial revisions because they deface the text *after* it was finished.[50]

Final intentions, then, should be conceptualized as the author's most complete intentions. I further propose that what is most complete and authoritative is best defined in terms of *the intended structure of the reader's response*. This view of author's final intention follows naturally from my definition of inferred intention as intended conventional response. Unlike Tanselle's use of active intention, inferred intention implies an aesthetic criterion: the interpretive framework of reader-response criticism.[51]

For the editor, the most important aspect of a reader-response approach is the temporal and convention-based reading model I have been developing. The convention-based component provides the basis for the definition of inferred intention and the temporal dimension presents the aesthetic criterion—the intended structure of the reader's response—for establishing the

---

50. Cf. George Watson's argument that when an author corrupts his own text, an editor should be able "to reject the last intentions of the author as *mutilations*": *The Study of Literature* (New York: Scribner, 1969), p. 129.

51. The best alternative to the concept of chronologically final intention has been suggested by Hershel Parker: When faced with especially problematic revisions, "an editor may be driven to theorizing about the precise time at which a given writer may be said to have the most 'authoritative' sense of his intentions and accomplishments for a particular work" ("Melville and 'Author's Final Intentions,'" p. 165). Parker does not develop this idea into a detailed theoretical position here, nor does he do so in a later essay where it is mentioned again— "Aesthetic Implications of Authorial Excisions: Examples from Nathaniel Hawthorne, Mark Twain, and Stephen Crane," in *Editing Nineteenth-Century Fiction*, ed. Jane Millgate (New York: Garland, 1978), p. 100. However, even if the guiding principles for editing were reconceived along the lines of Parker's suggestions, the editor would still have to discover that moment of the author's "most authoritative sense of his intentions and accomplishments," and he would have to do so primarily through a *critical interpretation* of the extant textual versions. Therefore, my proposals for an aesthetic criterion apply both to the traditional view of "author's final intention" and to Parker's new approach to the problem.

author's final intention. A reader-response approach forces the editor to investigate the intended reader, "the reader whose education, opinions, concerns, linguistic competences, etc., make him capable of having the experience the author wished to provide."[52] The editor must therefore be especially aware of the communicative conventions the author assumed he shared with his readers. Also, reader-response criticism's focus on the structure of response makes editors sensitive to temporal aspects of authorial intention: how the author uses earlier passages to set up later ones, how later scenes or actions are designed to fulfill earlier structural or thematic promises, how the final interpretive synthesis or unity depends on a certain ordering of the text. Insofar as it emphasizes the author's temporal design and makes use of any relevant effects described by other approaches (the unities and patterns of New Criticism, Myth Criticism, and the like), reader-response criticism approximates as closely as possible the author's position as reader of his own text. Such an approach helps the editor recapture the author as reviser. For in revision the author must become his own reader as he prepares his text to be read by others. As Henry James wrote while selecting and revising his fiction for the collected edition of his works: "The teller of a story is primarily, none the less, the listener to it, the reader of it, too."[53]

To return to Figure 1: an editor bases his decisions on critical interpretation and knowledge of historical, bibliographical, and other evidence about the author's final intention. Tanselle's discussion defines "authorial intention" but suggests no positive link between his definition and a framework for critical interpretation. What I am doing with inferred intention and reader-response criticism is providing just this theoretical connection. Now, in practical terms, how might an editor's attention to the structure of reader response interact with his knowledge of external evidence in establishing an author's intended text?

52. Stanley E. Fish, "Interpreting the *Variorum*," in *Is There a Text in This Class?*, pp. 160-61.
53. Henry James, *The Art of the Novel* (New York: Scribner, 1934), p. 63. See Walter Benn Michaels, "Writers Reading: James and Eliot," *MLN*, 91 (1976), 827-49.

There are three kinds of textual decisions that are central to the editor's attempt to establish the intended text. These decisions involve:

(1) Distinguishing separate versions of a work that should not be conflated through eclectic means and deciding if one version has priority over others. These decisions are based on critical considerations about the structure of the reader's response and on evidence regarding prepublication forms of the text, publication history, and external pressure on the author.

(2) Choosing a copy-text for a critical edition, a decision based entirely on Greg's theory and involving no critical interpretation.[54] However, choice of copy-text can have an effect on reader response. For example, the extant manuscript of *The Great Gatsby* retains Fitzgerald's sparse use of commas, while the first edition text is heavily punctuated as a result of house styling. By choosing the first edition as copy-text, an editor adopts its accidentals and thus loses the authorial rhythm of the manuscript's style.[55]

(3) Making corrections and choosing between textual variants. Making conjectural emendations in a text involves both bibliographical evidence and critical interpretation. For example, to establish the following passage, the editors of the Northwestern-Newberry edition of Melville's *Typee* relied on the structure of the reader's response in emending "nations" of the English first edition and "nation" of the American first edition to "matrons."

What, thought I, on first witnessing one of these exhibitions, would the nervous mothers of America and England say to a similar display of hardihood in any of their children? The

54. Greg's general theory of copy-text holds that "the choice of copy-text depends solely on its formal features (accidentals)." An editor chooses a copy-text as the basis for his critical edition and then emends authoritative readings into it: "whenever there is more than one substantive text of comparable authority, then although it will still be necessary to choose one of them as copy-text, and to follow it in accidentals, this copy-text can be allowed no over-riding or even preponderant authority so far as substantive readings are concerned" (Greg, p. 31, n. 18, and p. 29).
55. James L. W. West, III, "The SCADE Gatsby: A Review Article," *Proof,* 5 (1977), 246.

Lacedemonian *matrons* might have approved of it, but most modern dames would have gone into hysterics at the sight.[56]

The editors explain: "What the context calls for must be a synonym of 'mothers' (earlier in the paragraph) and 'dames' (later in the paragraph), which in Melville's hand could easily be misread as 'nations': 'matrons' alone satisfies all these requirements, and it is adopted as the word Melville probably wrote."[57] The use of "context" here indicates the editors' interpretation of the *Typee* paragraph as an intended structure of reader response; and this interpretation of the response structure constrains the emendation and serves as a background against which the editor uses the textual variants to pinpoint where the correction should be made. As with conjectural emendations, an editor's choice between existing variants involves him in critical interpretation and evaluation of all external evidence.

Establishing the Text

Editorial decisions about different textual versions and variant words or passages are decisions about "author's final intention." They involve cases of "revision" that force the editor to make choices about what text the author intended his audience to read. The textual examples that follow are limited to these cases.

"If, in practice, editors are not going to regard each version as necessarily a separate work," writes Tanselle, "then some rationale is required for distinguishing those instances of revision which are to be edited as separate works from those which are not."[58] A reader-response methodology provides such a rationale. In talking about different versions, we can focus on manuscript versions like those for Melville's *Billy Budd* or prepublication versions like those for Dreiser's *Sister Carrie* and

56. Harrison Hayford, Hershel Parker, and G. Thomas Tanselle, ed., *Typee* by Herman Melville (Evanston and Chicago: Northwestern University Press and The Newberry Library, 1968), p. 215, emphasis added.
57. Hayford, Parker, and Tanselle, "Discussions of Adopted Readings," in *Typee*, p. 332.
58. Tanselle, "Final Authorial Intention," p. 198.

Faulkner's *Sanctuary*.[59] Or we can discuss post-publication versions: Whitman's *Leaves of Grass,* Auden's poems, or James's New York Edition. All of these pre- and post-publication versions could be analyzed in terms of the structure of the reader's response. An author's radical restructuring of response would indicate that the editor is dealing with separate versions that should not be conflated into one critical text but should be edited separately.

Let me illustrate. Are the two versions of James's "Four Meetings" different works or merely refinements of one work? "Four Meetings" was originally published in *Scribner's Monthly* in 1877; James published a revised version in the New York Edition in 1909.[60] In both versions Caroline Spencer longs to see Europe more than anything else and saves for years to make the trip. She finally fulfills her dream, but after only forty-eight hours in Europe she gives all her money to a worthless cousin and must return to the United States. Five years later the narrator finds her still in New England, now waiting on a countess (her dead cousin's "wife") and having no prospects of ever returning to Europe.

From the two versions of the story, the reader forms radically different attitudes toward the narrator. The difference is most striking at the very end of the narrative. Both reader and narrator realize that the illusion of serving a countess is all that is left of Europe for Caroline, for she has given up all hope of returning to the Continent. In the 1877 version the narrator is careful not only to leave her illusion intact but also to refrain from intentionally embarrassing her about the loss of her dream.

59. See stages D and G, for example, in the genetic text provided in Harrison Hayford and Merton Sealts, Jr., ed., *Billy Budd, Sailor* by Herman Melville (Chicago: University of Chicago Press, 1962); John C. Berkey, James L. W. West III, Alice M. Winters, and Neda M. Westlake, ed., The Philadelphia Edition of *Sister Carrie* by Theodore Dreiser (Philadelphia: University of Pennsylvania Press, 1981); and Noel Polk, ed., *Sanctuary: The Original Text* by William Faulkner (New York: Random House, 1981).

60. *Scribner's Monthly*, 15 (November 1877), 44–56; *The Novels and Tales of Henry James*, vol. 16 (New York: Scribner, 1909), pp. 267–312. (Page numbers following the quotations in the next paragraph refer to these published versions.) Cf. the following discussion with that in Wayne C. Booth, *The Rhetoric of Fiction* (Chicago: University of Chicago Press, 1961), pp. 356–58, on James's revision of "The Aspern Papers."

When asking about the loan to her cousin, he corrects himself: "there was something too methodical in my questions" (p. 55). The 1909 version changes this to a hyperbolic and (in the circumstances) insensitive, "I kept her on the rack" (p. 305). In both versions the narrator resolves not to take away from Caroline the last connection to her original dream, even though it is illusory: the woman Caroline is waiting on is obviously not a European countess. At the end of the 1877 version he is true to his resolution (p. 56). But in the 1909 version he does exactly what he resolved not to do: he shows contempt for the countess (pp. 311–12). When the reader arrives at the narrator's comment that Caroline "was glad I was going" (which appears in the final paragraph of both versions), he makes very different interpretations. In reading the 1877 version, the reader thinks Caroline is glad because the narrator's presence reminds her of her past dream; in reading the 1909 version, he realizes that it is because of this reason *and* because of the narrator's obvious attitude toward the present remnant of that dream.

Once it has been established (as in the above example) that the reading experience has been radically changed, then another question arises: Does one version of a work have priority over another? There are two considerations in answering this question: external influence on the author and illogical or inconsistent restructuring of reader response.[61] In the "Four Meetings" example, there is no evidence of external pressure forcing James to make the revisions, nor do the revisions he made result in an illogical or inconsistent response structure. Both the original and revised texts provide coherent reading experiences that cannot be distinguished in terms of completeness or sophistication. Therefore, the editor cannot give either text priority over the other. In contrast, the second American editions of Melville's *Typee* and Crane's *Maggie* are examples of texts expurgated by their authors as a result of pressure from publishers after the

61. I should note here that all of the following textual examples from American literature depend on the conventions for reading classic representational fiction. A different reader-oriented proposal would have to be made for editing post-modernist fictions, which are not based on the principles of coherence and consistency governing traditional or what Barthes calls "readerly" texts: see Roland Barthes, *S/Z*, trans. Richard Miller (New York: Hill and Wang, 1974), p. 4.

appearance of more complete first editions.[62] Such external pressure invalidates the author's chronologically final intention, and modern editors are fully justified in rejecting the revised editions and giving priority to the earlier versions. The same principle holds for *The Red Badge of Courage,* even though Crane's editor applied pressure prior to publication of the text in book form. In this case the modern scholarly editor is justified in rejecting the expurgated first edition and basing his critical text on the more complete and consistent final manuscript.[63] These three textual situations provide good examples of a betrayal of the author's most complete intentions and a radical weakening of the structure of the reader's response.

Brian Higgins and Hershel Parker present an even better example in "Sober Second Thoughts: The 'Author's Final Version' of Fitzgerald's *Tender Is the Night,*" where they compare the 1934 version of *Tender* with the 1951 Cowley edition, which rearranged major sections of the book with only the slightest rewriting by Fitzgerald. Higgins and Parker criticize Malcolm Cowley for following directions of Fitzgerald's that are highly suspect on biographical grounds. The two textualists also argue that "as far as aesthetics went, Cowley barely asked such superficial critical questions as the effect of moving a particular scene about, much less more profound questions about how any literary work is constructed and how any piece of literature affects its readers." Higgins and Parker claim that, by the time Fitzgerald got to the original Book II, "almost every detail of what he chose to write was to some extent a consequence of what he had al-

---

62. Melville's publisher, John Wiley, demanded that the author delete criticism of the missionaries for the 1846 revised edition of *Typee;* and Ripley Hitchcock, Crane's editor at D. Appleton & Co., required Crane to clean up the language originally used in the 1893 edition of *Maggie* and to delete the central character's encounter with the "chuckling and leering" fat man for the 1896 edition of the book. For discussions of the *Typee* example, see Tanselle, "Final Authorial Intention," p. 193, and Parker, "Melville and 'Author's Final Intentions,'" pp. 161–62. For *Maggie,* see Robert Wooster Stallman, "Stephen Crane's Revision of *Maggie: A Girl of the Streets,*" *American Literature,* 26 (1955), 528–36; Joseph Katz, "The *Maggie* Nobody Knows," *Modern Fiction Studies,* 12 (1966), 200–12; and Hershel Parker and Brian Higgins, "Maggie's 'Last Night': Authorial Design and Editorial Patching," *Studies in the Novel,* 10 (1978), 64–75.

63. This is what Henry Binder has done in his edition of *Red Badge*—see nn. 14 and 17, above.

ready written and was designed to cause certain effects in the
mind of the reader who had already read certain scenes."[64]
Thus, when a large section of the original Book II was placed at
the beginning of the 1951 text with only minimal revisions, this
reordering "caused great damage, in the long run, to all parts of
the novel," resulting in much violent and unintended restructuring of what Higgins and Parker call the "reader's response."[65]
Higgins and Parker conclude that the 1934 version of *Tender* has
priority over the confused 1951 edition.

Though it was certainly not their primary goal, Higgins and
Parker effectively demonstrate how biographical evidence and
reader-oriented analysis can be used together to determine the
priority of one version of a work over another.[66] However,
sometimes the external influences are unclear, the historical evidence inconclusive. Then the analysis of the temporal response
structure must carry the weight of the argument about priority
of versions. This is the case with Hawthorne's "The Hall of Fantasy," which was published in its original form in the *Pioneer*
(1843) and then revised for inclusion in *Mosses from an old Manse*
(1846).[67] The major difference between the two versions is the
deletion from the original of passages referring by name to some
of Hawthorne's contemporaries. It is unclear why Hawthorne
made these excisions. Though various commentators have
speculated about his motivation, no decisive evidence exists.[68]

64. Brian Higgins and Hershel Parker, "Sober Second Thoughts: The 'Author's Final Version' of Fitzgerald's *Tender Is the Night,*" *Proof,* 4 (1975), 136, 139.
65. Ibid., pp. 152, 140. For specific examples, see especially pp. 139-40.
66. Cf. Higgins and Parker, "Maggie's 'Last Night,'" p. 73: "From his familiar-
ity with the writer's strategies for affecting the reader by words, passages, whole
scenes, chapters, and larger units of the work as originally written, the true
editor—the devoted textualist—will develop special alertness to the effects that
any subsequent alterations, whether authorial or not, have on those intended
responses."
67. *Pioneer,* 1 (February 1843), 49-55; Nathaniel Hawthorne, *Mosses from an
Old Manse* (New York: Wiley & Putnam, 1846), pp. 159-72—this 1846 version
was also used in the 1854 edition of *Mosses* published by Ticknor and Fields (pp.
199-215).
68. The textual editor of the Centenary Edition writes: "Although intended to
be cordial, the original text could be narrowly construed as critical, since one's
presence in the Hall is not necessarily a flattering mark. It seems clear that
Hawthorne removed these passages because of the ambiguity of tone, and what
might seem to be an air of personal criticism, despite the fact that he liked to

However, the differing structures of reader response do provide the foundation for a choice between the two versions.

In Hawthorne's tale the narrator and his friend walk through the Hall of Fantasy observing the various authors gathered there. One passage in the revised version reads:

> A few held higher converse, which caused their calm and melancholy souls to beam moonlight from their eyes. As I lingered near them—for I felt an inward attraction towards these men, as if the sympathy of feeling, if not of genius, had united me to their order—my friend mentioned several of their names. The world has likewise heard those names; with some it has been familiar for years; and others are daily making their way deeper into the universal heart.
>
> "Thank heaven," observed I to my companion, as we passed to another part of the hall, "we have done with this techy, wayward, shy, proud, unreasonable set of laurel-gatherers. I love them in their works, but have little desire to meet them elsewhere.[69]

In this passage the narrator's expression of affinity with the group of writers is immediately followed by the contradictory declaration that he actually wishes to avoid this "proud, unreasonable set" of authors. The reader cannot help but be confused as he reads first one and then the other paragraph; the confusion is a result of a long deletion between the two.[70] The omitted passage contains light satiric thrusts at some of Hawthorne's contemporaries. Hawthorne simply did not take the trouble to mend the gap left by the deletion.[71] The illogical restructuring of the reader's response in the *Mosses* version provides an aesthetic reason for giving the original version priority.

What these examples show and what the following cases will

---

honor his friends and fellow authors in print"—Fredson Bowers, "Textual Commentary," in *Mosses from an Old Manse,* vol. X of the Centenary Edition of the Works of Nathaniel Hawthorne, ed. Bowers and J. Donald Crowley (Columbus: Ohio State University Press, 1974), p. 539. In spite of this claim about Hawthorne's nonaesthetic revisions, the Centenary edition publishes the 1846 cut version.

69. Centenary *Mosses,* p. 175.

70. See the "Historical Collation," in ibid., pp. 635–37.

71. See Harold P. Miller, "Hawthorne Surveys His Contemporaries," *American Literature,* 12 (1940), 235.

further indicate is that editors can validly overrule the author's chronologically final intention. Put most contentiously: editors can take control of the intended text out of the author's hands if justified by an examination of historical evidence and the intended structure of the reader's response. We can apply this argument even to prepublication versions, as in choosing a text based on the manuscript of *The Red Badge of Courage* instead of the expurgated first edition. Another example is including the deleted raft episode in a new critical edition of *Huckleberry Finn.* In the latter case, Twain allowed his publisher to delete from his final manuscript a fifteen-page passage which Twain had previously taken from his novel in progress and published in *Life on the Mississippi.* But, as Peter Beidler argues, the deleted episode "very much belongs in its original context in Chapter XVI [of *Huckleberry Finn*]. It supplies narrative connections which are otherwise rather conspicuously missing. It affects our reading of the rest of the chapter by giving information about Cairo which Huck and Jim do not yet have."[72] Without the raft episode, the reader is unintentionally confused by the text. Here again a weakened response structure and nonaesthetic reasons for deletion argue for overruling an author's chronologically final intentions.

After distinguishing and evaluating different versions of a work, the editor must then choose between extant variants of words or passages within the same version. Here again reader-response criticism coupled with historical evidence can help make editorial decisions. Frank Norris's *A Man's Woman* provides a useful example. Published in 1900 by Doubleday & McClure, this novel was attacked for its brutal realism by many reviewers.[73] A passage in chapter III describing a surgical operation was particularly criticized. One reviewer called it "sickening and disgusting" and added that "such a description out-Zolas Zola, and has no legitimate place in a work of fiction."[74] As a result of such criticism, the publisher apparently required Nor-

72. Peter G. Beidler, "The Raft Episode in *Huckleberry Finn*," *Modern Fiction Studies,* 14 (1968), 20.
73. See Joseph Katz and John J. Manning, "Notes on Frank Norris's Revisions of Two Novels," *Papers of the Bibliographical Society of America,* 62 (1968), 257.
74. *Outlook,* 64 (3 March 1900), 486, quoted in ibid., p. 257.

ris to replace the passage in a republication of the novel (some-
time before 1903).[75] The two versions follow:

ORIGINAL

Street located the head of the thigh-bone with his fingers and
abruptly thrust in the knife, describing Sayre's cut, going down to
the bone itself. Farnham turned back the flap made by the semicir-
cular incision, and with a large, broad-bladed, blunt-edged knife,
slightly curved upon the flat, pulled the soft tissues to one side.
Street, without looking away from the incision, held the knife from
him, and Lloyd took it and laid it on the table with her left hand, at
the same time passing the bistoury to him with her right. With the
bistoury the surgeon, in half a dozen strokes, separated the sur-
rounding integuments from the diseased head of the bone. But by
this time the wound was full of blood. Street drew back, and Lloyd
washed it clear with one of the gauze sponges, throwing the sponge
in the pail under the table immediately afterward. When the operation was resumed the surgeon went into the incision again, but
this time with the instrument called the periosteal elevator, peeling
off the periosteum, and all the muscles with it, from the bone itself.
Meanwhile Lloyd had gone to the foot of the table and had laid
hold of the patient's leg just above the knee, clasping it with both
her hands. Dr. Street nodded to her, signifying that he was ready,
and Lloyd, exerting her strength, pulled down upon the leg, at the
same time turning it outward. The hip-joint dislocated easily, the
head of the bone protruding. While Lloyd held the leg in place
Farnham put a towel under this protruding head, and the surgeon, with a chain-saw, cut it away in a few strokes. And that was
all—the joint was exsected.   [New York: Doubleday & McClure,
1900, pp. 64–65]

REVISION

Promptly the operation was begun; there was no delay, no hesitation; what there was to be done had been carefully planned
beforehand, even to the minutest details. Street, a master of his
profession, thoroughly familiar with every difficulty that might
present itself during the course of the work in hand, foreseeing

75. Ibid., p. 259. A similar situation arose in the case of Norris's *McTeague*
(1899)—see ibid., pp. 256–57. However, in this earlier revision, no inconsistent
restructuring of reader response occurs (though the humor of the scene is considerably weakened).

every contingency, prepared for every emergency, calm, watchful, self-contained, set about the exsecting of the joint with no trace of compunction, no embarrassment, no misgiving. His assistants, as well as he himself, knew that life or death hung upon the issue of the next ten minutes. Upon Street alone devolved the life of the little girl. A second's hesitation at the wrong stage of the operation, a slip of bistoury or scalpel, a tremor of the wrist, a single instant's clumsiness of the fingers, and the Enemy—watching for every chance, intent for every momentarily opened chink or cranny wherein he could thrust his lean fingers—entered the frail tenement with a leap, a rushing, headlong spring that jarred the house of life to its foundations. Lowering close over her head Lloyd felt the shadow of his approach. He had arrived there in that commonplace little room, with its commonplace accessories, its ornaments, that suddenly seemed so trivial, so impertinent—the stopped French clock, with its simpering, gilded cupids, on the mantelpiece; the photograph of a number of picnickers "grouped" on a hotel piazza gazing with monolithic cheerfulness at this grim business, this struggle of the two world forces, this crisis in a life.

Then abruptly the operation was over.   [New York: Doubleday, Page & Co., 1903, pp. 64–65]

The variant passages are followed by these paragraphs:

The nurse and surgeons eased their positions immediately, drawing long breaths. They began to talk, commenting upon the operation, and Lloyd, intensely interested, asked Street why he had, contrary to her expectations, removed the bone above the lesser trochanter. He smiled, delighted at her intelligence.

"It's better than cutting through the neck, Miss Searight," he told her. "If I had gone through the neck, don't you see, the trochanter major would come over the hole and prevent the discharges."

"Yes, yes, I see, of course," assented Lloyd.

The incision was sewn up, and when all was over Lloyd carried Hattie back to the bed in the next room. Slowly the little girl regained consciousness, and Lloyd began to regard her once more as a human being. During the operation she had forgotten the very existence of Hattie Campbell, a little girl she knew. She had only seen a bit of mechanism out of order and in the hands of a repairer. It was always so with Lloyd.

Interpretive Conventions

The original portrayal of the operation, with its objective medical descriptions, is consistent with the impersonal discussion of the operation that follows it, a discussion indicating that Lloyd "had forgotten the very existence of Hattie Campbell," the patient, "a little girl she knew." The reader understands the narrator's point when he reads that "Lloyd began to regard her once more as a human being." However, the revised description of the operation unintentionally confuses the reader's response. The new passage contains the sentences: "His assistants [including Lloyd], as well as he himself, knew that life or death hung upon the issue of the next ten minutes. Upon Street alone devolved the life of the little girl." In this revised form, Lloyd does *not* forget the little girl. The result is an unintended contradiction in the response structure when the reader comes to the passage claiming that Lloyd had forgotten about Hattie during the operation. Furthermore, in the revision the operation is viewed melodramatically, not objectively, by Lloyd and the reader. Thus in the revised state the drama is anticlimactically followed by an insensitive discussion, whereas in the original the discussion is merely an extension of the impersonal professionalism of the operation. On the basis of the historical evidence and this analysis of the response structure, an editor would be fully justified in choosing the earlier variant passage for his critical text.

Several other textual situations provide similar examples where external evidence and intended reader-response structures conspire against the author's chronologically final intention.[76] What Parker claims for Melville is true for other authors

76. See, for example, Hawthorne's deletions in "The Gentle Boy" discussed by Seymour L. Gross, "Hawthorne's Revision of 'The Gentle Boy,'" *American Literature*, 26 (1954), 196–208, and Brian Higgins and Hershel Parker, "The Chaotic Legacy of the New Criticism and the Fair Augury of the New Scholarship," in *Ruined Eden of the Present: Hawthorne, Melville, and Poe*, ed. G. R. Thompson and Vergil Lokke (West Lafayette, Ind.: Purdue University Press, 1981), pp. 30–34; the two added paragraphs at the end of chapter 27 of the English edition of Melville's *White-Jacket* discussed in Parker, "Melville and 'Author's Final Intentions,'" p. 165; Howells's revision of Irish slurs in *An Imperative Duty* discussed by Martha Banta, "Introduction" to *The Shadow of a Dream and An Imperative Duty*, vol. 17 of A Selected Edition of W. D. Howells, ed. Martha Banta, Ronald

as well: "an editor of Melville finds a series of . . . ambiguous textual situations in which he may decide, contrary to Greg, that the author's final intentions should not be obeyed."[77] However, any such decision requires a principled justification, that is, "anyone arguing for the original reading must elaborate some alternative to the concept of letting the author himself have the last say about his texts."[78] In this chapter I have attempted to offer such an elaboration by combining the interpretive strategies of reader-response criticism with the textualist's procedures for historical reconstruction.

A reader-response criticism based on a temporal and convention-based reading model provides the accounts of authorial intent and author's final intention required by textual scholarship. Before I can apply this model of reading to American literary history, I must develop this chapter's preliminary account of communicative conventions. In my subsequent discussion of the reader's role in literary history, I will emphasize holistic interpretation and the conventions constraining it, but it should not be forgotten that the diachronic (temporal) and synchronic (convention-based) dimensions of reading are inextricably joined. The sequential acts by the reader include a final interpretive synthesis at the end of reading, and the temporal reading experience also includes several preliminary attempts at synthesis before the end is reached. Throughout the time-flow of reading, then, not just at its conclusion, the reader is continually trying to make a holistic sense of the text, but his attempts are continually revised as he proceeds further. The reader uses communicative conventions in all these attempts at sequential and holistic interpretation.

Gottesman, and David J. Nordloh (Bloomington: Indiana University Press, 1971), pp. viii–ix, and Hershel Parker, "The First Nine Volumes of a Selected Edition of W. D. Howells: A Review Article," *Proof*, 2 (1972), 325–27; and Howells's replacement of a character's anti-semitic remarks in *The Rise of Silas Lapham*, discussed by David J. Nordloh, "Textual Commentary," *The Rise of Silas Lapham*, vol. 12 of A Selected Edition of W. D. Howells, ed. Walter J. Meserve and David J. Nordloh (Bloomington: Indiana University Press, 1971), pp. 382–84.

77. Parker, "Melville and 'Author's Final Intentions,'" p. 161.
78. Parker with Bebb, "The CEAA," p. 141.

CHAPTER FIVE

A Typology of Conventions

> We must notice that the illocutionary act is a conventional act: an act done as conforming to a convention.
> —J. L. Austin, *How to Do Things with Words*

> But for every convention in the hand, there are two in the bush.
> —A. R. Louch, *Explanation and Human Action*

Since communication is only one kind of human activity accounted for by conventions, we can ask how communicative conventions relate to other conventions of social action. Exactly which conventions are relevant to reading and interpretation? Do the communicative conventions for speech acts and literary reading function in the same way in textual interpretation? To answer these questions, I will broaden my analysis and provide a general typology of conventions. The subsequent chapter will propose a comprehensive theory of interpretive conventions.

Kinds of Shared Practices

The term "convention" has been used in a variety of ways across several areas of study, including sociology, linguistic pragmatics, philosophy of language, social psychology, cultural anthropology, and literary criticism. Understood in its widest application, "conventions" refers to *shared practices*. The following schema distinguishes the three kinds of conventions relevant to the study of human action.

    (i)   Traditional conventions of precedent:
           working definition—descriptions recognizing (past) regularities in action and belief

representative terms—custom and ritual
examples—singing the national anthem before a football
game
central ritual of organized religion (such as the
Mass of Roman Catholicism)
genre and mode in literature
(ii) Regulative conventions of agreement or stipulation:
working definition—prescriptions regulating (future) action
representative terms—covenant and law
examples—football rules for penalties
central covenant of organized religion (such as
the Mosaic Law of Judaism)
propriety or censorship in literature
(iii) Constitutive conventions of meaning:
working definition—descriptions determining (present)
meaning
representative terms—systems constituting meaning
examples—football rules constituting a touchdown
systems of religious belief constituting sacrifices
communicative competence constituting
speech acts

Traditional conventions are based on precedent and manifested most explicitly in a society's customs and rituals.[1] For example, singing the national anthem before a sports event is a traditional convention in contemporary American society. David Lewis's definition of conventions in general applies to these traditional conventions of precedent: "Conventions are regularities in action, or in action and belief, which are arbitrary but perpetuate themselves because they serve some common interest. Past conformity breeds future conformity because it gives one a reason to go on conforming; but there is some alternative regu-

---

1. "Custom" refers to habitual action or expected behavior. Ritual is "a category of standardized behaviour (custom) in which the relationship between the means and the end is not 'intrinsic,' i.e. is either irrational or non-rational"; some other custom could easily have been used to fulfill the ritual's function, becoming the traditional convention in force—see Jack Goody, "Religion and Ritual: The Definitional Problem," *British Journal of Sociology*, 12 (1961), 159. Obviously, as traditional conventions become more formalized (as in religious rites) they come to resemble regulative conventions prescribing behavior.

larity which could have served instead, and would have perpetuated itself in the same way if only it got started."[2] Such conventions can loosely be translated into descriptive "rules" that account for conventional behavior and belief.[3] These rules or conditions make the content of the conventions explicit. For instance, we might describe the sequence of actions that make up a certain traditional ritual: Just before an American football game, the announcer asks the audience to stand; the audience stands; the band begins to play; etc.

A series of contrastive pairs suggests the basic difference between traditional and regulative conventions: descriptive vs. prescriptive, normal vs. normative, habitual vs. prescribed, regular vs. regulated, expected vs. obligatory. Traditional conventions easily "rigidify" into regulative conventions: we have always done it this way (a description), therefore we *should* continue to do it this way (a prescription).[4] The history of standing up for the national anthem is an example of this transformation pro-

2. David Lewis, "Languages and Language," in *Language, Mind, and Knowledge*, ed. Keith Gunderson (Minneapolis: University of Minnesota Press, 1975), pp. 4-5; for a more complete account of this kind of convention, see pp. 5-6, and also Lewis's earlier discussions in his *Convention: A Philosophical Study* (Cambridge: Harvard University Press, 1969). Cf. Stephen R. Schiffer, *Meaning* (London: Oxford University Press, 1972), especially pp. 148-55; pp. 129-30 of Schiffer's book suggested the terms "precedent" and "agreement (or stipulation)" in my typology of conventions. Traditional conventions are similar to what Bach and Harnish call "social regularities," which they define as a kind of behavior *A* fulfilling two conditions: (i) the members of a collectivity do *A* in certain recurrent situations; and (ii) it is mutually believed among these members that (i)—see Kent Bach and Robert M. Harnish, *Linguistic Communication and Speech Acts* (Cambridge: MIT Press, 1979), p. 272.

3. The term "rules," for all its misleading associations, does capture the sense of order that conventions establish as the ground for intelligibility, the basis of any theory of interpretive conventions of the kind I will propose based on this chapter's typology. See Lewis's discussion of rules ("an especially messy cluster concept") in *Conventions*, pp. 100-107; also see Hubert Dreyfus on orderly-but-not-rule-governed behavior in *What Computers Can't Do: A Critique of Artificial Reason*, 2d ed. (New York: Harper & Row, 1979), esp. pp. 271 and 286-87.

4. By "prescriptions" I mean to include proscriptions against doing something (negative prescriptions) as well as positive prescriptions to do something. Regulative or prescriptive conventions are "sanctioned norms" that often include "collective evaluations" of what behavior *ought* to be—see Jack P. Gibbs, "Norms: The Problem of Definition and Classification," *American Journal of Sociology*, 70 (1965), 589-93. Also, cf. the legal discussion of prescriptive rules in William Twining and David Miers, *How To Do Things With Rules* (London: Weidenfeld and Nicolson, 1976), esp. pp. 48-70.

cess in which a traditional custom becomes a binding practice.[5] Prescriptive conventions as rules regulating future actions are most formally manifested in covenants and laws. A simple illustration is rules for penalties in football, formal rules of behavior for which all players agree to be held accountable.

In contrast to prescriptive rules for penalties, there are descriptive rules that constitute a touchdown in American football. These constitutive conventions describe the conditions under which a certain action has meaning. John Searle has usefully contrasted the "regulative rules" of etiquette (regulative conventions) with the "constitutive rules" of achieving checkmate or making a touchdown (constitutive conventions).[6] "Constitutive rules do not merely regulate, they create or define new forms of behavior."[7] Without such constitutive conventions it would be impossible to make a touchdown, whereas without the regulative conventions of etiquette it would still be possible to eat mashed potatoes with your hands. "Constitutive rules often have the form: X counts as Y in context C."[8] Through a system of constitutive conventions, a football player's crossing of a certain line with a certain object *counts as* a touchdown. One pervasive set of constitutive conventions is that of language use, a system of conventions making speech acts possible.[9]

5. In 1923 and 1924, national flag conferences in Washington, D.C., drew up a code "prescribing the correct manner of displaying and respecting the flag. In 1942, by joint resolution, Congress adopted this code as federal law" (David Eggenberger, *Flags of the U.S.A.* [New York: Thomas Y. Crowell, 1959], p. 193). The regulative convention formalized into law reads: "When the national anthem is played and the flag is not displayed, all present should stand and face toward the music" (*United States Code*, 22 June, 1942, ch. 435, sec. 6, 56 Stat. 380).

6. John R. Searle, *Speech Acts: An Essay in the Philosophy of Language* (London: Cambridge University Press, 1969), pp. 33-42; see also John Rawls on "rules of practices" in "Two Concepts of Rules," *Philosophical Review*, 64 (1955), 26. J. R. Cameron provides a precedent for using the term "constitutive conventions" to refer to what Searle calls "constitutive rules"—see Cameron, " 'Ought' and Institutional Obligation," *Philosophy*, 46 (1971), 311, and "Sentence-Meaning and Speech Acts," *Philosophical Quarterly*, 20 (1970), 98-99.

7. Searle, *Speech Acts*, p. 33.

8. Ibid., p. 35.

9. For work in speech act theory, see above, Ch. 4, nn. 21 and 22. Also cf. Saussure's comments on the universality of language compared to other social institutions and his discussion of how signification is based on the "arbitrary convention" associating signifier with signified. He writes that "every means of expression used in society is based, in principle, on collective behavior or—what

This account of conventions does not rule on whether all action is conventional, that is, motivated by convention. However, all three kinds of conventions *can* function as motives: by providing precedents (traditional conventions); by stipulating the rules for action, agreed upon through voluntary covenant or imposed law (regulative conventions); and by describing the conditions under which a certain institutional act counts as such (constitutive conventions). This proposed account of conventions can be applied to a wide range of human activities and within a variety of disciplines. In what follows, I will use the typology to examine the kinds of conventions employed in literary study.

Literary Conventions

Literary criticism and theory have made wide use of the notion of convention. Literary conventions have most often been viewed as *traditional* conventions—accepted subjects and forms used by writers and recognized by readers. As traditional conventions, they are "habits of art" which provide compositional possibilities for authors and raise expectations in their audiences.[10] These conventions of precedent include both modal and generic conventions. Put most succinctly: modes are stylistic and thematic conventions that cross genres; for instance, symbolism, realism, and romanticism are modes that can be manifested in the lyric poem, the historical drama, and the war novel; genres are conventional categories of literary works.

Though studies of individual modes are common, theoretical

---

amounts to the same thing—convention." Ferdinand de Saussure, *Course in General Linguistics,* ed. Charles Bally and Albert Sechehaye, trans. Wade Baskin (New York: McGraw-Hill, 1966), pp. 67-74; the quotations are from pp. 74 and 68. For a useful history and philosophical analysis of the concept of "conventional meaning," see Bernard E. Rollin, *Natural and Conventional Meaning: An Examination of the Distinction* (The Hague: Mouton, 1976).

10. See Robert M. Browne, "Theories of Convention in Contemporary American Criticism," Ph.D. diss., Catholic University of America, 1956 (rpt. Folcroft Library Editions, 1971), esp. pp. 12-13. On the concept of convention (especially in literary theory) during earlier periods and in other countries, see Lawrence Manley, *Convention, 1500-1750* (Cambridge: Harvard University Press, 1980), and Harry Levin, "Notes on Convention," in *Perspectives of Criticism,* ed. Harry Levin (Cambridge: Harvard University Press, 1950), pp. 55-83.

treatments of mode in general have been scarce. For Paul Alpers, "mode is the literary manifestation, in a given work, of the writer's and the putative reader's assumptions about man's nature and situation."[11] Guided by such a definition, we might say that modal conventions determine the world view that a reader expects to share (or at least recognize) in the course of his reading within a specific mode. Northrop Frye defines *mode* as "a conventional power of action assumed about the chief characters in fictional literature."[12] Though at first it seems very different, Frye's definition of mode actually complements Alpers's: the "power of action" assumed about the chief character (Frye's definition) *particularizes* how "assumptions about man's nature and situation" (Alpers's definition) are expressed in a narrative. For example, in the naturalistic mode, the fact that a character has no power of freely chosen action signifies a deterministic view about man's nature and situation.

As revealing as their definitions are, neither Alpers nor Frye focuses on the conventional nature of modes. In contrast, Douglas Hewitt does emphasize this dimension, but he discusses only one specific mode (realism) within one specific genre (the Victorian novel). Still, some of his remarks have implications for an account of mode in general. For instance, he writes: "By 'realistic' . . . I refer to a formal convention. Like all conventions it is the result of compromise between various demands. But we often talk as though it is not a convention at all, as though it were a way of presenting a direct picture of a series of typical and lifelike experiences. As soon as we try to define it, however, we realize how many questions we are usually begging—how far we take for granted highly conventional and often highly complex features."[13] Once we admit, with Hewitt, that modal *conventions* of realism constitute that mode's verisimilitude, it becomes easier to recognize the conventional nature of all modes.

11. Paul Alpers, "Mode in Narrative Poetry," in *To Tell a Story: Narrative Theory and Practice* (Los Angeles: Wm. Andrews Clark Memorial Library, UCLA, 1973), p. 29.
12. Northrop Frye, *Anatomy of Criticism* (Princeton: Princeton University Press, 1957), p. 366; Frye observes there that "modes tend to succeed one another in a historical sequence": myth, romance, high mimetic (most epic and tragedy), low mimetic (most comedy and realistic fiction), and then ironic.
13. Douglas Hewitt, *The Approach to Fiction* (London: Longman, 1972), p. 47.

Literary theorists have discussed genre conventions much more often than those of mode.[14] Fredric Jameson typifies a well-established view of genres when he writes that they "are essentially contracts between a writer and his readers; or rather ... they are literary *institutions,* which like the other institutions of social life are based on tacit agreements or contracts."[15] Past literary practice determines such contracts; that is, genre conventions are traditional. They can be as general as those comprising all narratives, distinguishing such texts only from literary genres like lyric poetry; and genre conventions can be as specific as those constituting the many subgenres or formula fictions. Thus, general narrative conventions (like those described by William Labov for natural narratives) can apply to epics, novels, dramas, short stories, and ballads, while specific conventions distinguish such restricted (sub)genres as the Gothic romance, realistic war story, and detective fiction.[16] A typical description of a genre includes the historical precedents and the relevant conventions. For instance, Wellek and Warren's description of the Gothic novel fixes Horace Walpole's *Castle of Otranto* (1764) as the first in a long line of tales with several distinguishing conventions: "there is not only a limited and continuous subject matter or thematics, but there is a stock of devices (descriptive-accessory and narrative, e.g., ruined castles, Roman Catholic horrors, mysterious portraits, secret passageways reached through sliding panels; abductions, immurements, pur-

14. See Wolfgang Ruttkowski, *Bibliography of the Poetics of Literary Genres for the Student of Literature* (Munich: Max Hueber, 1973).

15. Fredric Jameson, "Magical Narratives: Romance as Genre," *New Literary History*, 7 (1975), 135; cf. René Wellek and Austin Warren, *Theory of Literature*, 2d ed. (New York: Harcourt, Brace, 1956), p. 216, and Harry Levin, *Gates of Horn* (New York: Oxford University Press, 1963), pp. 21–23.

16. Labov's study of oral narratives of personal experience led to the following conclusion about their conventional organization: "A complete narrative begins with an orientation, proceeds to the complicating action, is suspended at the focus of evaluation before the resolution, concludes with the resolution, and returns the listener to the present time with the coda"—William Labov, *Language in the Inner City* (Philadelphia: University of Pennsylvania Press, 1972), p. 369. See Mary Louise Pratt's use of these conventional narrative sections in an analysis of literary texts: *Toward a Speech Act Theory of Literary Discourse* (Bloomington: Indiana University Press, 1977), ch. 2. On subgenres see John G. Cawelti, *Adventure, Mystery, and Romance: Formula Stories as Art and Popular Culture* (Chicago: University of Chicago Press, 1976).

suits through lonely forests)."[17] A writer uses such preestablished genres in composing his work, and the generic conventions determine structural and thematic expectations for the reader.

Traditional literary conventions can also function as regulative conventions which stipulate what should and should not be written (or read). Such prescriptive conventions act as evaluative criteria: they become rules that every "good work of art" should follow. Traditional conventions of genre and mode can rigidify into these regulative conventions; classical and neoclassical insistence on purity of kinds and decorum within genres are examples of this transformation.[18] Also, regulative literary conventions include rules of propriety: prohibitions against portraying explicit sex, against cursing and blasphemy, and so on. In its crudest form, a prescriptive convention of literature is a form of censorship.

Recent literary theory has discussed constitutive conventions as much as traditional conventions and certainly more than regulative ones. Since constitutive conventions include those that make a text count as literary, it is not surprising that theorists refer to them in the perennial debate over the definition of literature. Some theorists attempt to isolate *unique* conventions that constitute literary discourse. For instance, Richard Ohmann argues for a speech act definition: "A literary work is a discourse whose sentences lack the illocutionary forces that would normally attach to them. Its illocutionary force is mimetic."[19] In Ohmann's view, speech act conventions are somehow void in literature; for example, a novelist is not committed to the truth of his assertions. According to Ohmann, literary speech acts are "quasi-speech acts," constituted by conventions that imitate speech act rules of ordinary discourse. We can distinguish literature from nonliterature because literary works consist of these quasi-speech acts. Ohmann's definition ends up sounding like essentialist definitions of literature and is vulnerable to the ob-

17. Wellek and Warren, *Theory of Literature,* p. 223.
18. See, for example, ibid., p. 220; and William K. Wimsatt, Jr., and Cleanth Brooks, *Literary Criticism: A Short History* (New York: Knopf, 1957), pp. 80–82.
19. Richard Ohmann, "Speech Acts and the Definition of Literature," *Philosophy and Rhetoric,* 4 (1971), 14; italics in original are deleted here.

jection now routinely raised against them: any "essential characteristics" found in literary language can also be found in nonliterary language, whether rhyme, metaphors, or fictivity. Discussing Ohmann's definition, Mary Louise Pratt notes that fictive speech acts are present not only in literature but in daily
discourse as well: in hyperbole, teasing, "kidding around," imita-
tions, hypothetical statements, speculations, plannings, and verbal musings of almost any kind.[20]

To avoid such objections, other theorists focus on the constitutive conventions that are merely *necessary* to literature; that is,
these theorists do not claim that such conventions are the exclusive property of literary discourse. Pratt, for example, rejects the
literature/nonliterature distinction insofar as it stands for a difference in essential characteristics between literary and "ordinary" speech. She argues that literature is composed of several
characteristics, none of which is unique to literary discourse. For
instance, she notes that "processes of selection and elimination
play a central role in defining and bringing into being the institution we call Literature" but that texts not generally considered literature also go through a similar conventional process.[21]
Furthermore, for Pratt, the literary speech situation consists as
much in a reader applying these conventions to a text's genesis
and history as it does in the text actually having that prepared
and preselected background: "The essence of literariness or
poeticality can be said to reside not in the message but in a
particular disposition of speaker and audience with regard to
the message, one that is characteristic of the literary speech situation."[22] Others have pushed the convention-based definition of
literature even further by emptying it of any specific ties to prior
speaker intention or intrinsic textual properties. These theorists
have argued persuasively that the category of literature is a
wholly conventional (not an essentialist) one: literature is defined by what a society has decided to call literary. Literature, in
this view, is not a set of characteristics held in common by verbal

20. Pratt, p. 91.
21. Ibid., pp. 117-18.
22. Ibid., p. 87.

objects; rather, it is an empty category filled by general conventional agreements within historical communities.[23]

Related to this last approach are those theories that describe the kinds of constitutive conventions underlying the activity of reading in the literary situation. They focus on the question: How do readers and critics make sense of literary texts? As we saw in Chapter 2, Stanley Fish answers this question with "communal interpretive strategies" while Jonathan Culler uses a notion of "reading conventions." I will build on these concepts in the next chapter, where I develop a theory of interpretive conventions. It is possible to combine this focus on interpretive (reading) conventions with an answer to the definitional question. Literature then becomes a conventional frame put around discourse, a frame that brings with it reading conventions for interpreting the framed discourse.[24] This answer avoids the problems of essentialist definitions by making "literariness" a function of the frame (and the reading conventions it makes available) rather than of unique objective characteristics in the text. This view accounts for the intuition that literary texts must somehow differ significantly from nonliterary texts. They do differ, but the distinction is a result of texts being framed and read differently and not a result of intrinsic differences in language. This fact helps explain how the "same" text (for example, the Bible) can be considered nonliterature in one historical community and literature in another and how new meanings can be "discovered" in a nonliterary text once it is treated as literature.

The proposed definition also remedies a problem with theories such as Culler's that define the institution of literature

---

23. Cf. Morse Peckham, *Man's Rage for Chaos: Biology, Behavior and the Arts* (Philadelphia: Chilton, 1965), pp. 68–70; George Dickie, *Art and the Aesthetic: An Institutional Analysis* (Ithaca: Cornell University Press, 1974), pp. 30–50; and Stanley E. Fish, "How Ordinary Is Ordinary Language?" *New Literary History*, 5 (1973), rpt. in *Is There a Text in This Class?*, pp. 108–9.

24. Cf. Susan Stewart, *Nonsense: Aspects of Intertextuality in Folklore and Literature* (Baltimore: Johns Hopkins University Press, 1979), p. 28: "Each frame [constructed for language] bears a set of procedures for interpretation that members manipulate in engaging the text."

solely in terms of reading conventions.[25] For instance, John Reichert effectively argues against Culler's view of literature as a conventional institution by pointing out that the literary reading conventions Culler describes (conventions of significance and unity, for instance) also function in reading nonliterature *as nonliterature*. Thus he objects to Culler's theory because it does not distinguish the institution of literature from the institution of writing in general.[26] I would claim instead that it is not just reading conventions that constitute literature; it is the conventional *framing* of a discourse as literature *plus* the reading conventions (used vigorously and together) that the framing brings along with it.[27]

This framing takes place within historical communities, a fact that has two important consequences. First, what is framed may change from culture to culture, from period to period, and the hierarchy of reading conventions brought along with the frame may change as certain conventions achieve priority and others lose status.[28] Second, the successful act of framing is communal, not individual.[29] The notion of community thus becomes crucial

25. Culler, *Structuralist Poetics* (Ithaca: Cornell University Press, 1975), pp. 115, 118. In *The Structure of Literary Understanding* (Cambridge: Cambridge University Press, 1978), Stein Haugom Olsen also focuses on the reading conventions making up the institution of literature (pp. 82–117). However, Olsen gives one convention absolute priority: "to impose some sort of structure on the text, to divide it into parts and to interrelate the parts in a pattern" (p. 82). By giving authority only to this convention of unity, he too narrowly limits the reading conventions relevant to literary interpretation.

26. John Reichert, *Making Sense of Literature* (Chicago: University of Chicago Press, 1977), pp. 155–65. Reichert makes a similar objection to Olsen's theory in his review of *The Structure of Literary Understanding, Comparative Literature,* 32 (1980), 210–13.

27. It remains an open question how many of Culler's literary reading conventions actually are used in reading texts considered nonliterary. However, my discussion of literary communication in Ch. 4 requires only that there are certain conventions for reading literature, not that they are *exclusively* those for reading literature.

28. See Morse Peckham, "'Literature': Disjunction and Redundancy," in *What Is Literature?*, ed. Paul Hernadi (Bloomington: Indiana University Press, 1978), pp. 223–24; Frank Kermode, "Institutional Control of Interpretation," *Salmagundi,* No. 43 (1979), pp. 83–84; and the works cited above, Ch. 2, n. 38.

29. Though I have been using the notion of framing to explain how a discourse is placed in the descriptive category of literature, a *successful* act of framing refers to establishing a discourse as literary either in the descriptive or in the honorific sense. That is, an individual (e.g., author, publisher, literary critic)

here. In sociology, three aspects characterize the term "community": geographic area, social interaction, and common ties.[30] In the modern age of rapid communication and transportation, geographic area has become less a distinguishing characteristic of community than social interaction and common ties. But even these latter factors must be reconceived in light of modern technology. Social interaction now takes place over the telephone and television, through rapidly distributed periodicals, and at annual conferences in addition to day-to-day, neighborhood contact. Common ties remain the most relevant general criteria for defining community. For my purposes, common ties can be conceptualized as shared traditions, imposed or agreed-upon behavior patterns, and common ways of making sense—that is, as traditional, regulative, and constitutive conventions.[31] As one sociologist of communities has written, community members "are in the same 'club' whose conventions constitute a

---

performs a successful act of framing only when he convinces a community to accept his framing as its own, and that acceptance can take the form either of including the discourse in the general descriptive category of literature or of placing the discourse within the privileged literary canon.

30. George A. Hillery, Jr., "Definitions of Community: Areas of Agreement," *Rural Sociology*, 20 (1955), 118–19. Recent discussions continue to take Hillery's analysis as authoritative; see Jessie Bernard, *The Sociology of Community* (Glenview, Ill.: Scott, Foresman, 1973), pp. 3–5, and Dennis E. Poplin, *Communities: A Survey of Theories and Methods of Research*, 2d ed. (New York: Macmillan, 1979), pp. 3–25

31. My view of historical communities here can be contrasted to the communities discussed by Bleich and Fish—see above, Ch. 1. First of all, historical communities are more unified, have more conventions in common for longer periods of time, than do Bleich's provisional discussion groups. Second, Fish's interpretive communities refer to only one aspect (though a most important one) of historical communities—shared constitutive conventions for making sense of reality. At particular moments on particular issues, a single historical community can function as a single interpretive community; for example, in 1942 most citizens of the United States used the same interpretive strategies to make sense of World War II (as a fight for freedom, etc.) and in the mid-nineteenth century a European community of astronomers used the same Copernican paradigm to interpret celestial motion (as a system of planets orbiting around the sun). More often, however, historical communities are made up of several conflicting interpretive communities: in the late 1960s, U.S. citizens had radically different ways of making sense of the Vietnam War and a historical community of the mid-nineteenth century could include astrologers, Fundamentalist Christians, and Copernican astronomers, all with radically different ways of interpreting the cosmos.

kind of boundary-maintenance device."[32] So understood, historical communities that fill the category of "literature" can be
whole societies, but more often they are societal groups based on
economic organization (for example, the network of authors,
publishers, periodical editors, and book reviewers), social rank
(for instance, intelligentsia and governing classes), or institutional and professional position (such as English professor).[33]

We might more fully understand conventions relevant to
literary study by looking at the following diagram, which places
literary conventions (traditional, regulative, and constitutive)
within a larger framework.

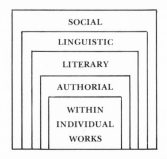

Disciplines such as sociology, social psychology, and cultural
anthropology focus on the most general *social conventions* of
human activity. The question "What is art?" can be answered at
this level, if art is viewed as a social institution constituted by
convention. Language is a social convention with its own set of
linguistic conventions: lexigraphic, syntactic, semantic, and pragmatic; the pragmatic component includes the communicative
conventions of speech act conditions and conversational postu-
lates. These conventions of language (form and use) are studied
in such disciplines as rhetoric, philosophy of language, communication theory, and linguistics (including sociolinguistics,
psycholinguistics, ethnography of speaking, and others). I have

32. Bernard, p. 9.
33. Cf. Dickie, pp. 31-38; Richard Ohmann, "The Social Definition of Literature," in Hernadi, pp. 89-101; and William J. Goode, "Community Within a
Community: The Professions," *American Sociological Review,* 22 (1957), 194-200.

just discussed *literary conventions* in examining modes and genres.[34] This level isolates the specific conventions for reading literature. A writer develops *authorial conventions* throughout the works making up his literary corpus. Examples range from characteristic word usages and individual symbolic systems to idiosyncratic plot or image patterns to particular variations on generic and modal conventions.

We may also speak of conventions developed *within individual works*. It might at first seem unsatisfying to refer to a "convention" established during the reading of a single literary text. Like genre conventions, however, conventions within a work are agreements or contracts set up between reader and author; they are the "ground rules" for that particular work and include provisions for allowable characters (hobbits or dentists), permissible narrator knowledge or intrusion (omniscient or limited points of view), possible plot twists (supernatural intervention or realistic cause-and-effect), and requirements of an implied reader. Specific conventions vary in different texts, but, as Douglas Hewitt writes, "what we do demand is consistency to its convention within each work."[35] Readers sometimes recognize such conventions immediately at the beginning of a narrative; in other cases they are learned slowly during the reading experience. For example, in my analysis of "Rappaccini's Daughter" in Chapter 3, I demonstrate how Hawthorne's discourse strategies teach the reader certain conventions of judgment that Hawthorne relies on the reader to use in making the final ethical judgment required by the narrative's ending.

With this typology of conventions and the various definitions of genre, mode, and so forth as background, I can now propose a comprehensive theory of interpretive conventions. The payoff for all this hermeneutic wind-up will be a detailed examination of the disguised interpretive work within American literary history.

34. For an especially interesting comparison between the levels of social and literary conventions, see Elizabeth Burns's discussion of the "rhetorical" and "authenticating" conventions of the theatre—in *Theatricality: A Study of Convention in the Theatre and in Social Life* (New York: Harper & Row, 1972), chs. 4–7.
35. Hewitt, p. 58.

CHAPTER SIX

Interpretive Conventions

> All reading is translation, and all attempts to communicate a reading seem to court reduction, perhaps inevitably.
>
> —Harold Bloom, *Poetry and Repression*

> The process of diachronic translation inside one's own native tongue is so constant, we perform it so unawares, that we rarely pause either to note its formal intricacy or the decisive part it plays in the very existence of civilization.... In short, the existence of art and literature, the reality of felt history in a community, depend on a never-ending, though very often unconscious, act of internal translation.
>
> —George Steiner, *After Babel*

To talk about interpretation is a difficult task in the present context of American literary theory. In the scholarly journals, there seems to be little agreement over the general aims or specific methods for interpreting literature. Instead, old and new hermeneutic theories constantly attack each other's most basic assumptions, and the majority of approaches even disagree over the definition of "interpretation" itself. Whenever anyone sets out to discuss interpreting, he runs the risk of getting lost in the general confusion of the ongoing debate. To avoid such dangers in my discussion of conventions and interpretation, I will try to make my own assumptions as clear as possible, beginning with a discussion of conflicting views of the interpretive process.

Interpretation

As we saw in Chapter 2, validity in interpretation remains a central concern of the American critical tradition. Reader-response and text-oriented critics argue most violently over the limits of acceptable interpretation; we hear charges of "solipsist" and "relativist" from one side, "elitist" and "reductivist" from the other. But the most publicized controversies have been stirred by the post-structuralists who reject *all* notions of interpretive validity. Such sweeping rejections have forced many otherwise dissimilar American critics to close ranks against the "intruders." This closing of ranks is not fully evident in print as yet, but I think the following is an accurate picture of the American critical situation: On the subject of interpretation, there is today a silent majority view being challenged by a growing and vocal minority. These two opposed hermeneutic stances, most commonly called traditional and deconstructive, can be personified by two of the participants in the ongoing debate over interpretation: M. H. Abrams and J. Hillis Miller.[1] A discussion of their respective positions will help me focus on *the problem of a hermeneutic definition.* I will use Abrams as an early and articulate representative of the silent majority opinion among professional critics and teachers of literature in the United States.[2] Miller's role as a representative of a vocal minority is more problematic, not only because that minority has again and again attacked the very concept of representation (in all its senses), but also because some members of that minority claim Miller has tamed their radical deconstructive stance.[3] Still, insofar as one can talk about

1. See especially M. H. Abrams, "The Deconstructive Angel," *Critical Inquiry,* 3 (1977), 425–38, and "How to Do things with Texts," *Partisan Review,* 46 (1979), 566–88; and J. Hillis Miller, "Tradition and Difference," *Diacritics,* 2, No. 4 (1972), 6–13, and "The Critic as Host," in *Deconstruction and Criticism* (New York: Seabury, 1979), pp. 217–53.

2. Admittedly, the majority's silence has never been complete. Even before Abrams's responses, there was E. D. Hirsch's counterattack on the "cognitive atheists"; see his *Aims of Interpretation* (Chicago: University of Chicago Press, 1976), which includes revised versions of essays published earlier in the decade. And it now appears that a growing and diverse reaction is gaining momentum in print: see, for example, Cleanth Brooks, "The New Criticism," *Sewanee Review,* 87 (1979), 592–607; Gerald Graff, *Literature against Itself* (Chicago: University of Chicago Press, 1979); and John Reichert, *Making Sense of Literature* (Chicago: University of Chicago Press, 1977). Cf. Frank Lentricchia's comments on the "traditionalist opposition" to deconstruction in America in *After the New Criticism* (Chicago: University of Chicago Press, 1980), pp. 159–60.

3. William Cain provides a useful description of Miller's more conservative assumptions in "Deconstruction in America: The Recent Literary Criticism of J.

a post-structuralist "position," Miller's theoretical statements (though not necessarily his critical practice) effectively demonstrate the antitraditionalist perspective in American literary theory.

M. H. Abrams bases his critical enterprise on the assumption that he can interpret an author's sequence of sentences and discover its "core of determinate meanings." He argues that if an interpretation is "sound," it "approximates, closely enough for the purpose at hand, what the author meant." This "sound" or correct interpretation may not capture all of the author's meaning, but it will at least be able to approximate some of it and exclude other meanings that are improbable. Abrams defines interpretation as an activity that "undertakes to determine what an author meant."[4]

In contrast, J. Hillis Miller rejects these constraining concepts of authorial origin and determinate meaning as the basis for interpretation. He sees Abrams's traditionalist project as impossible: for Miller, all origins are lost, all texts radically indeterminate. Miller embraces the hermeneutic theory he sees in Nietzsche, Derrida, and other deconstructionists: "The same text authorizes innumerable interpretations . . . there is no 'correct' interpretation." Miller's deconstructive project tries to follow out "the play of relations, repetitions, and differentiations within a work."[5] His aim is not to establish a determinate meaning but to continue self-consciously embroidering an indetermi-

---

Hillis Miller," *College English*, 41 (1979), 367–82. Also see Jonathan Culler, "The Critical Assumption," *SCE Reports*, 6 (1979), 81–82.

4. Abrams, "The Deconstructive Angel," pp. 426, 431. Cf. Hirsch, *Aims*, p. 49: "a text cannot be *interpreted* from a perspective different from the original author's. . . . Any other procedure is not interpretation but authorship." The hermeneutic project of recovering an author's intended meaning usually forms the first step in the work of literary historians and many American critics. As I mentioned in Ch. 4, even when the prohibition against the Intentional Fallacy appeared to dominate, critics often employed a rhetoric alluding to authorial intention or referred directly to "what the author meant" in order to decide a difficult interpretive crux; and the Intentional Fallacy itself underwent much attack and reformulation in literary theory—see the works cited in Ch. 4, nn. 3 and 4, and in G. Thomas Tanselle, "The Editorial Problem of Final Authorial Intention," *Studies in Bibliography*, 29 (1976), 170–71.

5. Miller, "Tradition and Difference," pp. 11–12.

nate one. He employs several strategies to accomplish this, including the use of etymologies for "key words" in the texts he deconstructs (or, as he sometimes puts it, the texts that deconstruct themselves). Such key words oscillate "painfully within the reader's mind. However hard he tries to fix the word in a single sense it remains indeterminable, uncannily resisting his attempts to end its movement."[6]

Miller's definition of interpretation has two complementary aspects: interpretation is an unfolding, unraveling, unweaving of the textual web *and* it is a self-conscious embroidering of its own. Miller's deconstructive use of etymologies demonstrates both of these hermeneutic aspects. By tracing a word's etymological roots, an interpreter both unravels a signifying thread in the text and simultaneously in his retracings leaves behind a web of his own making—the critical text. "The critic's attempt to untwist the elements in the texts he interprets only twists them up again in another place and leaves always a remnant of opacity, or an added opacity, as yet unraveled."[7] Miller views interpretation, then, as a kind of free yet self-defeating unraveling of the text.

In Abrams's and Miller's opposed theories of interpretation, we have two positions that are not only irreconcilable but incommensurate—the two debaters talk past each other. That is, their theories disagree at so many points that they do not appear to be discussing even the same general subject. This incommensurability of position is reflected in their mutually exclusive def-

---

6. Miller, "Stevens' Rock and Criticism as Cure," *Georgia Review,* 30 (1976), 11. Of course there is nothing about etymology that restricts its use to deconstructive criticism. Past literary critics have made use of etymology to recapture obscure word usages or to tease out additional complementary meanings for a word. Such practices, however, worked toward a unified or coherent meaning for a passage or a larger text. What distinguishes deconstructionists' use of etymology is their attempt to disrupt coherent sense, to show that a text is indeterminate by focusing on the contradictory meanings revealed in a word's history.

7. Miller, "Critic as Host," p. 247; cf. Miller, "Stevens' Rock and Criticism as Cure, II," *Georgia Review,* 30 (1976), 337: "The interpretation or solving of the puzzles of the textual web only adds more filaments to the web. . . . Criticism is the production of more thread to embroider the texture or textile already there. This thread is like the filament of ink which flows from the pen of the writer, keeping him in the web but suspending him also over the chasm, the blank page that thin line hides."

initions of interpretation: for Abrams interpretation is the discovery of the author's determinate meaning, but for Miller it is
unrestricted textual unraveling. From their assumed definitions,
Abrams can say that what Miller does might be interesting but it
is not interpretation; Miller can respond that Abrams's traditional project ignores what interpretation is really all about.

Faced with such basic disparities, the literary theorist wishing
to discuss hermeneutics must recognize that when such radically
opposed critics use the word *interpretation* they are never talking
the same "language." Every implicit and explicit definition of
interpretation can be viewed as an *argumentative* definition that
promotes the user's own hermeneutic theory. Armed with this
recognition, the literary theorist can attempt to locate some
common ground in these arguments and then suggest a more
comprehensive (and therefore useful) hermeneutic definition.
However, the kind of definition required here is not one that
attempts to synthesize the two different positions on the nature
of interpretation. Rather, what is needed is a definition that (1)
accounts for both Abrams's and Miller's definitions (explaining
how the term *interpretation* can be used to refer to such strikingly
different activities); (2) leaves room for the different hermeneutic arguments (that is, does not define one position out of existence from the start—as Abrams and Miller do to each other);
and (3) provides a direction for future discussions of the interpretive process.
A definition of interpretation as "acceptable and approximating translation" fulfills all these requirements. Let me demonstrate this claim first by explaining the definition in detail and
then by using it to clarify the Miller-Abrams debate.

Interpretation = acceptable and approximating translation.
The *OED* gives as one meaning of *interpret:* "the action of
translating; a translation or rendering of a book."
Interpret is derived from the Latin *interpretari*—to explain, ex-
pound, translate, understand—from *interpres:* an agent between
two parties, a broker, a negotiator, explainer, expounder, trans-
lator.

All interpretation is translation:

> we translate one meaning into another
> > one text into another
> > one phenomenon into another
> > one interpretation into another
> > one translation into another
> > > dark clouds become a warning of rain
> > > [kat] becomes "cat"
> > > "Je t'aime" becomes "I love you"
> > > a sequence of words becomes a poem
> > > a novel becomes an allegory of initiation
> > > the ritual of initiation becomes a symbol of
> > > > biological rebirth
> > > and on and on.[8]

Can interpretation therefore be infinite translation? Potentially, yes. Practically, no. Interpretation as translation is a version of the hermeneutic circle: every beginning is already an interpretation, and potentially we could circle around and around within an ever-expanding spiral of translation.[9] But we don't. We stop. We do not break out of the hermeneutic circle; we simply are satisfied with some translation within the circle. It makes sense. It is an acceptable approximation.

Interpretation in communication, for example, is always acceptable and approximating translation. We try to approximate the speaker's meaning as we create it for ourselves.[10] Translation

---

8. Recent literary theory provides some support for my use of the term "translation" in defining the interpretive process. For example, Susan Sontag, in her attack on critical interpretation, assumed that the "task of interpretation is virtually one of translation" (*Against Interpretation and Other Essays* [New York: Farrar, Straus & Giroux, 1965], p. 5). More positively, George Steiner has recently argued for a similar centrality of translation in his view of interpreting in *Against Babel: Aspects of Language and Translation* (New York: Oxford University Press, 1975), esp. chs. 1 and 5. Cf. Jonathan Culler, "Foreword" to *The Poetics of Prose* by Tzvetan Todorov (Ithaca: Cornell University Press, 1977), p. 10.

9. Cf. discussions of C. S. Peirce's theory of sign interpretation: e.g., "To respond interpretively to a sign is not to react to it automatically but is, in one sense of the term, to 'translate' it into another sign, which calls for further interpretation by virtue of being a sign" (Douglas Greenlee, *Peirce's Concept of Sign* [The Hague: Mouton, 1973], p. 108).

10. This is what interpretive (reading) conventions allow us to do—see the

toward a conventionally acceptable approximation is the form of most interpretive strategies. However, translations could approximate unendingly; indeed, this is the claim of deconstruction with its celebration of infinite sign-substitution, here exemplified by Miller's strategy of using etymologies.[11]

The term "approximation" marks an area of much debate in recent literary theory—the general problem of mimesis. Does a copy reflect, transform, or destroy its original? Versions of the most general "mimetic" position are that art imitates nature, that literary works resemble their sources, that correct interpretations reflect authorial intention. As my description of Miller's project suggests, post-structuralists have recently attacked such views. The myth of presence, the denial of origins, the displacement of centers, disbelief in correct interpretations, misreading of intention—such deconstructive catch-phrases indicate the recent antimimetic stance. The term "approximating" in my definition, however, remains neutral in relation to this mimetic-deconstructive debate. Mimetic theorists can use the definition and say that a copy always approximates (resembles) its original. Deconstructive critics can also use the definition and claim that approximation and copy are antithetical concepts: a copy imitates its source, an approximation transforms it. Though "approximating" as a defining term violates neither of these hermeneutic positions, it does point to a perspective on the continuing debate: a copy is an approximation of its source only in relation to some criteria of evaluation. For example, according to the criteria applied, the expurgated first edition of *The Red Badge of Courage* could be interpreted as a near approximation, an improved stylization, or a complete destruction of the story told in the final manuscript.[12] Now, the "criteria" applied by the

---

discussion of inferred intention in Ch. 4, and of communicative interpretation later in the present chapter.

11. Cf. Derrida's "abandonment of all reference to a *center*, to a *subject*, to a privileged *reference*, to an origin, or to an absolute *archia*" which restricts the "play" of "infinite substitutions": Jacques Derrida, "Structure, Sign, and Play in the Discourse of the Human Sciences," in *Writing and Difference*, trans. Alan Bass (Chicago: University of Chicago Press, 1978), pp. 278–93.

12. For a demonstration of this premise, see the critical judgments cited below in Ch. 7, esp. nn. 5, 59, and 62, and Conclusion, n. 4.

deconstructive critic *presuppose* that all copies destroy their sources, that all origins are unavailable; traditional mimetic critics assume just the opposite. What determines these criteria are conventions shared among groups of interpreters. This can be made clear by returning to the Abrams-Miller debate.

In a theoretically indeterminate field of translations, some take on a privileged status. They are conventionally agreed upon and become the "standard" translations, the range of "correct" interpretations.[13] The existence of the "correct" interpretation is not a problematic issue; it is "correct" if it is conventionally agreed upon, that is, if the reading conventions producing it are dominant in a communal context. Therefore, the explicit form of the Abrams-Miller debate is misleading: Abrams keeps saying, "There are correct interpretations," but actually means, "I accept standard translations (and the fact that there *are* such approximations)"; while Miller argues, "There are no correct interpretations," but means "I reject standard translations (and the fact that there *should* be such approximations)." Both critics view interpretation in a way congruent with my definition of interpreting as acceptable and approximating translation; the decisive disagreement is over the status of the acceptable approximation. Abrams wants the author's meaning to be the object of interpreting (the goal toward which his translation approximates), while Miller uses the approximating translations of etymologies to carry out his interpretive free play. For Abrams, acceptable approximation is a goal in itself ("we are satisfied that we have approximated the author's meaning").[14] For Miller, acceptable (etymological) approximation is merely a tool for his version of deconstructive criticism, which purportedly aims at undermining all stable meaning.

In tracing out the verbal roots or any thread in the web of the text, Miller's deconstructive critic finally arrives at an impasse, not being able to go any further but unable to find an ultimate grounding. This aporia, this impasse in interpreting the text, cannot be avoided. It "may only be veiled by some credulity

---

13. The "correct" interpretation is a part of what Stanley Fish calls a "standard story": see Fish, *Is There a Text in This Class?*, pp. 199–200.

14. Abrams, "The Deconstructive Angel," p. 438.

making a substance where there is in fact an abyss, for example, in taking consciousness as a solid ground. The thinly veiled chasm may be avoided only by stopping short, by taking something for granted in the terminology one is using rather than interrogating it, or by not pushing the analysis of the text in question far enough so that the impossibility of a single definitive reading emerges."[15] What Miller calls "stopping short" here is a form of acceptable approximation. For example, the phenomenological critics Miller alludes to use consciousness as an acceptable ground for their approximating interpretations. Miller rejects all such acceptable approximations, while Abrams makes one of them his goal. Miller refuses to stop short,[16] while Abrams sees such a move as the proper role of literary interpretation (*if*, of course, the stopping short is accomplished at the author's probable meaning, *the* acceptable approximation of Abrams's translating).

My view of interpretation as acceptable and approximating translation defines a common area of agreement between Abrams and Miller: their own definitions are argumentative ones that assume a view of interpretation as translation and then *legislate* more specific claims about the nature of the interpretive process. On the other hand, my formulation leaves room for both hermeneutic arguments and, in fact, provides a perspective on both by clarifying the ways in which they remain opposed. Furthermore, it provides questions for future hermeneutic discussions: In interpretation, what is translated into what? What is approximated (or not approximated)? What are the grounds of the acceptable? In my Conclusion I will return to the issues suggested by these questions. But now I will focus on perhaps

15. Miller, "Ariadne's Thread: Repetition and the Narrative Line," *Critical Inquiry*, 3 (1976), 74.

16. Or, I should say, Miller *claims* not to stop short. In fact, he does stop short in not applying his deconstructive premises to the institutional context of literary study. For example, though his version of deconstruction rejects many of the interpretive constraints of traditional projects such as Abrams's, Miller continues to reify "the literary canon as it now stands": see Cain, "Deconstruction in America," p. 379; also see Henry Sussman's excellent comments on the institutionalization of deconstruction in "The Deconstructor as Politician: Melville's *Confidence-Man*," *Glyph*, No. 4 (1978), pp. 52–54. Cf. Miller, "Theory and Practice: Response to Vincent Leitch," *Critical Inquiry*, 6 (1980), 612–13.

the most debated topic in recent literary hermeneutics: What exactly constrains the production and acceptance of interpretations? That is, what is the mechanism in interpretation that determines how the translating process works and how the resulting approximations are found acceptable?

Interpretive Conventions and Literary Meaning

The most important hermeneutic constraints are what I call "interpretive conventions": shared ways of making sense of reality. They are communal procedures for making intelligible the world, behavior, communication, and literary texts. Interpretive conventions can be as simple and short-lived as the instructions to a baby-sitter: "When Mary Nell cries, it means she wants her bottle." They can be as long-lasting and singleminded as Augustine's successful rule of faith: if a scriptural passage "seems to commend either vice or crime or to condemn either utility or beneficence," it should be taken as "figurative" and "subjected to diligent scrutiny until an interpretation contributing to the reign of charity is produced."[17] And they can be as complex and multipurpose as Freud's psychoanalytic techniques, which can interpret authors in their writings, characters in their fictional acts, or readers in their responses. Interpretive conventions like these are group-licensed strategies for constructing meaning, describable in terms of conditions for intelligibility. These conventions provide the mechanism for the acceptable and approximating translation in the interpretive process; they are the grounds not only for producing interpretations but also for accepting them.

This concept of interpretive conventions develops out of Culler's theory of reading conventions and Fish's notion of interpretive strategies. My account encompasses Culler's reading conventions (and the use I have been making of them in previous chapters), but interpretive conventions are not primarily filled out by structuralist descriptions. Nor are they restricted to read-

17. Augustine, *On Christian Doctrine*, trans. D. W. Robertson, Jr. (New York: Liberal Arts Press, 1958), p. 93. See the discussion of this "rule of interpretation" in Stanley E. Fish, "Interpreting the *Variorum*," in *Is There a Text in This Class?*, p. 170.

ing and interpreting literary texts; for they are also used in "reading" the extraliterary world.[18] Interpretive conventions most closely resemble Fish's communal interpretive strategies, the specification of which Fish leaves open enough to allow various ways of describing shared interpretive practices. Yet my account differs from Fish's in that I particularize the dynamics of interpretive conventions by using the typology proposed in the previous chapter.

That chapter distinguishes three kinds of conventions— traditional, regulative, and constitutive. A basic assumption in a theory of interpretive conventions is that in interpretation all these conventions constitute meaning: from the complex conventional nature of language use to the various features of genre and mode in literature to the binary signification of football rules. We have already seen how a traditional convention, standing for the national anthem, becomes prescriptive. It also becomes constitutive; that is, compliance or noncompliance with a traditional or regulative convention *signifies:* not standing up for the national anthem *counts as* disrespect for the flag, the nation, etc.[19] More generally, traditional and regulative conventions become constitutive any time they are used to make sense of an action, past or present, whether that action is communicative or not.[20]

18. For example, Kuhn's concept of paradigms as "shared exemplars" for interpreting nature is closely related to certain kinds of interpretive conventions—see Thomas S. Kuhn, *The Structure of Scientific Revolutions,* 2d ed. (Chicago: University of Chicago Press, 1970), esp. pp. 174–210; and see my discussion of Kuhn's theory in Ch. 1, above.

19. Cf. Kent Bach and Robert M. Harnish, *Linguistic Communication and Speech Acts* (Cambridge: MIT Press, 1979), p. 95: "Rule violations, if committed with recognizable [reflexive] intentions, can communicate the agent's contempt for society, his disrespect for those present, or even his acknowledgment that the rules can be relaxed." The point Bach and Harnish seem to miss here is that reflexive intentions are recognizable primarily *because* of the rule (regulative convention) violation. And of course it is not just rule violation that signifies; rule following can also convey meaning: in our example, standing (potentially) signifies respect.

20. Ethnomethodological studies make similar claims: "Aside from determining the *occurrence* of certain responses under suitable conditions, rules [or regulative conventions] are also invoked [as constitutive conventions] to clarify the *meaning* of actions retrospectively.... Indeed, it is a readily demonstrable fact that a good deal of the sense we make of the things happening in our presence

Though their basic hermeneutic function is the same, the three kinds of conventions make the production of meaning possible in different ways. Traditional conventions allow interpreters of an action to fit that act into the context of a mutually believed regularity described by the convention. Interpreters use regulative conventions either to infer the reflexive intention of someone who obeys or disobeys a binding rule or to make sense of the motivation for an action that accords with the behavior sanctioned by the convention. Constitutive conventions define (and therefore describe and regulate) institutional actions that would not be possible (or identifiable) apart from the conditions specified by the convention; interpreters know that an action has a certain meaning if it is performed according to a certain constitutive convention. By calling traditional and regulative conventions constitutive in interpretation, I mean to indicate their potential usefulness for accomplishing meaning-production; I am not suggesting that once so used the three kinds of conventions are no longer distinguishable. In interpretation, traditional and regulative conventions become constitutive conventions only in the sense that all three make meaning possible for interpreters.

All interpretive conventions are intersubjective and often (but not always) intertextual. Intertextuality involves the relation of one text to other texts.[21] To naturalize an object-text is to relate it to a textual network in order to make sense of the object-text; in fact, the relationship *is* the sense made for that text. One form of literary naturalization relates a present text to the traditional conventions of past literature, genre and modal conventions thus becoming constitutive of meaning.[22] In this case, genre and

---

depends on our ability to *assign them* to the phenomenal sphere of influence of some rule"—Egon Bittner, "The Concept of Organization," *Social Research,* 32 (1965); rpt. in *Ethnomethodology: Selected Readings,* ed. Roy Turner (Baltimore: Penguin, 1974), p. 77.

21. On intertextuality, see Julia Kristeva, *Semiotikè: Recherches pour une sémanalyse* (Paris: Seuil, 1969), p. 378; Michael Riffaterre, *Semiotics of Poetry* (Bloomington: Indiana University Press, 1978), pp. 115–50; and Jonathan Culler, *Structuralist Poetics* (Ithaca: Cornell University Press, 1975), p. 139.

22. As I noted in Ch. 2, Culler defines "naturalization" as a way of bringing a text "into relation with a type of discourse or model which is already, in some sense, natural and legible" (*Structuralist Poetics,* p. 138). He goes on to describe

modal conventions not only provide a reader with expectations as traditional conventions, they also function intertextually as constitutive conventions to enable the reader to make sense of literary texts. Conventions within an author's entire corpus and within individual works serve a similar dual function: they constitute part of both sequential and holistic interpretation, creating meaning immediately during the time-flow of reading and retrospectively after the whole text has been read.

Interpretive conventions account for both communicative interpretation and interpretive free play. By communicative interpretation I mean the attempt by readers to recover the intention of the author. As I argued in Chapter 4, intention in literary acts can be recovered only through communicative conventions; insofar as intention (as a state of mind) is not expressed or manifested conventionally, it is to that extent not recoverable. When communicative conventions are used by an interpreter to make sense of a spoken utterance or written discourse, they function as interpretive conventions. The traditional hermeneutic project of searching for an author's original meaning translates the text into an approximation of authorial intention, and the production and acceptability of this approximation depend upon the interpretive conventions in force.[23]

---

five levels of naturalization, "five ways in which a text may be brought into contact with and defined in relation to another text which helps to make it intelligible" (p. 140); one of these ways is the use of "genre conventions" (p. 147). Cf. Culler, "Semiotics as a Theory of Reading," in *The Pursuit of Signs* (Ithaca: Cornell University Press, 1981), pp. 58–59.

23. Those communication-intention theories of meaning (alluded to in Ch. 4, n. 21) that deny the wholly conventional nature of inferring intention would seem to reject the importance I am giving interpretive conventions here. Without giving a full-dress rebuttal of these theories, I can suggest how they do in fact use conventions (especially interpretive conventions) in their account of communication despite their anti-conventionalist stance.

In "Intention and Convention in Speech Acts," *Philosophical Review*, 73 (1964), 439–60, P. F. Strawson rejects conventions as a basis for most illocutionary acts. He restricts convention-based illocutionary acts to those performed within institutional practices like marriage ceremonies (pronouncing a couple husband and wife) and legal trials (giving a verdict). However, he also extends the category of conventional acts to include introductions and surrendering. The last of these acts, surrendering, "may be said to be (to have become) an act performed as conforming to an accepted convention" (p. 443). The parenthetical "to have become" is crucial here: Strawson implies the act of surrendering—"by saying

In contrast to communicative interpretation, interpretive free play gives no special status to authorial intention. However, such interpretive free play can also be accounted for by invoking interpretive conventions. For example, in the approaches of post-structuralists such as Jacques Derrida and Julia Kristeva, "interpretation is not a matter of recovering some meaning which lies behind the work and serves as a centre governing its structure; it is rather an attempt to participate in and observe the play of possible meanings to which the text gives access."[24] But even in the analysis of a *système décentré*, which entirely ignores authorial intention, conventions continue to function in the

---

'*Kamerad*' and throwing up your arms"—was (in my terms) a traditional convention that became constitutive. But this transformation process is true for other practices as well, practices that Strawson calls nonconventional acts such as warning (p. 444). Putting aside the historical question whether such conventions did evolve from traditional to constitutive, we can find a convincing convention-based account of all the speech acts Strawson calls nonconventional: see John Searle, *Speech Acts* (London: Cambridge University Press, 1969), especially his account of "warning" in terms of conventional speech act conditions, p. 61. Cf. the attack on Strawson's account of nonconventional illocutionary acts in Quentin Skinner, "Conventions and the Understanding of Speech Acts," *Philosophical Quarterly*, 20 (1970), 118–38.

The distinction that Strawson captures in his account is not (as he thinks) a distinction between speech acts that are based on constitutive conventions and those that are not, but between conventional acts within extralinguistic institutions and conventional acts outside such institutions. (Cf. Searle, "A Classification of Illocutionary Acts," *Language in Society*, 5 [1976], 14.) Bach and Harnish make an error similar to Strawson's when they reject Searle's conventionalist account. In its place, they substitute a Gricean inferential process, which they represent in their "speech act schema" (*Linguistic Communication*, pp. 76–77; for Grice's analysis of meaning, see above, Ch. 4, n. 31). For my purposes here, the revealing features of the Bach-Harnish schema are the mechanisms guaranteeing that the hearer takes all the inferential steps to achieve uptake. All these mechanisms resemble the assumptions and strategies that make up interpretive conventions: general presumptions (pp. 60–61), "conversational presumptions" (p. 62), "conversational and social rules" (pp. 104–5), and especially "inference strategies" (p. 77). Like interpretive conventions, all of these mechanisms for aiding inference are shared by groups of speakers and hearers, and though bound by context, they are trans-situational, stable enough to be used in different contexts. This observation is not a criticism of Bach and Harnish's account (which excludes such mechanisms from its restricted concept of "convention"); I am simply trying to show that what I call interpretive conventions play a central role even in intention-communication theories that claim to be anticonventional.

24. Culler, *Structuralist Poetics*, p. 247. See Kristeva, *Semiotikè*, p. 284, and Derrida, *Writing and Difference*, pp. 278–93. Also, cf. J. Hillis Miller's American version of deconstruction discussed earlier in the present chapter.

practice of interpretation. As Culler points out, "Anything can be related to anything else, certainly: a cow is like the third law of thermodynamics in that neither is a waste-paper basket, but little can be done with that fact. Other relations, however, do have thematic potential, and the crucial question is what governs their selection and development. Even if 'emptied' by a radical theory, the centre will inevitably fill itself in as the analyst makes choices and offers conclusions."[25] In other words, some procedure governing selection and development of relations will be adopted in interpretive free play; the center will be filled (perhaps only temporarily) by shared rules for the game (like using etymologies or deconstructing basic oppositions). These shared hermeneutic strategies function as interpretive conventions, making (and destroying) meanings. Thus, in both traditional and post-structuralist criticism, there will always be some interpretive conventions at work.

This theory of interpretive conventions accounts for a wide range of hermeneutic activity. When applied to literary study, we can use the theory to explain the sense critics make of a text in critical discourse (using different and shared sets of critical conventions) as well as the sense readers are constantly making as they read (through different and shared reading conventions).[26] Thus such a theory of interpretive conventions can be elaborated into a hermeneutic theory, a paradigm for criticism, and a model of reading.

Speech Act Philosophy Once Again

I can further explain the proposed theory of interpretive conventions through a brief comparison to some recent work in speech act philosophy. Such a comparison will clarify the two most general ways conventions become constitutive of meaning: through convention-violation and convention-application. For instance, a communicative act that violates a traditional or regu-

---

25. Culler, *Structuralist Poetics,* pp. 250–51.
26. For a detailed examination of the assumptions and critical moves constituting the interpretive conventions of one recent critical approach, see Steven Mailloux, "Learning to Read: Interpretation and Reader-Response Criticism," *Studies in the Literary Imagination,* 12, No. 1 (1979), 93–108.

lative convention can be made to signify by virtue of that violation, and various kinds of acts can be made sense of by applying
conventions to their performance. Exploring certain moments
in the work of H. P. Grice and John Searle will demonstrate
these two ways of using interpretive conventions.

We can begin with Grice's theory of "conversational implica-
ture," which provides a revealing example of how the violation
of a regulative convention can constitute a hearer's interpretation of the speaker's meaning. Grice describes a set of conversational guidelines that are assumed to be in force in any speech
exchange. The most general of these is the Cooperative Principle: "Make your conversational contribution such as is required,
at the stage at which it occurs, by the accepted purpose or direction of the talk exchange in which you are engaged."[27] Grice
distinguishes four categories of maxims that fall under this general principle: maxims of quantity—be only as informative as
required; quality—be truthful; relation—be relevant; and
manner—be perspicuous. As Michael Hancher has pointed out,
"these rules are all regulative, not constitutive."[28] When used by
a hearer to *interpret* a rule-violation, however, these maxims do
become constitutive of meaning. Grice argues that a speaker can
"flout" a maxim by blatantly failing to fulfill it and that such
flouting gives rise to "conversational implicatures" if the speaker
is obviously still adhering to the Cooperative Principle.[29] For
example, if a teacher says, "This is the best class I have ever
had," to students who have just received failing grades from that
teacher, the class will interpret the utterance as flouting the
maxim of quality and thus implicating an ironic reading of the
statement. Here we have interpreters using the violation of a
regulative convention to infer the speaker's reflexive intention,
regulative conventions becoming constitutive of meaning.[30]

27. H. P. Grice, "Logic and Conversation," in *Speech Acts: Syntax and Semantics 3*, ed. Peter Cole and J. L. Morgan (New York: Academic Press, 1975), p. 45.

28. Michael Hancher, "Beyond a Speech-Act Theory of Literary Discourse," *MLN*, 92 (1977), 1090.

29. Grice, "Logic and Conversation," p. 49. I should note in passing that when Grice calls these conversational implicatures "non-conventional" (p. 45), he is using "conventional" in a more restricted sense than the one I have developed here.

30. Cf. Mary Louise Pratt, *Toward a Speech Act Theory of Literary Discourse*

We can learn more about interpretive conventions by examining Searle's detailed analysis of speech acts. A good place to begin is with the fact that interpreting can be viewed as an illocutionary act like asserting, ordering, promising, and so on. In his tentative taxonomy of speech acts (which Searle and others revise), J. L. Austin calls "interpret" an *expositive* (an act of exposition) that might well be taken as a *verdictive* (an act "giving a finding as to something—fact, or value—which is for different reasons hard to be certain about").[31] Unfortunately, such general taxonomic descriptions do not really clarify the precise nature of interpreting (and they were not intended to do so).

More helpful is Searle's notion of constitutive rules, which helps describe exactly how specific interpretive conventions work. According to Searle, a promise is made possible by constitutive rules that specify the conditions upon which promising logically depends for its existence. Similarly, meaning is made possible by constitutive conventions that specify the conditions upon which interpretation (meaning-making) logically depends for its existence. To be even more precise: constitutive rules describe the "necessary and sufficient" conditions for the "successful and non-defective performance" of an act such as promising.[32] In the same way, constitutive conventions describe the conditions for the successful and nondefective—that is, valid—performance of interpretation. The interpretive conventions in force in a particular context determine this valid interpretation, just as the speech act conventions in force determine the nondefective act of promising. Both kinds of conventions are

---

(Bloomington: Indiana University Press, 1977), chs. 5 and 6, where the author presents several examples of how readers can use Grice's conversational maxims to make sense of literary texts.

31. J. L. Austin, *How to Do Things with Words,* ed. J. O. Urmson (New York: Oxford University Press, 1962), pp. 150–60. Bruce Fraser lists "interpret" under *acts of evaluating* in his taxonomy—see "Hedged Performatives," in Cole and Morgan, p. 191; and in "Describing and Interpreting as Speech Acts," *Journal of Aesthetics and Art Criticism,* 36 (1978), 484, Michael Hancher uses Searle's taxonomy to class "interpreting" as a *representative,* an illocutionary act that commits "the speaker (in varying degrees) to something's being the case, to the truth of the expressed proposition" (Searle, "A Classification of Illocutionary Acts," p. 10).

32. Searle, *Speech Acts,* p. 54.

context-sensitive, socially determined, and potentially change-
able; and when a hearer uses speech act conventions to make
sense of a speaker's utterance, they function as interpretive conventions. However, speech act conventions are more stable than
most other interpretive conventions, especially those of the latter
used in literary study (as the history of criticism testifies).

Searle grounds his speech act analysis on the distinction between regulative and constitutive rules: "Regulative rules regulate a pre-existing activity, an activity whose existence is logically
independent of the rules. Constitutive rules constitute (and also
regulate) an activity, the existence of which is logically dependent on the rules."[33] Thus Searle contrasts the regulative rules
of etiquette and fishing with the constitutive rules of chess and
speech acts. It should be noted that he is not referring to the
interpretation of these activities here but to their performance.[34]
Certain acts are made possible by constitutive conventions: promising, playing chess, making a touchdown. But, I would argue,
interpretation of *all* action is made possible only through constitutive conventions. We make sense of acts by invoking interpretive conventions (traditional, regulative, and constitutive);
such conventions constitute meaning.

Stanley Fish employs Searle's regulative/constitutive distinction in a critique of the use of speech act theory by literary critics.
For example, Fish writes that Wolfgang Iser

> equivocates between two senses of "convention": the stricter sense
> by which illocutionary acts are constitutive rather than regulative,
> and the looser sense (roughly equivalent to "accepted practice")

33. Ibid., p. 34.
34. As long as Searle restricts his discussion to the performance (and not the
interpretation) of acts, he can maintain his sharp distinction between regulative
and constitutive conventions. However, he does not always restrict himself in this
way: see *Speech Acts*, pp. 35–37. In "Speech Acts or Fluid Language," *Journal of
Literary Semantics*, 5 (1975), 15–30, David H. Hirsch launches a frontal attack on
Searle's speech act theory through a wholesale rejection of the regulative/
constitutive distinction. I do not agree with most of Hirsch's attack nor with his
complete rejection of the regulative/constitutive distinction. At least one example
Hirsch uses in his critique (p. 27) owes its force to his unacknowledged move
from a focus on an act's performance to a focus on its interpretation. The same
move is made by Christopher Cherry in his critique of Searle, "Regulative Rules
and Constitutive Rules," *Philosophical Quarterly*, 23 (1973), 312.

employed by literary critics when they talk, for example, of the conventions of narrative. The equivocation is important to Iser ... because he wants to assert a parallel between a violation of speech act conventions and a violation of the conventions of literature or society. But the parallel will not hold because in one case a violation amounts to non-performance, while in the other the convention (which rather than constituting the activity is merely a variation on it) is either replaced or modified.[35]

Like Searle most of the time, Fish is talking primarily about the performance of an act and not its interpretation. He is therefore correct in saying that the constitutive conventions of an illocutionary act are not the same as the traditional conventions ("accepted practice") of writing narratives: violation of the former results in nonperformance, while violation of the latter will simply provide variations on storytelling. If we shift the focus from performance to interpretation, however, traditional conventions become constitutive: "accepted practice" becomes a way of making sense of a literary act in the same way that speech act conventions are used to interpret an utterance. In literary interpretation, part of a text's meaning emerges in the reader's perception of whether the text follows or violates traditional conventions.

The purpose of Chapters 5 and 6 has been to propose a comprehensive theory of interpretive conventions in order to provide a more detailed convention model to discuss the use of "the reader" in doing literary history, the subject to which we now turn.

35. Fish, "How To Do Things with Austin and Searle: Speech Act Theory and Literary Criticism," in *Is There a Text in This Class?*, pp. 222–23. Michael Hancher makes a similar critique of Mary Louise Pratt's collapsing of the regulative/constitutive distinction ("Beyond a Speech-Act Theory of Literary Discourse," pp. 1085–87).

CHAPTER SEVEN

Literary History and Reception Study

> Literary history has been much too busy trying to prove that past writers shouted loud enough to be heard by posterity. We should be more interested in knowing how far their voices carried in their own generation, and—equally important—whether their generation talked back.
>
> —William Charvat, "Literary Economics and Literary History"

> As the mediating, long-forgotten element in literary history, the reader can no longer be ignored.
>
> —Hans Robert Jauss, "Theses on the Transition from the Aesthetics of Literary Works to a Theory of Aesthetic Experience"

The *Literary History of the United States* has gone through four editions since its first publication in 1948, and these editions, the latest in 1974, testify to the staying power of a once dominant approach to doing American literary history. The introduction to *LHUS* summarizes the approach succinctly: "History as it is written in this book will be a history of literature within the margins of art but crossing them to follow our writers into the actualities of American life. It will be a history of the books of the great and the near-great writers in a literature which is most revealing when studied as a by-product of American experience."[1] In his review of the first edition, René Wellek took issue with the kind of extrinsic literary history implied by this introductory statement. He wrote that "the most serious

---

1. "Address to the Reader," in *Literary History of the United States*, vol. 1, ed. Robert E. Spiller et al. (New York: Macmillan, 1948), p. xvii. New one-volume editions of *LHUS* were published in 1953, 1963, and 1974.

deficiency" of *LHUS* was its "failure to provide a continuous and coherent history of poetic styles, prose-genres, devices and techniques—in short, a history of literature as art."[2] In place of an account that emphasized political, cultural, and intellectual backgrounds, Wellek and others argued for an "internal literary history," one that stressed "the development of literature as literature."[3]

Aspects of this intraliterary project have since become essential to doing American literary history. Many journals now routinely publish detailed accounts and analyses of traditions, devices, and genres. Descriptions of "traditional conventions" maintain a prominent place within this intrinsic literary history. Before questioning this now established approach, let me illustrate its activities by discussing the traditional literary conventions Stephen Crane used and modified in writing *The Red Badge of Courage*.

Conventions and American Literary History

Crane composed *The Red Badge of Courage* as an ironic tale of a young soldier's egotistical self-deceptions. To accomplish this portrayal, he showed Henry Fleming to be as deluded in his attitude toward his heroic acts as he was in his earlier rationalizations about running from battle. Throughout the story, the narrator consistently undercuts Henry's unfailing egotism, both his lack of concern for others and his belief in his own uniqueness (either as victim or prophet). The novel concludes with a masterfully ironic coda in which Henry's final evaluation of his past conduct appears as just one more self-delusion. This is the *Red*

2. René Wellek, "The Impasse of Literary History," *Kenyon Review*, 11 (1949), 504.
3. René Wellek, "The Concept of Evolution in Literary History," in his *Concepts of Criticism*, ed. Stephen G. Nichols (New Haven: Yale University Press, 1963), p. 52; Wellek (with Austin Warren), *Theory of Literature* (New York: Harcourt, Brace, 1949), p. 255. Also see the following: Norman Holmes Pearson's statement that the "most useful referent" of literary history is "the individual and traditional forms making up the body of literature which it studies": "Literary Forms and Types; or, A Defense of Polonius," in *English Institute Annual, 1940* (New York: Columbia University Press, 1941), p. 66; Cleanth Brooks's prediction that "the new history of literature should be more truly a history of *literature:*

Badge that Crane wrote. However, it is not the book that D. Appleton & Co. published in October 1895. A cut-down version of Crane's final manuscript, the text of the Appleton first edition resulted from wholesale expurgations but no extensive rewriting.

Appleton did not print several passages that can still be found in the extant pages of Crane's final manuscript as well as others that existed on pages now missing. Crane marked some of these deletions in the manuscript itself; for example, he crossed out passages at the ends of chapters 7, 10, and 15 in pencil or blue crayon and removed the folio pages of chapter 12. Other passages (such as those in chapters 16 and 25) were left uncanceled in the manuscript but were not published in the first edition.[4] Crane cut all this material from the story at the insistence of his Appleton editor, Ripley Hitchcock.[5] The result was a radically different story from the one Crane had originally written. The Appleton *Red Badge* seems to present a realistic account of a young soldier's growth to maturity.

Henry Binder has recently demonstrated that Crane's most complete intentions are realized more fully and more consistently in the final manuscript than in the Appleton first edition. Binder is especially effective in showing the incoherence of the Appleton final chapter, the section that most critics use as crucial

---

that is, it should be better able to deal with literary structures and modes more closely than have the literary histories of the past": *The Well Wrought Urn* (1947; New York: Harcourt, Brace, 1975), p. 238; and R. S. Crane's advocacy of a "narrative history of forms" in his *Critical and Historical Principles of Literary History* (Chicago: University of Chicago Press, 1971)—this essay was written in 1950 but remained unpublished for seventeen years, according to Sheldon Sacks, "Foreword," p. 5.

4. Most of the manuscript is preserved in the Stephen Crane Collection of the Clifton Waller Barrett Library at the University of Virginia, and four pages of the original chapter 12 are distributed among the Houghton Library at Harvard, the Butler Library at Columbia, and the Berg Collection at the New York Public Library. The final manuscript and an earlier draft are reproduced in *The Red Badge of Courage: A Facsimile of the Manuscript*, ed. Fredson Bowers, vol. II (Washington, D.C.: NCR/Microcard, 1972).

5. See Henry Binder's convincing argument in "The *Red Badge of Courage* Nobody Knows," *Studies in the Novel*, 10 (1978), 17–23. Also cf. Donald Pizer, "*The Red Badge of Courage* Nobody Knows: A Brief Rejoinder," *Studies in the Novel*, 11 (1979), 77–81, and Henry Binder, "Donald Pizer, Ripley Hitchcock, and *The Red Badge of Courage*," *Studies in the Novel*, 11 (1979), 216–23.

proof that Henry Fleming has undergone a change in character. Binder illustrates how the referents for key words and passages are illogically missing and how important characters lose their original functions because of the cuts. What he proves quite decisively is that "the excisions were perfunctorily made by a process of cutting out large or small pieces and splicing loose ends together with almost no attempt at rephrasing places where the deletions left the text obscure or incomplete."[6] As a result of his study, Binder decided to follow Hershel Parker's suggestion and reconstruct the version of *Red Badge* presented in the final manuscript.[7] This new critical edition of Crane's novel is now available in *The Norton Anthology of American Literature.*[8]

There are, then, two texts currently called *The Red Badge of Courage.* The reconstruction of the final manuscript is the version closest to Crane's most complete intentions, but reprints based on the expurgated Appleton first edition contain the version most widely read. Both of these texts can be located in the tradition of the nineteenth-century war novel, as an examination of the traditional conventions of that genre will show.

The historical romance dominated war fiction during the first half of the nineteenth century.[9] Most historical romances pictured war as an idealized setting for attaining glory. They gave officers the roles of courageous heroes and relegated the common soldier to accepting his patriotic duty and the authority of those over him. If any barbarity tainted the battle descriptions, it was used to show the enemy's cruelty.[10] These conventions persisted throughout the nineteenth century. But after the Civil

6. Binder, "The *Red Badge* Nobody Knows," p. 17.

7. Hershel Parker, rev. of *The Red Badge of Courage: A Facsimile Edition of the Manuscript* and the Virginia edition of *Red Badge, Nineteenth-Century Fiction,* 30 (1976), 562.

8. Ed. Ronald Gottesman et al. (New York: Norton, 1979), II, pp. 802–906.

9. Typical American examples were James Fenimore Cooper's *The Spy* (1821) and William Gilmore Simms's romances of the Revolutionary War (1835–56). See Wayne C. Miller's useful study, *An Armed America, Its Face in Fiction: A History of the American Military Novel* (New York: New York University Press, 1970), Ch. 1.

10. Such was the case in John Esten Cooke's *Surry of Eagle's-Nest: or, The Memoirs of a Staff-Officer Serving in Virginia,* a 1866 romance which also contained another popular traditional convention, the romantic love interest. See Miller, *An Armed America,* pp. 82–83.

War many war novels began modifying the conventions, presenting in particular more realistic detail among the romantic idealizations.[11]

A departure from all variations on the historical romance was the realisitic war novel, which made its appearance with Tolstoy's *Sebastopol* (1854-55; English translation, 1887). This kind of antiromance idealized neither war nor combatant. A fallible antihero, the common soldier, replaced the traditionally courageous officer of historical romance. At the opening of a typical realistic war novel, the central character often appeared vainglorious, and the traditional martial attitudes of romance were sometimes parodied. Surrounded by the brutality of warfare, the youthful "hero" showed himself afraid in battle and only later became brave; he did not come to war with inborn courage but acquired it in the heat of battle. The realistic war novel thus established a new genre plot convention: growth from cowardice and inexperience to courage and manhood. As Eric Solomon has observed, "By the time American novelists began writing about the Civil War, a European tradition of irony and realism, and a motif of the development, through war, from innocence to maturity, had been established through the war fiction of De Vigny, Stendhal, Zola, and Tolstoy."[12] In a promotional flyer to book dealers, Appleton directed its edition of *Red Badge* into this realistic tradition: "For an equally searching and graphic analysis of the volunteer in battle, one is tempted to turn to certain pages of Tolstoy."[13]

The Appleton text of *Red Badge* does seem to exhibit all of the genre conventions that characterize the realistic war novel typified by *Sebastopol*.[14] Henry Fleming is an enlisted man whose

11. "Romanticism" and "realism" are relative terms placed along a spectrum of verisimilitude with abstract stylization and idealization near one end and photographic realism near the other, the values along the spectrum being defined by conventional agreement. Another way of putting this is to say that realism, like romanticism, is a modal convention. See Douglas Hewitt's description of this convention quoted above, in Ch. 5, p. 131.

12. Eric Solomon, *Stephen Crane: From Parody to Realism* (Cambridge: Harvard University Press, 1966), p. 69.

13. This bookseller's order blank, discovered by Henry Binder, is reprinted in *Studies in the Novel*, 10 (1978), 4-5.

14. See Lars Åhnebrink, *The Beginnings of Naturalism in American Fiction*

romantic visions of war ("a Greeklike struggle") are soon dispelled in the actualities of combat. At the outset he dreams of heroic accomplishments but then feels grave doubts about his ability to act courageously in battle. As it turns out, he stands and returns fire during the first attack only to flee in terror during the second. Then after wandering for some time in the woods, he is returned to his regiment by a stranger and fights courageously the next day, becoming the company flag-bearer. In the final chapter, Henry feels "a quiet manhood, nonassertive but of sturdy and strong blood."[15]

On the basis of the Appleton text, most contemporary reviewers saw *Red Badge* as a realistic war novel in the tradition of Tolstoy, perhaps exceptional in its psychological realism or impressionistic style but wholly traditional in its use of the convention of initiation and growth in its young hero. However, the maimed state of the Appleton text did not allow reviewers and later critics to see the originality of what Crane had actually written. The manuscript version is antiromantic, but it is also the ultimate extension of ironic realism in that it rejects the convention of initiation. In the manuscript Henry experiences no growth, no movement from innocence to maturity or illusion to enlightenment. Certain passages not published in the Appleton first edition clearly indicate that Henry has learned nothing by the end of the novel.[16] There were obvious precedents for the story told in the Appleton text within the tradition of nineteenth-century war fiction, but what Crane wrote in the

---

(Cambridge, 1950; rpt. New York: Russell & Russell, 1961), pp. 344–60; and J. C. Levenson, Introduction to *The Red Badge of Courage: An Episode of the American Civil War,* ed. Fredson Bowers (Charlottesville: University Press of Virginia, 1975), pp.xl–xlvi.

15. Stephen Crane, *The Red Badge of Courage: An Episode of the American Civil War* (New York: Appleton, 1895), p. 232. A facsimile of the first impression of the Appleton first edition has been published by Charles E. Merrill Publishing Co. (Columbus, O., 1969), introduced by Joseph Katz.

16. The most significant deletions included passages referring to Henry's propensity for self-delusion portrayed in cosmic terms (final manuscript pp. 188, 191–92); the words that show Henry thinking that death was only "for others" (final manuscript p. 192); and the last Jimmie Rogers episode which exposed Henry's continued egotism (final manuscript p. 187). See Binder, "The *Red Badge* Nobody Knows," pp. 27–31.

manuscript transcends the tradition. The manuscript indicates that Crane's original conception was truly unique, reacting against both the historical romance's idealization of war and the realistic novel's convention of successful initiation.

Aesthetics of Reception

The foregoing discussion closely resembles the traditional discourse of intrinsic literary history. It takes a text and locates it in the developing context of a literary movement (realism) and a narrative genre (the war novel). Such a historical placement is usually the first step in any literary history, and this is often as true for extrinsic literary histories as it is for intrinsic accounts.[17] A study like *The Machine in the Garden* illustrates this last point nicely.[18] In writing his cultural history, Leo Marx set out to discover responses to industrialization in nineteenth-century American literature and found the recurrent use of a contrast between machine and natural landscape. However, before investigating further the "interplay between literature and the extraliterary experience of the age," Marx had to decide how this interplay was affected by the "interior history of literature itself." He therefore examined the tradition of the pastoral, "the interior development of its forms and conventions." He concluded that "the conventional features of a work must be acknowledged and understood before the cultural historian can answer such important questions as: what made the convention relevant at the time? what modifications did the age make in the conventions? how can the modifications be explained?"[19] Here Marx affirms that intrinsic literary history, as an account of traditional conventions, must precede the kind of extraliterary investigation he wished to pursue.

17. René Wellek writes that the "establishment of the exact position of each work in a tradition is the first task of literary history" (*Theory of Literature*, p. 249).
18. Leo Marx, *The Machine in the Garden: Technology and the Pastoral Ideal in America* (New York: Oxford University Press, 1964). I have chosen to use Marx's book as an example of extrinsic approaches primarily because of some excellent observations he makes on his study in "American Studies—A Defense of an Unscientific Method," *New Literary History*, 1 (1969), 75–90.
19. Marx, "American Studies," pp. 85–86.

Interpretive Conventions

Such intrinsic and extrinsic literary histories are illuminating as far as they go. But unfortunately they do not go far enough. What these accounts conceal is the interpretive work of readers and critics that constitutes the basis of all literary history. Such traditional histories ignore what Ingarden called the different "concretizations" of a literary work, that is, the various realizations which arise from individual readings of the text throughout its history. Ingarden spoke of the "life" of a literary work as being "*in* its concretizations."[20] Recognition of this "life" calls for a different kind of intrinsic and extrinsic literary history, one that places the reader at the center of historical research. In other words, the traditional history of production must be supplemented by a history of literary reception.

In the *Theory of Literature,* Wellek (influenced by Ingarden) had in fact acknowledged the importance of *both* histories when he described the two tasks of literary historians: the "tracing of the development of works of art" in terms of genres, styles, and the like, and the description of the historical "process of interpretation, criticism, and appreciation" of the work's structure which changes "while passing through the minds of readers, critics, and fellow-artists."[21] In this definition of tasks, Wellek gives equal importance to histories of production and reception. However, the history of production completely dominates his general discussion of literary history and has always done the same in actual histories of American literature. Accounts of reception have usually been relegated to the history of taste, which is ultimately seen as secondary, even marginal, within American literary study.[22]

German aesthetics of reception has recently proposed an alternative to the production model of traditional literary history.

20. Roman Ingarden, *The Literary Work of Art,* trans. George G. Grabowicz (Evanston: Northwestern University Press, 1973), p. 350.

21. Wellek, *Theory of Literature,* pp. 244–45.

22. This does not mean that American literary study has produced no useful reception histories. It does mean that such histories (1) are often treated as being of minor importance and (2) are usually written with no self-consciousness about the historical conditions of reception. The most significant exception to (2) is Michael Meyer, *Several More Lives to Live: Thoreau's Political Reputation in America* (Westport, Conn.: Greenwood Press, 1977).

This *Rezeptionsästhetik* stresses "the dialectical unity of production and reception,"[23] writes Peter Hohendahl; but it emphasizes even more the neglected pole of this dialectic, the process of reception or consumption. "Just as production mediates consumption—in the area of supply, distribution, and formation of attitude in the recipient—so does consumption mediate production: the reader's concretization transforms a model into a living work, and those needs of the public articulated in the reception condition the direction and extent of literary production."[24] American literary history has generally ignored this dialectic between the author and his reading public. William Charvat's outstanding study, *The Profession of Authorship in America, 1800–1870*, is the proverbial exception that proves the rule of a production-centered tradition in American literary history.[25]

Hans Robert Jauss has stated the case for an alternative tradition most forcefully: "If literary history is to be rejuvenated, the prejudices of historical objectivism must be removed and the traditional approach to literature must be replaced by an aesthetics of reception and impact."[26] The most important assumption of this *Rezeptionsästhetik* is its belief in the openness of the literary text. As Jauss puts it, "A literary work is not an object which stands by itself and which offers the same face to each reader in each period." He rejects the claims "that literature is timelessly present and that it has objective meaning, determined once and for all and directly open to the interpreter."[27] Instead, he and others in reception aesthetics take very seriously Ingarden's con-

23. Peter Uwe Hohendahl, "Introduction to Reception Aesthetics," *New German Critique*, No. 10 (1977), p. 56.
24. Ibid., p. 62. Cf. Hans Robert Jauss, "Theses on the Transition from the Aesthetics of Literary Works to a Theory of Aesthetic Experience," in *Interpretation of Narrative*, ed. Mario J. Valdés and Owen J. Miller (Toronto: University of Toronto Press, 1978), p. 138.
25. William Charvat, *The Profession of Authorship in America, 1800–1870*, ed. Matthew J. Bruccoli (Columbus: Ohio State University Press, 1968). See also Charvat, *Literary Publishing in America, 1790–1850* (Philadelphia: University of Pennsylvania Press, 1959).
26. Hans Robert Jauss, "Literary History as a Challenge to Literary Theory," *New Literary History*, 2 (1970), 9.
27. Ibid., pp. 10, 19. Also see "Interview/Hans R. Jauss," *Diacritics*, 5, No. 1 (1975), 53.

cept of concretizations.[28] Different concretizations are allowed by the "fundamental openness of literary texts . . . which forms the basis for the concept and the process of reception."[29]

Reception aesthetics assumes a text's fundamental openness and focuses on the history of concretizations this openness permits. Of course, the "historical life of a literary work is unthinkable without the active participation of its audience."[30] A second basic assumption of Jauss's *Rezeptionsästhetik* is that readers' "horizons of expectations" determine their active participation. According to Jauss, the response and impact of a literary work should be described "within the definable frame of reference of the reader's expectations: this frame of reference for each work develops in the historical moment of its appearance from a previous understanding of the genre, from the forms and themes of already familiar works, and from the contrast between poetic and practical language." The third factor he lists "includes the possibility that the reader of a new work has to perceive it not only within the narrow horizon of his literary expectations but also within the wider horizon of his experience of life."[31]

Jauss's theory of reception, then, recognizes both intra- and extraliterary horizons of expectations. The intraliterary horizon

28. In fact, the aesthetics of reception takes the concept *more* seriously than did Ingarden. For example, Jauss uses Felix Vodička's version of the concept, and Vodička has "historicized" Ingarden's use of it. According to Ingarden, "the work, in the polyphonic harmony of its qualities, still had the character of a structure independent of temporal changes in the literary norm; but Vodička disputes the idea that the esthetic values of a work could be given complete expression through an optimal concretization": Jauss, "History of Art and Pragmatic History," in *New Perspectives in German Literary Criticism: A Collection of Essays,* trans. David Henry Wilson et al., ed. Richard E. Amacher and Victor Lange (Princeton: Princeton University Press, 1979), p. 461. Cf. the critique of Ingarden in Hohendahl, "Introduction to Reception Aesthetics," pp. 33-35, and see above, Ch. 2, p. 52.

29. D. W. Fokkema and Elrud Kunne-Ibsch, *Theories of Literature in the Twentieth Century: Structuralism, Marxism, Aesthetics of Reception, Semiotics* (New York: St. Martin, 1977). p. 158.

30. Jauss, "Literary History," p. 8.

31. Ibid., pp. 11, 14. Cf. the concept of "horizon" in Hans-Georg Gadamer, *Truth and Method* (original German ed. 1960; 2d ed. 1965; English trans. London: Sheed & Ward, 1975), pp. 269-70. Jauss carefully notes similarities and differences between his and Gadamer's use of "horizons" in their theories ("Literary History," pp. 20-23).

is the background of genres, forms, and themes against which a text is read at any historical moment. The text can either fulfill or disappoint these expectations, and if it disappoints, it can help change the content of the horizon. The extraliterary horizon of social expectations also influences reception and impact; and as with the intraliterary, the effect of literature can change the extraliterary horizon as well. It is this power to change social expectations that defines "the society-forming function of literature" for Jauss. "The horizon of expectations of literature is differentiated from the horizon of expectations of historical life by the fact that it not only preserves real experiences but also anticipates unrealized possibilities, widens the limited range of social behavior by new wishes, demands, and goals, and thereby opens avenues for future experience."[32] Literature changes society by changing readers' social expectations.

Reception aesthetics as a whole stresses the interdependence of the intra- and extraliterary horizons of expectations. The histories of reception that result from this stance are analogous (and complementary) to the combination of intrinsic and extrinsic forms of traditional literary history. What would a parallel to an exclusively intrinsic literary history look like and what purpose would such intraliterary reception studies serve? The analyses in the next two sections will answer this question. In these analyses, the emphasis is not on the political or cultural constraints on reading and criticism nor on the effects of literature on society, but rather on the literary conventions that influence evaluation and interpretation. In the same way that intrinsic literary history precedes (but does not replace) extrinsic accounts, the reception study I propose is assumed by *Rezeptions-ästhetik*.

The two kinds of interpretive work I describe underlie the various literary histories now being written, both traditional accounts of production and newer accounts of reception. For between the text's production and its impact in reception stands its interpretation by readers and critics. As we have seen, interpretive conventions determine the shape and content of this initial

32. Jauss, "Literary History," pp. 32–33. He further clarifies his notion of "horizon of expectations" in "Theses," pp. 140–42.

step in literary consumption. Traditional literary history completely ignores this interpretive work by readers and critics when it locates conventions in texts that are viewed as stable and fixed in writing for all time. Literary conventions thus play merely a passive role: readers and critics must simply recognize them, and literary historians need only pick them out and place them in the context of movements, genres, and periods as they build up their historical accounts. Traditional literary history pays no attention to the *active* role played by conventions in evaluation and interpretation during different historical periods. Even current histories of reception often emphasize the *effect* of the text's meaning and value rather than the interpretive activity that produces that meaning and value. For example, in reconstructing the horizon of social norms for a group of French lyrics of 1857, Jauss discusses the effect of their reception on the socialization process in bourgeois society; but his "horizon analysis" leaves completely unexplained the interpretive work of readers that would have to be performed *before* such a socialization effect could take place.[33]

To uncover this concealed hermeneutic activity in literary history, I will examine two instances of reception. The first demonstrates how traditional conventions can become prescriptive or evaluative, a fact that accounts for a curious difference between the initial American and British responses to Melville's *Moby-Dick*. In the second example, I analyze the critical history of the Appleton *Red Badge of Courage*. The reception of this text is an especially clear illustration of disguised interpretive work because the text is incomplete and must obviously be supplemented by its readers before its meaning can be discovered. Here traditional literary conventions become constitutive conventions.

Traditional Conventions as Prescriptive

While working on his sixth book, Herman Melville wrote to his friend, Evert Duyckinck, "I don't know but a book in a man's

---

33. Jauss, *"La Douceur du Foyer:* The Lyric of the Year 1857 as a Pattern for the Communication of Social Norms," *Romanic Review,* 65 (1974), 201–29.

brain is better off than a book bound in calf—at any rate it is safer from criticism."[34] Despite such wry protestations, Melville allowed Bentley to publish *The Whale* in London on 18 October 1851; and Harpers published *Moby-Dick; or The Whale* in New York around 14 November.[35] The title was not the only difference between the first English and American editions. The "Etymology" and "Extracts" appeared in an "Appendix" after the final chapter in the third volume of the English edition, rather than at the beginning of the book as in the American. More important to the critical reception were the alterations made in the American proofs from which the English edition was set. Besides Melville's own revisions of the proofs he sent to England, Bentley or his reader also made several changes in the text: deleting Chapter 25 for its disrespect toward royalty; changing "God" to "G-d" and "damn" to "d—n"; and expurgating passages considered irreverent or indecent. Because they worked with the unexpurgated version, the American reviewers criticized Melville much more often than did their British counterparts for the "indelicacies" and "profane jesting" in his book. Also crucial to the critical response was the epilogue missing from the first English edition. Still, these textual variations alone do not explain all the differences between the American and the British evaluations of Melville's novel. To locate one of these differences and its specific causes, I must first outline the general critical reception given the book on both sides of the Atlantic. Such a survey is needed to counteract past claims about a predominantly negative reaction from contemporary reviewers.[36]

34. Letter dated 13 December 1850, in *The Letters of Herman Melville*, ed. Merrell R. Davis and William H. Gilman (New Haven: Yale University Press, 1960), p. 117.

35. See Jay Leyda, *The Melville Log*, vol. I (New York: Harcourt, Brace, 1951; rpt. with supplement, New York: Gordian Press, 1969), pp. 430, 433.

36. See, for example, John Freeman, *Herman Melville* (London: Macmillan, 1926), p. 130; O. W. Riegel, "The Anatomy of Melville's Fame," *American Literature*, 3 (1931), 196; F. O. Matthiessen, *American Renaissance* (New York: Oxford University Press, 1941), p. 251, n. 5; Alexander Cowie, *The Rise of the American Novel* (New York: American Book, 1948), p. 384; Howard P. Vincent, *The Trying-Out of Moby-Dick* (Boston: Houghton Mifflin, 1949), p. 3; and Alan Wykes, *A Concise Survey of American Literature* (New York: Library Pub., 1955), p. 70. Willard Thorpe was one of the first modern scholars to debunk this "legend that

The response to *The Whale* and *Moby-Dick* actually ranged from enthusiastic praise to extravagant condemnation in both England and America. Two of the most influential British papers, the *Athenaeum* and the *Spectator,* were highly critical in their comments, while *Blackwood's* apparently ignored *The Whale* entirely. The *Athenaeum* bluntly indicated its displeasure with Melville's performance: "Our author must be henceforth numbered in the company of the incorrigibles who occasionally tantalize us with indications of genius, while they constantly summon us to endure monstrosities, carelessness, and other such harassing manifestations of bad taste as daring or disordered ingenuity can devise."[37] Melville's "extravagances," his "raving and rhapsodising" were favorite targets for the London *Morning Chronicle* and others: "mad (rather than bad) English," complained the *Athenaeum* (p. 7). However, opposed to such censure were reviews like the one in *John Bull:* "few books which professedly deal in metaphysics, or claim the parentage of the muses, contain as much true philosophy and as much genuine poetry as the tale of the *Pequod's* whaling expeditions" (p. 9). The London *Morning Post* sounded even more enthusiastic: "we cannot hesitate to accord to Mr. Melville the praise of having produced one of the cleverest, wittiest, and most amusing of modern books" (p. 30). The London *Morning Advertiser* went so far as to claim that no work "more honourable to American Literature" had "yet reflected credit on the country of Washington Irving, Fenimore Cooper, Dana, Sigourney, Bryant, Longfellow, and Prescott" (p. 7). An examination of the other known English reviews simply confirms this picture of a radically divided opinion of *The Whale,* high praise on the one hand, violent attack on the other.

Unlike their British counterparts, the majority of American reviews were very brief notices, many giving no evidence of a close or even complete reading of *Moby-Dick.* The longer reviews and the more perceptive shorter ones appeared just as divided

---

the reviewers demolished *Moby-Dick,*" in his "Introduction" to *Herman Melville: Representative Selections* (New York: American Book, 1938), p. cxxii.

37. Rpt. in *Moby-Dick as Doubloon,* ed. Hershel Parker and Harrison Hayford (New York: Norton, 1970), p. 8. Page citations in the text of this section refer to *Doubloon.*

in their evaluations as the British notices. The *Literary World* pronounced *Moby-Dick* "a most remarkable sea-dish" (p. 49), while the *Spirit of the Times* called it "a work of exceeding power, beauty, and genius" (p. 64). "It will add to Mr. Melville's repute as a writer, undoubtedly," wrote the *Evangelist* (p. 41). In contrast, *To-day* complained, "the book appears to us rather drawn out, and could easily afford considerable paring down" (p. 86). The strongest criticism came from the *Democratic Review*, which concluded its comments: "if there are any of our readers who wish to find examples of bad rhetoric, involved syntax, stilted sentiment and incoherent English, we will take the liberty of recommending to them this precious volume of Mr. Melville's" (p. 84).

This brief survey of contemporary reviews presents only part of the available evidence disproving those twentieth-century accounts which assumed that Melville's novel was a critical failure at its birth.[38] The true picture shows a more positive and more divided critical reception. Though similar in their split opinions, American and British reviewers differed in their reasons for praise and blame. One difference followed from the British reviewers' greater professionalism, which gave their comments a sophistication and precision found in only a few American notices. This distinction between the two groups of critics had a rather curious (and as yet unexplained) consequence: the British reviewers' professionalism sometimes prejudiced their comments on *The Whale* as much as it benefited them.[39] How exactly did this happen?

38. Earlier corrections in addition to Thorpe's, can be found in David Potter, "Reviews of *Moby-Dick*," *Journal of the Rutgers University Library*, 3 (1940), 62–65; John C. McCloskey, "*Moby Dick* and the Reviewers," *Philological Quarterly*, 25 (1946), 20–31; and Hugh W. Hetherington, "Early Reviews of Moby-Dick," in *Moby-Dick Centennial Essays*, ed. Tyrus Hillway and Luther S. Mansfield (Dallas: Southern Methodist University Press, 1953), pp. 89–122. The most complete surveys of the contemporary reception are Hugh W. Hetherington, *Melville's Reviewers* (Chapel Hill: University of North Carolina Press, 1961), and Hershel Parker's section of the "Historical Note" in the forthcoming Northwestern-Newberry edition of *Moby-Dick.*

39. Of course, calling some British reviewers "prejudiced" here is a function of the twentieth-century reevaluation of *Moby-Dick*. That is, Melville's novel is a "masterpiece" only in relation to our present horizon of expectations, just as the British evaluations were determined by their horizons.

The British critics were guided by tested literary standards, based on a thorough knowledge of traditional literary conventions.[40] For some, this *descriptive* knowledge rigidified into *prescriptive* rules; traditional conventions became regulative. The advantage of such literary prescriptions was that a reviewer could more clearly and rigorously specify the faults of inartistic works. But in cases of unprecedented masterpieces, these conventional precepts failed.[41]

There was, then a built-in conservatism in some British evaluations of *The Whale* due to the use of these traditional conventions turned prescriptive. For example, the *Athenaeum* could not tolerate the untraditional combination of extravagant adventure story and technical whaling information, a combination which it called "an ill-compounded mixture of romance and matter-of-fact." To explain its criticism, the *Athenaeum* gave first a general precept, "There is a time for everything in imaginative literature;—and according to its order, a place—for rant as well as for reserve"; then its specific objection followed: "The voice of 'the storm wind Euroclydon' must not be interrupted by the facts of Scoresby and the figures of Cocker. Ravings and scraps of useful knowledge flung together salad-wise make a dish in which there may be much surprise, but in which there is little savour" (p. 7). The *Spectator* proceeded in a similar fashion, first giving

40. Cf. Hetherington, *Melville's Reviewers*, p. 14: "The British reviewers tended to be more thorough and analytical, to be more concerned with aesthetic values, to be more aware of literary conventions."

41. This fact supports Jauss's claim that the "aesthetic value" of a literary work resides in the extent it challenges the contemporary horizon of expectations; see Jauss, "Literary History," p. 14. However, Jauss does not stress that a text can challenge expectations and still be considered worthless later; e.g., novels by Melville's fellow Young American, Cornelius Mathews, certainly challenged contemporary expectations about American novels, but his books are still considered failures today. The crucial point is not simply whether a work challenges contemporary expectations, but whether such a challenge is valued in *later* horizons of expectations. This is the case for *Moby-Dick*, whose 1850s reception was rejected by twentieth-century critics. These later critics differed from nineteenth-century reviewers not only because they utilized different regulative conventions (e.g., about indecency and blasphemy in fiction writing), but also because they used different traditional conventions: *Moby-Dick* became a brilliant example of a new horizon of intraliterary expectations for the novel, instead of a rejected transgression against the old horizon, as it was for some contemporary British reviewers.

the regulative convention and then Melville's transgression: "It is a canon with some critics that nothing should be introduced into a novel which it is physically impossible for the writer to have known.... Mr. Melville hardly steers clear of this rule"; then it added, "and he continually violates another, by beginning in the autobiographical form and changing ad libitum into the narrative" (p. 12). The London *Examiner* complained that "all the regular rules of narrative or story are spurned and set at defiance. For a great part of the book it is Ahab the captain monologuizing in a wild mad way; then it is the seaman Ishmael; and then Mr. Melville himself." The reviewer then observed that it is Melville "who has kindly taken up the narrative which must otherwise have gone to the bottom with Ishmael and everybody else concerned" (pp. 24–25). Indeed, the unintentional absence of the epilogue in *The Whale* certainly added to the dissatisfaction with "rule-breaking" on Melville's part. The *Spectator, New Quarterly Review,* and *Dublin University Review* all noticed the inconsistent ending. The remark of the *Literary Gazette* was typical: "How the imaginary writer, who appears to have been drowned with the rest, communicated his notes for publication to Mr. Bentley is not explained" (p. 61).

The British preoccupation with literary conventions led them naturally to ask: In what traditional genre should *The Whale* be placed? Since three-decker novels were common, the *Literary Gazette* thought that the book was "professing to be a novel" (p. 60). With a similar assumption, the *Britannia* wrote that it was "at a loss to determine in what category of works of amusement to place it. It is certainly neither a novel nor a romance, although it is made to drag its weary length through three closely printed volumes, and is published by Bentley, who, *par excellence,* is the publisher of the novels of the fashionable world, for who ever heard of novel or romance without a heroine or a single love scene?" (p. 22). Similarly, the *New Quarterly Review* observed: "Many, doubtless, will cavil at the application of the term 'novel' to such a production as this, seeing that no tale of love is interwoven with the strange ana of which it is compounded" (p. 78). The London *Morning Chronicle* exemplified this bewildered side of the British response when it commented that Melville's book was a "strange conglomeration of fine description, reckless fancy, rhapsodic mistiness, and minute and careful Dutch painting" (p. 77). On the other hand, the London *Weekly News* had no problem categorizing *The Whale:* it is "the most powerful and original contribution that Herman Melville has yet made to the Romance of Travel" (p. 55). The admiring London *Leader* was puzzled but not frustrated when it asserted, "The book is not a romance, nor a treatise on Cetology. It is something of both: a strange, wild work with the tangled overgrowth and luxuriant vegetation of American forests, not the trim orderliness of an English park" (p. 26). Perhaps this understated comment from the *Dublin University Magazine* most typified the reaction of its British counterparts with their concern for traditional and regulative literary conventions: "All the rules which have been hitherto understood to regulate the composition of works of fiction are despised and set at naught. Of narrative, properly so called, there is little or none; of love, or sentiment, or tenderness of any sort, there is not a particle whatever; and yet, with all these glaring defects, it would be vain to deny that the work has interest" (p. 86).

In their analyses of *Moby-Dick,* most American reviewers were less specific than *The Whale*'s commentators in England. However, because they were also less concerned with literary traditions, they did not become as frustrated with the strange mixture of genres that made up Melville's masterpiece. In fact, the imaginative American labels for *Moby-Dick* seem a celebration of its diversity. "Such a salmagundi of fact, fiction and philosophy, composed in a style which combines the peculiarities of Carlyle, Marryatt and Lamb, was never seen before," exclaimed the New York *Commercial Advertiser* (p. 53). The *Literary World* called *Moby-Dick* "an intellectual chowder of romance, philosophy, natural history, fine writing, good feeling, bad sayings" (pp. 49–50). "It appears to be a sort of hermaphrodite craft—half fact and half fiction," wrote the Boston *Evening Traveller* in a brief approving notice (p. 32). The New York *Daily Tribune* coined the term "Whaliad" for what the Washington *National Intelligencer* called "a prose Epic on Whaling" (pp. 47, 68). Finally, *Harper's New Monthly Magazine* labeled *Moby-Dick* "a romance, a tragedy, and a natural history, not without numerous gratuitous suggestions on psychology, ethics, and theology. Beneath the whole story, the subtle, imaginative reader may perhaps find a pregnant allegory, intended to illustrate the mystery of human life" (p. 57).

Not preoccupied by the literary precepts of the British professionals and having the "Epilogue" in their edition, the American reviewers made no complaints about Melville's "violation" of conventional narrative rules. The only two American reviewers to raise the issue at all did not allow traditional-turned-prescriptive conventions to dominate their evaluations of Melville's unique work. Noting that "no man can serve two masters, even in fiction," the reviewer for *Peterson's* felt that the "philosophical romance" had spoilt "a skilfully told narrative of sea-adventures." But he added: "Still the demerit of 'Moby-Dick' is only comparative. It is not an indifferent work, but a very superior one, after all" (p. 84). This prescriptive restraint was even better illustrated by the sophisticated critic of the Washington *National Intelligencer:* "Nor do we propose . . . to haul Mr. Herman Melville over the coals for any offences committed against the code of Aristotle and Aristarchus: we have nothing to allege against his admission among the few writers of the present age who give evidence of some originality" (p. 66). Though the American reviewers critical of *Moby-Dick* found reasons to justify their critiques, traditional conventions turned prescriptive were certainly not among them.

What we find illustrated in the contrast between these British and American reviews is one reception in which traditional conventions became prescriptive (and thus evaluative) and another reception in which they did not. But the exact way conventions worked in the British judgments needs a bit more specification. The British use of these regulative conventions accomplished very economically the two movements of evaluation: making precise distinctions within a work and at the same time raising the work to the level of abstraction or general value—in the words of one recent theorist, "moving simultaneously to finer points with reference to the text and more abstract points with reference to the value of the text."[42] Through traditional-

---

42. Susan Stewart, "Some Riddles and Proverbs of Textuality: An Essay in Literary Value and Evaluation," *Criticism*, 21 (1979), 103.

turned-prescriptive conventions, British reviewers could define exactly how a new book worked (or didn't work) and how it succeeded (or failed) in its general relation to the established canon. Here the act of evaluation reveals itself as a consequence of interpretation. Evaluation follows from the translation of the work from one context (the analyzed specifics of a text's dynamics) to another context (the text in relation to a valued set of traditional conventions); and interpretive work is clearly involved both in the analysis of the text and in the placement of the analyzed work in the context of literary history. Thus in the British reviews of *The Whale*, evaluation becomes a complex extension of interpretation.[43]

The same extension can be seen if we look at the critical history of the Appleton *Red Badge of Courage*. In the British reception of *The Whale*, traditional genre conventions became criteria for evaluation, and Melville's novel was sometimes found wanting. In the case of *Red Badge*, critics have used traditional *modal* conventions as evaluative criteria and praised Crane for initiating or perfecting the use of these modal conventions— impressionism, ironic realism, deterministic naturalism, and modern symbolism. Such modal conventions can be exhibited across different genres, throughout a single text, and even in fragments of texts. This latter fact explains how the expurgated Appleton version could still be widely praised for its impressionism, realism, etc.[44]

But another question arises: What interpretations of *Red Badge* do such evaluations assume? That is, what holistic meanings have its enthusiastic readers constructed for the Appleton

43. The intraliterary reception study I have presented in this section can be contrasted to examinations of the extraliterary factors affecting the reviews of Melville's novels. See John Stafford, *The Literary Criticism of "Young America": A Study in the Relationship of Politics and Literature, 1837–1850* (Berkeley: University of California Press, 1952), and Perry Miller, *The Raven and the Whale: The War of Words and Wits in the Era of Poe and Melville* (New York: Harcourt, Brace & World, 1956).

44. See Edwin H. Cady, *Stephen Crane*, 2d ed. (New York: Twayne, 1980), pp. 119–40; Donald Pizer, "Stephen Crane," in *Fifteen American Authors before 1900: Bibliographic Essays on Research and Criticism*, ed. Robert A. Rees and Earl N. Harbert (Madison: University of Wisconsin Press, 1971), pp. 112–18; and Marston LaFrance, "Stephen Crane Scholarship Today and Tomorrow," *American Literary Realism*, 7 (1974), 129, 131–33.

text? Put even more pointedly: if the Appleton edition is illogical and inconsistent (as Binder has shown), how have *Red Badge* critics been able to make any sense of it, let alone call it an American classic?

Traditional Conventions as Constitutive

The following discussion is limited to critical arguments that focus on Crane's use of two genre conventions—growth of protagonist and attitude of narrator toward characters—because most holistic interpretations of *Red Badge* focus on Crane's use (or misuse) of these conventions. In the course of the discussion, I will show how generic, modal, and authorial conventions constitute the interpretations of the Appleton text. *Red Badge* criticism clearly illustrates how traditional literary conventions become constitutive conventions: to make sense of the expurgated Appleton text, critics have been forced to rely on conventions of past literary practice to supply the present meaning of an incoherent text.

Critics of *Red Badge* fall into one of three general categories: (1) those who, seeing few if any interpretive problems, make sense of the Appleton text by concluding that Henry grows and that the narrator's attitude toward him moves from ironic undercutting to various degrees of sympathetic approval; (2) those who cannot make sense of the text because of its apparent contradictions; and (3) those who make sense of the text by concluding that Henry experiences no growth and that the narrator's attitude is consistently ironic.

The overwhelming majority of *Red Badge* critics fall into the first category; they interpret the Appleton text according to the traditional conventions of the nineteenth-century realistic war novel and therefore see Henry as growing in the course of his war experience. There is, however, an extremely wide divergence of opinion among these critics over the terms of his growth, whether from cowardice to bravery, innocence to experience, or ignorance to insight.

Those critics who believe that Henry grows from a cowardly civilian to a courageous soldier view *Red Badge* as a war story in its narrowest sense. Most contemporary reviewers belonged to this group. For example, in the *Saturday Review* Sydney Brooks spoke of Henry Fleming as "a raw youth" who "develops into a tried and trustworthy soldier," and the reviewer for *The Bookman* saw in the novel "a genuine development of the untried civilian into the capable and daring soldier."[45] In his 1925 preface to *Red Badge*, Joseph Conrad referred to Crane's "war book" and "the problem of courage," seeing Henry as a "symbol of all untried men."[46] More recently, critics such as Lars Åhnebrink have written of Henry's "development into a real war hero" and about "the process of conquering fear" analyzed in the novel.[47]

A more complex growth in Henry is posited by critics who interpret him as growing in experience from innocence to maturity but make no explicit reference to his gaining self-knowledge. In 1895, William Dean Howells called Henry a "tawdry-minded youth" and praised Crane's skill "in evolving from the youth's crude expectations and ambitions a quiet honesty and self-possesion manlier and nobler than any heroism he had imagined."[48] In a similar vein but decades later, V. S. Pritchett wrote about Henry as "a green young recruit" who "loses his romantic illusions and his innocence in battle and acquires a new identity, a hardened virtue."[49] In 1945, R. B. Sewall interpreted the ending as a complete "moral victory" for Henry, whose "victory over fear" seems to have made up for his past sins (running from battle and deserting the tattered soldier). However, Sewall was also the first critic to voice objections to the ending of the Appleton text; he found Henry's final "state of

45. "In the School of Battle: The Making of a Soldier," London *Saturday Review*, 11 January 1896, p. 43; and London *Bookman*, 9 (January 1896), 131. On the evidence for attributing the *Saturday Review* notice to Brooks, see Richard M. Weatherford, ed., *Stephen Crane: The Critical Heritage* (London: Routledge & Kegan Paul, 1973), p. 99.

46. Joseph Conrad, "His War Book: A Preface to Stephen Crane's 'The Red Badge of Courage,'" in his *Last Essays* (Garden City, N.Y.: Doubleday, Page, 1926), 121–23. Also see Conrad's earlier comment on *Red Badge:* "The subject of that story was war, from the point of view of an individual soldier's emotions" ("Stephen Crane: A Note Without Dates," *The London Mercury*, 1 [December 1919], 192).

47. Åhnebrink, p. 351.

48. *Harper's Weekly*, 26 October 1895, p. 1013.

49. V. S. Pritchett, "Two Writers and Modern War," in *The Living Novel* (London: Chatto & Windus, 1946), p. 174.

complacency" to be "undeserved and arbitrary" in terms of "Henry's moral struggle as Crane has represented it."[50]

Of recent comments on *Red Badge*, Donald Pizer's interpretation is the most interesting example from this group of critics who see growth in experience but not necessarily in self-knowledge. For Pizer, Henry "emerges at the end of the battle not entirely self-perceptive or firm-willed—Crane is too much the ironist for such a reversal—but rather as one who has encountered some of the strengths and some of the failings of himself and others." Pizer never specifically states that Henry gains an insight into himself; he only describes the youth's growth negatively—Henry is *not* the same as he was—and implies that the difference *may* be limited self-knowledge. Pizer surmises that "something has happened to Fleming which Crane values and applauds," and then suggests that this "something" is partly Henry's movement from isolation to "oneness with his fellows." Whether Pizer thinks Henry himself actually realizes this is not clear: "Henry is still for the most part self-deceived at the close of the novel, but if he is not the 'man' he thinks he has become, he has at least shed some of the innocence of the child."[51] Sensitive to irony as an authorial convention exhibited throughout Crane's canon, Pizer is careful not to claim too much

50. R. B. Sewall, "Crane's *The Red Badge of Courage*," *The Explicator*, 3, No. 7 (1945), Item 55.

51. Donald Pizer, *Realism and Naturalism in Nineteenth-Century American Literature* (Carbondale: Southern Illinois University Press, 1966), pp. 26–30. Recognizing that "Fleming's self-evaluations contrast ironically with his motives and actions throughout the novel," Pizer also claims that "Fleming's own sanguine view of himself at the close of the novel—that he is a man—cannot be taken at face value" (p. 28). This last assertion and Pizer's later published comments on *Red Badge* suggest that the ambiguity I see in his critical text might actually be what he unambiguously saw in Crane's literary text. In "A Primer of Fictional Aesthetics," *College English*, 30 (1969), Pizer clearly states that "ambivalence dominates the closing portion" of *Red Badge* and that "the author's evaluation of his central character" is a "mystery" which "is left unsolved at the close of the novel" (pp. 576–77). In his 1969 review of Crane scholarship, Pizer lists his own interpretation as one of those supporting the thesis that Henry "has gained from his experiences but he is nevertheless deluded in his understanding of what he has gained" (Pizer, "Stephen Crane," p. 125). And in "*The Red Badge* Nobody Knows: A Brief Rejoinder," Pizer supports interpretations that see the last chapter as "ambivalent and ambiguous" (p. 80). The statements noted here suggest that his later interpretations (and aspects of his original one) should be grouped with those that claim growth *and* irony at the end of *Red Badge* (see below).

for the story in the Appleton text; the ambiguities of his interpretation are to some extent the result of an intelligent critic reading a maimed text.

Also in the first category of critics who see growth in *Red Badge* are still others who interpret Henry's change as an explicit movement from illusion to enlightenment. In 1925, Joseph Hergesheimer put it simply: *Red Badge* is the "story of the birth, in a boy, of a knowledge of himself and of self-command."[52] There has been a great diversity of opinion about what precisely is Henry Fleming's insight into himself. A contemporary reviewer saw Henry's "agony of fear" turning into a "recognition of the universality of suffering."[53] In 1934, Harry Hartwick claimed that the youth "reaches the conclusion that the chief thing is to resign himself to his fate, to participate in Darwin's 'survival of the fittest,' to play 'follow the leader' with Nature, and to confront this mad, implacable world with 'intestinal fortitude' and a brave smile; in one word, to become a stoic."[54] In 1951, R. W. Stallman spoke of a "spiritual change" in which Henry "confesses to himself the truth" about his previous pride and "puts on new garments of humility."[55] Still later, Eric Solo-

52. Joseph Hergesheimer, Introduction to *The Red Badge of Courage* (New York: Knopf, 1925), p. xi.

53. N[ancy] H. B[anks], "The Novels of Two Journalists," New York *Bookman*, 2 (November 1895), 219.

54. Harry Hartwick, "The Red Badge of Nature," in *The Foreground of American Fiction* (New York: American Book, 1934), p. 27.

55. R. W. Stallman, Introduction to the Modern Library Editon of *The Red Badge of Courage* (New York: Random House, 1951), pp. xxxi–xxxii. This introduction was part of a longer essay that Stallman published as "Stephen Crane: A Revaluation," in *Critiques and Essays on Modern Fiction, 1920–1951*, ed. John W. Aldridge (New York: Ronald Press, 1952), pp. 244–69. The *Critiques and Essays* article contains a footnote in which Stallman points out that although Henry "progresses upwards toward manhood and moral triumph," "the education of the hero ends as it began; in self deception." Henry is "deluded" in "believing he has triumphed in facing up" to the battle of life "shorn of all romantic notions" (p. 255, n. 5). Also see Stallman's comments in his *Stephen Crane: An Omnibus* (New York: Knopf, 1952), pp. 221–23. These later interpretations suggest a revision of his first published analysis of *Red Badge;* but see Stanley B. Greenfield, "The Unmistakable Stephen Crane," *PMLA*, 73 (1958), 562–72, esp. n. 16, and Stallman's reply to Greenfield in a 1961 "postscript" to a reprinting of his 1951 Introduction to *Red Badge*, in the Norton Critical Edition of *The Red Badge of Courage*, ed. Sculley Bradley, Richmond Croom Beatty, and E. Hudson Long (New York: Norton, 1962), p. 254.

mon argued that "the standards by which Henry's development is measured are those of group loyalty rather than fear and courage." At the end of the novel, Henry's "self-interest and pride are not obliterated but transformed as he identifies himself as a member of his group." For Solomon, Henry "has learned the essence of man's duty to man, as well as the fact that life (like war) is not a romantic dream governed by absolutes, but a matter of compromises. . . . At least war has shown the young soldier his true self, and the acquisition of self-knowledge is no small accomplishment."[56] The list of critics with various opinions on Henry Fleming's self-insight could easily be extended.

Among these critics, Edwin Cady provides one of the most perceptive discussions of the early ironic distance between the narrator and Henry. Cady shows how, as a civilian, Henry was a "perfect neo-romantic"; how the youth's romantic egotism is undercut by "ridicule and irony"; how false are both his "irresponsibility" for his acts on the one hand and his sense of a "prophetic role" on the other; and how nature "varies with his psychic states."[57] However, Cady interprets Henry as gaining a certain understanding and modesty in the final section of the Appleton text: "In the end he sees that he is neither a hero nor a villain, that he must assume the burdens of a mixed, embattled, impermanent, modest, yet prevailing humanity."[58] Cady makes some use of the manuscript; but he misjudges the importance of the deleted chapter 12 (where Henry in railing against the universe is most obviously a fool),[59] and he entirely misses the interpretive significance of the excisions made in the last chapter.[60]

Also among the critics who see Henry as growing through self-knowledge are some who mention problems they have in interpreting the ending of the Appleton text. For example,

56. Solomon, pp. 82, 87, 97.
57. Cady, pp. 122–30.
58. Ibid., p. 142.
59. Ibid., p. 130. Cady does recognize that this chapter "derided the naturalistic diagnosis of Fleming's condition together with Henry's Dreiser-like urge to proclaim its gospel"; but he claims that "since the relative slackness of the previous chapter makes it clear that discursive patches mar *The Red Badge*, it is not surprising that Crane suppressed his intended Chapter XII. He was right to do so. . . ."
60. Ibid., p. 141. See note 16, above.

Interpretive Conventions

George Johnson wrote that Henry "supposedly learns to abide incongruity and find the world meaningful," but he also noted a "dramatic falseness" in this "implicitly optimistic close."[61] Mordecai Marcus interpreted Henry as revolting against both his cowardly and fierce behavior and accepting "the perilous but unavoidable human lot." Marcus also mentioned, however, a "general weakening of interest and cohesion in the last eight chapters" and noted that the conclusion "jars slightly with some of the preceding narrative, especially with the ironic treatment of Henry," the reasons being (in part) the "suddenness of Henry's insight" and "traces of irony in the final chapter." Marcus then swept these problems aside when he confusingly argued that restoring the deleted passages would make the final chapter "quite ambiguous and would suggest that Crane regarded Henry ironically to the very end."[62] That is, Marcus first complained that the ending of the Appleton text was "slightly jarring" but then rejected the solution that would remedy that "jarring."

Finally, within this large category of critics who interpret Henry as growing, there are some who see both growth *and* irony at the end of the Appleton text (what Pizer has called "purposeful ambivalence").[63] Whereas most of the critics I have discussed assume that once Henry grows the narrator's attitude toward him changes, this last group interprets Henry as growing in some respects but emphasizes that the narrator preserves a degree of ironic distance to the end. For example, Larzer Ziff noted that "at the very close Crane makes Henry's newly acquired cockiness so great that it becomes ambiguous when we remember his shortcomings and his rationalizations," and J. C. Levenson remarked that "residual egotism makes the ending

61. George W. Johnson, "Stephen Crane's Metaphor of Decorum," *PMLA,* 78 (1963), 251.
62. Mordecai Marcus, "The Unity of *The Red Badge of Courage,*" in *The Red Badge of Courage: Text and Criticism,* ed. Richard Lettis, Robert F. McDonnell, and William E. Morris (New York: Harcourt, Brace, 1960), pp. 193–95. Marcus wrote further that Crane's "final problem was to make us accept some intellectual self-transcendence in Henry so that our sympathies—no matter how they have been tried—will remain with him. Crane's success with this problem was, I think, only moderate" (p. 195).
63. Pizer, "Stephan Crane," p. 125.

184

ambiguous."[64] Stanley Greenfield made the most frequently cited case for Crane's having a "duality of view" at the conclusion of *Red Badge*. Greenfield argued that Henry grows in both attitude and behavior and that his final evaluation of his past conduct is not undercut. "There is no vain delusion about the past," wrote Greenfield; but then he added, "As for the future—well, that is a different matter, highly ambiguous."[65] As ambiguous as these critics see the ending, they always interpret a degree of growth in Henry and should properly be placed among those who make a sense of the Appleton text (indeed the intended ambiguity they find *is* the sense they make).

All critics in the large first category, though differing radically in specifics, do make sense of the Appleton text by interpreting Henry Fleming as growing in bravery, experience, or knowledge. A second category of critics could *not* make sense of the Appleton version and therefore concluded that Crane's artistic skills were limited and the writer's problems in *Red Badge* proved too much for him.[66] One such dissenter, John Shroeder, argued that Crane's novel was "more confused than its critics have been willing to admit." He found "false directions and incoherencies" and called aspects of the book "diffuse and inchoate." Concerning the last chapter, Shroeder thought that Crane "had his own doubts about the validity of Henry's transformation." Giving a nonironic reading to the penultimate sentence, "He turned now with a lover's thirst to images of tranquil skies, fresh meadows, cool brooks—an existence of soft and eternal peace," Shroeder

64. Larzer Ziff, *The American 1890s* (New York: Viking, 1966), p. 199, and Levenson, p. lxxiii.

65. Greenfield, p. 571.

66. Of course, critics in this second category ultimately do make a sense of the text (e.g., by saying that Crane couldn't handle his materials or Crane didn't know what he wanted), but this is a different kind of interpretation than that of the first and third categories of critics. The second category cannot provide a coherent meaning for the story and therefore tries to explain the lack of coherence by moving "beyond" the text to the artistry of its creator (overlooking the possibility of an expurgated text as an explanation) and judging that the artistic skill was defective. Thus we have another example of evaluation being an extension of interpretation. The second group's explanation is a result of two interpretations: (1) the text makes no sense; and (2) it makes no sense because of a failure on Crane's part. Both these interpretations determine the negative evaluation of Crane's artistic ability and the text he created.

commented that "Crane seems to have forgotten everything that has gone before in his own book."[67]

Another dissatisfied critic, Richard Chase, wrote that themes of "spiritual death and rebirth" and of "advancing maturity" are "only sketchily there, if at all" in the Appleton text. Crane "seems half-hearted about carrying things through to the moral conclusion." Indeed, the lack of extensive rewriting does indicate that Crane was half-hearted in making the cuts, but this is not what Chase is getting at. According to Chase, Crane inclined toward dramatizing the discrepancy between Henry's illusion and actual fact but instead tried to draw a moral "in the vague and pretentious language of the last five paragraphs" (which Chase does not interpret ironically).[68] James Colvert made a more detailed attack on the Appleton novel, complaining that "the problems raised in the story are not clearly defined or resolved. As a consequence the ending is confused and unconvincing." Like Shroeder and Chase, Colvert apparently believed that Crane was following the traditional genre convention of growth for his main character. With this assumption firmly in place, Colvert explained his objections:

> We are told that Henry Fleming is a changed man, but we are not told how he is supposed to have met the conditions implicitly required of him in the first sixteen chapters. In the first part of the story Henry is the target of the narrator's relentless ironic criticism, scored for his delusions of grandeur, his assumption that he somehow merits a special place in the regard of the universe. And though Crane labors in the final chapter to convince us that his hero has rid himself of these delusions, the deterioration in the quality of the writing—the *appearance of a tendency toward incoherence*—shows that the task is too much for him. The tone shifts inappropriately, the irony is erratic and often misdirected, and the hero is permitted certain assumptions inconsistent with his previous characterization and Crane's established attitudes toward him.[69]

67. John W. Shroeder, "Stephen Crane Embattled," *University of Kansas City Review*, 17 (1950), 123–28.

68. Richard Chase, Introduction to *The Red Badge of Courage* (Boston: Houghton Mifflin, 1960), pp. x–xiii.

69. James B. Colvert, "Stephen Crane's Magic Mountain," in *Stephen Crane: A*

Colvert's criticisms of the Appleton text leave very little of Crane's artistry for us to respect. In fact, this group of critics who found only incoherence in the final chapter actually demonstrates the damaging effect of the forced excisions and not a deficiency in the author's skill.

All the interpretive chaos in *Red Badge* criticism, including the hesitations and confusions within individual readings, is a direct result of the expurgations made for the Appleton edition, expurgations that have allowed the text to mean many things to some critics and nothing to others. But if such critical chaos is due to a maimed text, how do we account for those critics who construct a sense for the novel in which Henry does not grow and the narrator's attitude is consistently ironic? That is, if the problems in interpreting the Appleton text are caused by the missing passages, how can a small third category of Crane critics not only interpret that text but, in fact, provide a sense that closely resembles what Crane originally presented in the manuscript? How did Charles Walcutt and John Berryman, for example, interpret Henry as not growing and the narrator's attitude as ironic toward Henry throughout?[70]

Collection of Critical Essays, ed. Maurice Bassan (Englewood Cliffs, N.J.: Prentice-Hall, 1967), pp. 95–96, emphasis added.

70. Charles Walcutt, *American Literary Naturalism, A Divided Stream* (Minneapolis: University of Minnesota Press, 1956), pp. 74–82, and John Berryman, "Stephen Crane: *The Red Badge of Courage*," in *The American Novel: From James Fenimore Cooper to William Faulkner,* ed. Wallace Stegner (New York: Basic Books, 1965), pp. 86–96. Walcutt's consistently ironic interpretation has been seconded by Jay Martin, *Harvests of Change* (Englewood Cliffs, N.J.: Prentice-Hall, 1967), pp. 64–65; Clark Griffith, "Stephen Crane and the Ironic Last Word," *Philological Quarterly,* 47 (1968), 85–86, 88–90; and in part by Miller, *An Armed America,* p. 72, and Chase, p. xv. However, "most critics have not accepted such an extreme view of Crane's attitude toward Fleming" (Pizer, "Stephen Crane," p. 124). Berryman's interpretation might at first seem to be closer to that of Greenfield (intended ambiguity) or Colvert (unintentional confusion) than to Walcutt's. Berryman admitted, "I do not know what Crane intended. Probably he intended to have his cake and eat it too—irony to the end, but heroism too" (p. 90). Berryman went on, however, to tip the balance more toward irony: "It seems impossible not to conclude that the splendid burst of rhetoric with which the novel concludes is just that *in part*—a burst of rhetoric—and that Crane retained many of his reservations about his hero" (p. 91). Finally, the force of the hedging "*in part*" seems gone entirely when Berryman concluded that "we are left after all with a *fool* . . ." (p. 91), making Berryman's interpretation approach close to Walcutt's (as Miller recognized in *An Armed America,* p. 72).

One demonstrable answer is the critic's use of modal conventions—stylistic and thematic conventions that convey a particular interpretation of experience. For a critic who claimed that the modal conventions of naturalism governed *Red Badge,* the possibility of Henry's self-betterment would be very remote indeed, since the youth would be viewed as a mere pawn of external and internal forces. Thus, in *American Literary Naturalism, A Divided Stream,* Walcutt argued that Crane is a naturalist who "makes us see Henry Fleming as an emotional puppet controlled by whatever sight he sees at the moment." Guided by the modal conventions of naturalism, Walcutt decided that Henry "has not achieved a lasting wisdom or self-knowledge" and therefore fails to grow.[71] But apparently the use of modal conventions is not sufficient in itself to determine an interpretation that sees Henry not growing at all; Pizer, for example, also invoked modal conventions in his interpretation.[72] Nor are authorial conventions enough: Marston LaFrance was as sensitive as Berryman to ironic conventions throughout the Crane canon, yet he still interpreted Henry as attaining "authentic self-knowledge and a sense of manhood after long and fierce battles with his own moral weaknesses."[73]

I can, however, point to another literary convention and its use in *Red Badge* criticism—a convention of narrative consistency that guides the telling of stories in novels and related genres.[74] One corollary of this regulative convention can be roughly stated: There should be no radical (unexplained) change in the attitude of the narrator toward his protagonist. What Berryman

71. Walcutt, pp. 79, 82.

72. Pizer, *Realism and Naturalism,* pp. 12-14, 24-32.

73. Marston LaFrance, *A Reading of Stephen Crane* (London: Oxford University Press, 1971), p. 123.

74. This convention can be viewed as a traditional genre convention turned regulative. Its form is generic in that it holds within narrative genres, but its specific content develops during the reading of particular texts. For example, novel readers expect that the narrator's attitudes toward characters or the probabilities within the created world will remain the same (unless reasons are explicitly or implicitly given to account for changes); but each individual novel establishes what the actual attitudes or probabilities will be in that particular fiction and its telling. Thus the convention of narrative consistency is an example of a traditional genre convention that makes possible conventions (or contracts) within individual works.

and Walcutt have done in their interpretations of the Appleton text is to use this narrative convention to supply what "wasn't there"; they merely extended to the conclusion the narrator's ironic attitude established early in the novel. For example, Berryman noted that a "pervasive irony is directed toward the youth—his self-importance, his self-pity, his self-loving war rage." As a result of his sense of this early irony, at one point in his reading of the last chapter, Berryman protested, "But *then* comes a sentence in which I simply do not believe": "He turned now with a lover's thirst to images of tranquil skies, fresh meadows, cool brooks—an existence of soft and eternal peace." This sentence, which Shroeder took so literally, is interpreted by Berryman on the basis of the ironic conventions of the earlier chapters.[75] Walcutt was even more explicit about how his reading of the earlier sections determined his refusal to interpret Henry as growing in the final chapter: Henry's self-evaluation in the final section is "a climax of self-delusion. If there is any one point that has been made it is that Henry has never been able to evaluate his conduct."[76]

This last account of how a small number of critics could interpret the expurgated Appleton text ironically to its end also helps explain what happened with the critics who found the text incoherent: they simply refused to extend into the final chapter the interpretive conventions established early in the novel. For these dissatisfied critics, a genre convention that they assumed Crane to be following at the end (growth through war experience) was at odds with a convention developed early in the novel (ironic distance), and they resolved the inconsistency (which they had supplied in responding to a mutilated text) by judging Crane's artistic skill at fault. But then what happened with the large first category of critics, most of whom made a nonironic, "coherent" sense of the ending? We could simply say that they ignored relevant discrepancies in the story (relevant, that is, according to the terms of their own interpretations) which cannot be conven-

75. Berryman, pp. 89, 91.
76. Walcutt, p. 81. Cf. Michael J. Hoffman, *The Subversive Vision: American Romanticism in Literature* (Port Washington, N.Y.: Kennikat Press, 1972), pp. 138–39; and Clinton S. Burhans, Jr., "Judging Henry Judging: Point of View in *The Red Badge of Courage,*" *Ball State University Forum,* 15 (1974), 45–48.

tionally accounted for without the manuscript evidence.[77] But we could also further surmise that because their attention was deflected by the length of the battle descriptions between the obvious early narrative irony and the last chapter, these critics were able to accept a radical change in the narrator's attitude toward Henry Fleming; and because of the traditional convention that heroes in realistic war novels grow (and that outward heroism in battle indicates internal maturation), they could accept Henry as growing.

In this way the interpretations of the Appleton text can all be accounted for by the ability (or inability) of critics to invoke traditional and regulative conventions. Only those most sensitive to the conventions Crane was employing could come close on the basis of the expurgated Appleton text to a knowledge of his originality in transcending the tradition of the realistic war novel. But even these critics could not fully appreciate Crane's achievement because significant scenes are irretrievable without the manuscript.[78]

My concluding perspective on *Red Badge* criticism focuses on the convention of irony, an interpretive convention that has functioned in complex and subtle ways in attempts to make sense of the Appleton text. All *Red Badge* critics invoke an ironic convention to interpret the first part of the story, but the largest number drop the convention by the last chapter as they interpret Henry as growing and the narrator's attitude toward him as changing. Those that continue to invoke the convention do so in three different ways. Some critics (Colvert, Chase, Shroeder) do not use the ironic convention consistently to the end, "seeing"

---

77. See Binder, "The *Red Badge* Nobody Knows," pp. 24–26.

78. Lost to the readers of the Appleton text are such scenes as those in the original chapter 12, where Crane masterfully undercuts Henry's cosmic self-justifications. The power of the thoughts expressed in this chapter has encouraged some critics to underestimate the importance of the character expressing those thoughts—see O. W. Fryckstedt, "Henry Fleming's Tupenny Fury: Cosmic Pessimism in Stephen Crane's *The Red Badge of Courage*," *Studia Neophilologica*, 33 (1961), 265–81. Also lost to Appleton readers is the final Jimmie Rogers scene (see n. 16, above). Thus Berryman (pp. 90–91) could wonder why Crane's deep concern for "Human Kindness" plays no part in the Appleton *Red Badge*. In the manuscript, which contains the final Jimmie Rogers episode, concern for others (or lack of it) does play a part.

residual irony only in places and interpreting Henry as achieving an undeserved or incoherent self-knowledge. Others (Greenfield, Ziff, Levenson) agree that Henry grows in the Appleton text, but by continuing to invoke the ironic convention consistently, they resolve potential textual problems through the use of a popular modern interpretive convention, the "discovery" of purposeful ambivalence: Crane intended growth *and* irony, a positive change in Henry with an apparent residue of continued self-delusion. Still other critics (Walcutt, Berryman) use the ironic convention to eliminate any growth in Henry, resolving all potential textual problems by positing a consistent ironic attitude in the narrator which undercuts any apparent change in the main character.

The incomplete state of the Appleton ending requires critical choices in the use of interpretive conventions, choices that force critics to "write" their own texts that they call *The Red Badge of Courage.* One group writes a traditional realistic war novel of the nineteenth century; another constructs an inconsistent artistic failure; another makes a twentieth-century ironic tale of purposeful ambivalence; and still another creates a story that comes surprisingly close to the experimental novel that Crane actually intended. The interpretive work of each critic can best be revealed through the kind of literary history I have illustrated in these last two sections. Such an intraliterary history of reception provides a necessary supplement to the current histories of literary production and consumption.

CONCLUSION

Reading "the Reader"

> Ultimately, man finds in things nothing but what he himself
> has imported into them.
> —Friedrich Nietzsche, *The Will to Power*

> It is in words and language that things first come into being
> and are. —Martin Heidegger, *An Introduction to Metaphysics*

Most reader-response critics and theorists fail to examine the status of their own discourse on reading, and this fact
determines the direction of my concluding remarks. Throughout this book I have pushed to the background a problem implicit in its title: Who (or what) is "the reader" in American
fiction study? Functionally within my discourse, "the reader" is
an interpretive device for literary theory, practical criticism, textual scholarship, and literary history. I have tried to demonstrate
how the reader perspective can change American literary study
by helping to achieve certain goals and resolve particular problems within the activities that constitute the discipline. I will conclude my consideration of "the reader" in the study of American
fiction by examining the significance of the quotation marks
around the term. To do this, I must make a detour through a
series of questions that will eventually lead to my destination of
reading "the reader."

There is (at least) one question left over from the last chapter:
Though a theory of interpretive conventions accounts for the
general agreement and disagreement concerning the Appleton
Red Badge, what does it say about the details of disagreements
within agreements? Why, for example, do critics who agree on a
nonironic reading of the conclusion disagree over exactly how

Henry Fleming grows, when the growth begins, what causes it, and other such issues? The answer is that a hierarchy of interpretive conventions functions in every act of interpretation; and in this hierarchy, more general conventions at a higher level leave room for more particular ones at lower levels. A metacritical analysis can focus on any level of the hierarchy. My analysis described only the most controversial level of agreement and disagreement in *Red Badge* criticism. If the focus shifts to the level of detail *within* an area of agreement, the same kind of account can be produced. The group of critics agreeing on the growth of Henry usually rejects interpretive conventions of irony in making sense of the final Appleton chapter. Within that group are subgroups sharing interpretive assumptions about what constitutes growth, how such growth begins, what causes it, and so on, and it is these subgroups (which could be described in the same detail as the larger groups) that account for the disagreement within agreement. At each level of generality or detail, interpretive conventions of different kinds account for the particular interpretations made of the expurgated Appleton text.

But is there a point where what is left of the original text of *Red Badge* takes over the interpretation? That is, though interpretive conventions help the critic supplement the expurgated Appleton version and supply what is missing, what does the text that is still there contribute to the meaning of the novel? How exactly does the Appleton text constrain its interpretation? The chaos of *Red Badge* criticism leads me to conclude that the incomplete and contradictory Appleton edition does not significantly constrain its interpretation at all. Rather, as a mutilated text, it is totally constituted by readers' and critics' hierarchies of interpretive conventions, their assumptions and strategies. Such a claim leads to other, more difficult, questions.

Henry Binder says the critics who supply a nonironic interpretation of *Red Badge* misread an incoherent Appleton text, and I say those critics can do so because they use a traditional literary convention as an interpretive convention to supply what is missing—a coherent meaning in which Henry Fleming grows. Furthermore, I argue that those critics who supply an ironic reading are also filling in something that is not actually there in the Appleton text by consistently employing an interpretive convention of irony. Both Binder's argument and my own account assume that a clear, unambiguous irony is absent from the end of the Appleton version and that it is present in the final manuscript. But what determines if it is there or not in either the Appleton or manuscript texts?

Let's say we argue that irony is explicit *in* certain sentences and that the presence of ironic passages in larger sections of a text determines that text's ironic meaning. (This indeed seems to be Binder's assumption and my own in the last chapter.)[1] Such an argument immediately runs into problems. How can the same sentence in the Appleton text be interpreted ironically *and* nonironically? This is in fact what has happened in the history of *Red Badge* criticism with that sentence from the final chapter: "He turned now with a lover's thirst to images of tranquil skies, fresh meadows, cool brooks—an existence of soft and eternal peace." John Shroeder and R. B. Sewall interpret it as straightforward, while John Berryman and Neil Schmitz see it as ironic.[2] W. M. Frohock disagrees with both of these readings and claims that the sentence is neither a literal statement about life nor an ironic comment on Henry's perceptions; it is simply a renewal of the bucolic stereotype Crane has been using to elegize (not parody) the pastoral ideal destroyed by war.[3] Instead of taking these conflicting interpretations as proof that irony does

1. Most traditional accounts of verbal, structural, and dramatic irony make a similar assumption about irony *in* texts. Even intentionalist theories of irony share this assumption, at least when they talk about textual clues, stylistic signals, internal contradictions, and the like. See, for example, D. C. Muecke, *The Compass of Irony* (London: Methuen, 1969), pp. 58–59, 75–81, and *Irony* (London: Methuen, 1970), pp. 54–55; Wayne C. Booth, *The Rhetoric of Fiction* (Chicago: University of Chicago Press, 1961), pp. 316–18, and *A Rhetoric of Irony* (Chicago: University of Chicago Press, 1974), pp. 52–57, 61–73.
I am especially grateful to Stanley Fish and Jane Tompkins for conversations helping to clarify some of the issues I am raising in this conclusion.

2. John W. Shroeder, "Stephen Crane Embattled," *University of Kansas City Review*, 17 (1950), 126; R. B. Sewall, "Crane's *The Red Badge of Courage*," *The Explicator*, 3, No. 7 (1945), Item 55; John Berryman, "Stephen Crane: *The Red Badge of Courage*," in *The American Novel*, ed. Wallace Stegner (New York: Basic Books, 1965), p. 91; and Neil Schmitz, "Stephen Crane and the Colloquial Self," *Midwest Quarterly*, 13 (1972), 445.

3. W. M. Frohock, "*The Red Badge* and the Limits of Parody," *Southern Review*, N.S. 6 (1970), 147–48.

not reside *in* passages, perhaps we should take this troublesome sentence as an instance in which complete explicitness of irony is missing, because the sentence is inherently ambiguous.

But can irony ever be completely and unarguably explicit? One way of answering this question is to begin restoring the deleted "ironic" passages to the Appleton text, sentence by sentence, and note at which point the final chapter becomes indisputably ironic. But it is *always* possible to read the chapter nonironically no matter how many "ironic" passages are restored (just as it has always been possible to read the chapter as ironic no matter how many "ironic" passages were deleted—as Walcutt, Berryman, and others have demonstrated). This suggests two things: (1) adding more "ironic" passages resolves "inherent" ambiguity only when a critic has already adopted an ironic interpretive convention for the context of the passages; and (2) complete explicitness of irony is an impossibility.

But these facts are as true for the interpretation of the "coherent" final manuscript as they are for the interpretation of the "incoherent" Appleton first edition. To support this claim, all we need do is note how critics who have read the manuscript, and even those who have focused on the deleted passages, differ in their readings. For example, Binder reads the manuscript's final chapter as a skillful ironic coda in which the narrator demonstrates Henry's continued self-delusion and lack of growth. Donald Pizer also interprets the chapter ironically but sees the irony as heavy-handed and defends the deletions. Mordecai Marcus argues that the final manuscript chapter is actually neither all irony nor all nonirony; without the deletions it is ambiguous. Eric Solomon reads the final chapter as a straightforward, nonironic portrayal of Henry's new maturity. And while James Colvert interprets one eventually deleted passage as obviously ironic, Thomas Lorch interprets a similar passage as explicitly nonironic.[4] These various interpretations of

4. Henry Binder, "The *Red Badge of Courage* Nobody Knows," *Studies in the Novel,* 10 (1978), 27–31; Donald Pizer, "*The Red Badge of Courage* Nobody Knows: A Brief Rejoinder," *Studies in the Novel,* 11 (1979), 80–81; Mordecai Marcus, "The Unity of *The Red Badge of Courage,*" in *The Red Badge of Courage: Text and Criticism,* ed. Richard Lettis, Robert F. McDonnell, and William E. Morris (New

the manuscript are just as contradictory as the meanings "discovered" in the Appleton first edition.

All these conflicting interpretations of *Red Badge*'s two texts suggest that irony resides not in the text (whether a sentence or a whole chapter) but in the critic's interpretive conventions. And if irony and nonirony are not in texts but in interpretive conventions, then ambiguity in *Red Badge* must also be a function of an interpretation rather than of the text since the ambiguity is merely the indecision between interpretations of irony and nonirony. But what are we really talking about here? "Irony," "nonirony," and "ambiguity" are simply labels for *meanings,* meanings that in *Red Badge* arise out of the contradictions (or confirmations) among Henry's present self-evaluations, his past behavior and thoughts, and the narrator's attitude toward both. *Red Badge* and its critics demonstrate that a meaning is never so explicit that responsible critics cannot find evidence in the text to contradict it. Moreover, *Red Badge* criticism can serve as a synecdoche for all literary criticism, whose history shows that a work's meaning can never be made so distinct or clear that it cannot be explained away nor so literal that it cannot be taken as figurative.[5] Throughout this history, literary meaning remains a construction determined by the interpretive conventions of the critical discourse employed.

This series of questions and answers forces me to extend the conclusion of my *Red Badge* discussion in the last chapter. Not only is the Appleton text constituted by the interpretive conventions of its readers, but so is the final manuscript. Critics "write" different Appleton texts and even different manuscript recon-

---

York: Harcourt, Brace, 1960), p. 195; Eric Solomon, *Stephen Crane: From Parody to Realism* (Cambridge: Harvard University Press, 1966), pp. 96–97; James B. Colvert, "Stephen Crane's Magic Mountain," in *Stephen Crane: A Collection of Critical Essays,* ed. Maurice Bassan (Englewood Cliffs, N.J.: Prentice-Hall, 1967), pp. 97–98; and Thomas M. Lorch, "The Cyclical Structure of *The Red Badge of Courage,*" *CLA Journal,* 10 (1967), p. 237, n. 3.

5. See Harold Garfinkel, "Remarks on Ethnomethodology," in *Directions in Sociolinguistics: The Ethnography of Communication,* ed. John J. Gumperz and Dell Hymes (New York: Holt, Rinehart and Winston, 1972), pp. 315–21; and Stanley E. Fish, "Normal Circumstances, Literal Language, Direct Speech Acts, the Ordinary, the Everyday, the Obvious, What Goes without Saying, and Other Special Cases," *Critical Inquiry,* 4 (1978), rpt. in *Is There a Text in This Class?,* pp. 269–92.

structions according to their interpretive strategies and assumptions about American literature, naturalism, publishing, Crane, *The Red Badge of Courage,* and so on. And a similar hermeneutic situation holds for all the texts I have discussed—from "Rappaccini's Daughter" and *Moby-Dick* to "Four Meetings" and *A Man's Woman.* In fact, literary texts and their meanings are never prior to the employment of interpretive conventions; they are always its results. Texts do not cause interpretations, interpretations constitute texts.

But, of course, this deconstruction of the prior and independent text does not stop the questions. There is a commonsense objection to the claim for an absolute priority of interpretation over literary works. Though interpretive conventions do influence how a text is read, must there not *be* a text to be read in the first place? Such a commonsense attitude is manifested in a long tradition of literary theory that has attempted to describe the nature of this prior and independent text. These textual theories posit constraints in the literary work that control (or should control) interpretation. Wolfgang Iser's functionalist model of the text participates in this tradition, and an examination of his model will help demystify the foundations of all such textual theories.

We have seen that Iser's functionalist model consists of blanks between the textual perspectives (narrator, characters, plot, and fictitious reader), and these blanks restrict the configurative meaning the reader puts together from the text within the theme-and-horizon structure of reading. The underlying basis of the interpretive constraints Iser proposes is the negating relationship among the perspectives. Negation characterizes the connections that the reader projects to fill the blanks between segments, and it describes the horizon's relation to the theme during any moment in the time-flow of reading. The reader's "process of formulation is continually guided by negation."[6] In each case, what is negated (challenged, modified, or the like) is one perspective by another. And for Iser a perspective's specific negating function in any particular text is an uninterpreted

6. Wolfgang Iser, *The Act of Reading* (Baltimore: Johns Hopkins University Press, 1978), p. 214.

given in that text, constraining the reader's assembly of meaning. For example, he lists four basic types of perspective arrangements for narrative fictions.[7] It is not necessary to describe how each of these arrangements functions; what is important here is that these relations among perspectives, as they appear in any particular narrative text, are not the stable, intersubjective givens Iser supposes. Whether the hero's perspective cancels a minor character's or vice versa is always an interpretation and never the textual given that Iser assumes. Any particular perspective arrangement is a construct varying according to an ongoing critical interpretation. This means that such arrangements cannot serve as *prior* textual constraints on the critic's interpretive work because they are already its *products*.

Of course, I can go even further and say that not only is the negative relation between the hero and a minor character an interpretive construct but so is the "fact" that a certain character is designated "the hero" and another only "a minor character." To cite just one of many available examples: interpreters have proposed Ahab, Ishmael, and the White Whale himself as the hero of *Moby-Dick;* which character is so designated depends entirely on the critic's interpretation of Melville's novel as a whole. And the same kind of interpretive foundation underlies the apparently more basic "given," the individual character in a text.[8] And so on. It's interpretation all the way down.

However, the textual theorist must start somewhere. Once such a theorist posits the category of a "prior and independent

7. Ibid., pp. 100–103.
8. Cf. semiotic claims that a character is not a psychological entity but merely a "structural category . . . a pure syntactic function, without any semantic content." Readers fill this category by organizing the set of attributes predicated for it by the narrative. This "organization may be the object either of explicit indications by the author (the 'portrait') or of a series of indications addressed to the reader, who has to accomplish the task of reconstitution; finally, it may be imposed by the reader himself, that is, it may not even be present in the text" (Oswald Ducrot and Tzvetan Todorov, *Encyclopedic Dictionary of the Sciences of Language,* trans. Catherine Porter [Baltimore: Johns Hopkins University Press, 1979], p. 222). Also cf. Derrida's deconstruction of the ontological concept underlying the notion of an individual character: "The concept of *subjectivity* belongs *a priori and in general* to the order of the *constituted*"—Jacques Derrida, *Speech and Phenomena,* trans. David B. Allison (Evanston: Northwestern University Press, 1973), p. 84, n. 9.

text," he must begin filling it with textual elements, givens that will constrain its interpretation. These "givens" form the foundation of any theory of the literary work. Iser's foundation is the negative relation between textual perspectives; with this "given" he supports his functionalist model of the text and his whole phenomenology of reading.[9] The metatheory I am suggesting here—a kind of "constitutive hermeneutics"—helps explain why there have been so many conflicting accounts of the nature of literature in terms of the essential, given elements that make it up: different interpretive assumptions constitute different "objective" elements.[10]

This is especially true for such radically different literary theories as those of M. H. Abrams and J. Hillis Miller. Both the traditional literary historian and his deconstructionist adversary base their hermeneutic projects on the assumption of a prior and independent text. Abrams, of course, believes in an independent text that embodies the author's meaning which is subsequently discovered by an interpreter. Miller too believes in texts that are prior to interpretation, though his texts are of a

9. In a recent interview Iser claims, "What is given is textual segments": *Diacritics* 10, No. 2 (1980), 72. In a dismantling of Iser's theory complementary to my own, Stanley Fish starts with Iser's claim about textual segments and shows that "there can be no category of the 'given' if by given one means what is there before interpretation begins": "Why No One's Afraid of Wolfgang Iser," *Diacritics*, 11, No. 1 (1981), 8.

10. The philosophical precedents for constitutive hermeneutics range from Book Three of Nietzsche's *Will to Power* to Hubert Dreyfus's use of Heidegger in his *What Computers Can't Do: A Critique of Artificial Reason,* 2d ed. (New York: Harper & Row, 1979). In recent literary theory, see Kenneth S. Abraham, "Statutory Interpretation and Literary Theory: Some Common Concerns of an Unlikely Pair," *Rutgers Law Review,* 32 (1979), 676–94; Fish, *Is There a Text in This Class?,* introduction, chapter headnotes, and chs. 6–16; Susan Horton, *Interpreting Interpreting: Interpreting Dickens's* Dombey (Baltimore: Johns Hopkins University Press, 1979); Steven Mailloux, "Learning to Read: Interpretation and Reader-Response Criticism," *Studies in the Literary Imagination,* 12, No. 1 (1979), 93–108, and rev. of *Directions for Criticism, Journal of Aesthetics and Art Criticism,* 37 (1978), 97–100; Walter Benn Michaels, *American Epistemologies: Literary Theory and Pragmatism* (Baltimore: Johns Hopkins University Press, forthcoming); and Susan A. Stewart, *Nonsense: Aspects of Intertextuality in Folklore and Literature* (Baltimore: Johns Hopkins University Press, 1979). Related work in the social sciences can be found in *Interpretive Social Science: A Reader,* ed. Paul Rabinow and William M. Sullivan (Berkeley: University of California Press, 1979); and *Ethnomethodology: Selected Readings,* ed. Roy Turner (Baltimore: Penguin, 1974).

very different kind from Abrams's; they are texts that have their play of relations "within" them, texts that "authorize" innumerable interpretations, texts that are "the crossroads of multiple ambiguous meanings."[11]

Furthermore, both Abrams and Miller believe in the power of the literary text over its interpreters. What needs to be recognized here is that their interpretive theories function to constitute this textual power, and the specific ways they accomplish this depends entirely upon the assumptions and strategies of the theoretical discourse employed. Abrams's theory constitutes texts that have a *coercive* power; his texts constrain the reader's interpretation and impose on the unprejudiced critic a determinate meaning. Miller's theory constitutes texts that have a *preemptive* power; his texts deconstruct themselves with no help from readers or critics: "The critic... still has his uses, though this use may be no more than to identify an act of deconstruction which has always already, in each case differently, been performed by the text on itself."[12] In both of these hermeneutic theories, interpretation becomes supplemental (rather than primary), in that it is extraneous to a text that already contains its determinate or indeterminate meaning within itself; both textual constraints and self-deconstructions are taken as noninterpreted givens in prior and independent texts. Abrams's and Miller's theories, which differ so completely in other respects, share this valorization of the power-full text, a valorization that con-

11. J. Hillis Miller, "Tradition and Difference," *Diacritics* 2, No. 4 (1972), 11–12.

12. J. Hillis Miller, "Deconstructing the Deconstructers," *Diacritics*, 5, No. 2 (1975), 31; also see Miller, "Stevens' Rock and Criticism as Cure, II," *Georgia Review*, 30 (1976), 330–31. William Cain sees Miller's claims as more inconsistent than I suggest here—see Cain, "Deconstruction in America: The Recent Literary Criticism of J. Hillis Miller," *College English*, 41, (1979), 367–82. Miller's most recent work on the "ethics of reading" further complicates his position. For example, he writes of the ethical necessity of "first subjecting oneself to the words on the page.... There is in literary study a linguistic imperative which shapes what a critic or teacher says about a text. ... This imperative in the language forces the critic or teacher to repeat, sometimes in spite of himself, the heterogeneity, the resistance to a monological reading, which is present in any literary work": "Theory and Practice: Response to Vincent Leitch," *Critical Inquiry*, 6 (1980), 613–14. In this most recent formulation, the power of the text Miller constitutes becomes more coercive than preemptive.

tinues to dominate contemporary literary theory and criticism.[13]

Indeed, even at a time of repeated attacks on most traditional literary concepts, it remains extremely difficult to give up the notion of an independent text. We have seen how a psychological reading theorist as aggressive as Norman Holland keeps falling back on concepts such as the "raw materials" or givens in the text. Even Jonathan Culler's theory of reading conventions (to which my study owes so much) occasionally slips back into the traditional rhetoric of the prior and independent text. For example, in one place he writes, "The work has structure and meaning because it is read in a particular way, because these potential properties, *latent in the object itself,* are actualized by the theory of discourse applied in the act of reading."[14] Here we might draw a distinction between Culler's theory in which (at least in this passage) he sees reading conventions as only minimally enabling and a constitutive hermeneutics which sees inter-

13. The power referred to here is hermeneutic, not political, though in the end the effect of the first becomes the second; cf. Edward W. Said, *Orientalism* (New York: Pantheon, 1978). I should also note that a constitutive hermeneutics need not jettison the definition of *interpretation* proposed in Ch. 6. Interpretation can still be viewed as "acceptable and approximating translation" but with these qualifications: (1) every translation is actually a construction producing what it claims to approximate; (2) the position from which any translation is judged to be a close or remote approximation depends entirely on the interpretive conventions constituting that position; and (3) the acceptability of any translation is determined by the interpretive conventions with authority in a historical community. With these clarifications, the definition both captures the "commonsense" view of interpretation (a belief in a prior and independent text that the interpretation translates) and recognizes the claims of a constitutive hermeneutics which holds that the commonsense view is the enabling fiction of all practical criticism.

14. Jonathan Culler, *Structuralist Poetics* (Ithaca: Cornell University Press, 1975), p. 113, emphasis added. For purposes ultimately different than mine, two other commentators have used this quotation to show an inconsistency in Culler's theory; see Gerald Graff, *Literature against Itself* (Chicago: University of Chicago Press, 1979), p. 198, and Frank Lentricchia, *After the New Criticism* (Chicago: University of Chicago Press, 1980), p. 107. Both these theorists, however, see many more remnants of the traditional valorization of the text in Culler's book than I do; see Graff, p. 167, and Lentricchia, p. 108. In any case, that valorization does continue in Culler's later work when he writes: "On the one hand, the responses of readers are not random but are significantly determined by the constituents of texts, yet on the other hand the interpretive orientation of a response is what gives certain elements significance within a work": "Semiotics as a Theory of Reading," in *The Pursuit of Signs* (Ithaca: Cornell University Press, 1981), p. 59.

pretive conventions as maximally constitutive. For Culler, conventions are necessary though (at times) not sufficient for reading; that is, literary competence enables the reader to naturalize the text by actualizing the potential conventions *in* that text. In a constitutive hermeneutics, the interpretive conventions are *everything;* they constitute the text in every one of its aspects.

There are some reader-oriented critics who would agree with the claims I have just made about the dependent status of texts upon constituting interpreters. For in place of texts, most of these critics would assert the priority of "the reader." Theories of the reader, however, do not escape the interpretive problematic I have described for theories of the text. Most reader response critics simply do not see that "the reader," like "the text," is constituted by the descriptive discourse of which it is a part. The givens of the reading experience are no more independent of the constituting power of theoretical discourse than are the givens of the text. For this reason, there are as many different kinds of readers reading as there are kinds of discourse about "the reader": psychoanalytic, phenomenological, structuralist, and so on.

To sharpen this point, I will briefly examine the specific concepts of "the reader" in some of the reading theories discussed earlier in this book.

There is a strong temptation to divide reader-response critics into two competing groups: those (like Norman Holland and David Bleich) who examine the reactions of *actual* readers and those (like Wolfgang Iser and the early Stanley Fish) who rely on the concept of an *ideal* reader. As a strategy for characterizing different kinds of critical enterprises, this distinction is a useful first step. However, most people interested in reader criticism mistakenly posit an absolute distinction between actual and ideal readers. Such a move is misleading insofar as it suggests a distinction between real and hypothetical readers and one between neutrally described and critically constructed reading experiences. In fact, all readers are hypothetical and all reading experiences critically constructed. More exactly: in reader-response criticism, the description of reading is always an interpretive construct based on assumptions about who a reader is and what he or she does while reading.

To examine this claim, we can begin with the notion of an "implied reader," a reader required by the text. This reader is the most obvious interpretive construct in reader-response criticism. In the same way that a critic interprets the text's unity or the narrative voice, he can also interpret the reader implied by the text. For example, Iser interprets the implied reader of *Vanity Fair* as having the role of a social critic who judges the novel's characters and their sham attitudes. Iser claims that the actual reader is "invited" to take on this role.[15] The "implied reader" then is the reader that the text requires; which is to say, he is the reader that the critic interprets the text as requiring. Iser's analysis is an interpretation, whether we say it is an interpretation of the text or the author's intention or the implied reader's experience.

The "ideal reader" is merely an abstracted version of the "implied reader." He is not a reader of a specific text but one implied by all literary texts; or put another way, he is a hypothetical reader with the general ability to comprehend literature. Thus, we find the "informed reader" of Fish's affective stylistics and Culler's closely related notion of "literary competence," defined as "what an ideal reader must know implicitly in order to read and interpret works in ways which we consider acceptable, in accordance with the institution of literature." Culler points out that the "ideal reader is, of course, a theoretical construct, perhaps best thought of as a representation of the central notion of acceptability."[16] We have, then, a specific text's *implied reader,* which is really only a textual interpretation (or part of one) using a reader vocabulary. And we have an *ideal reader* who is also an interpretive construct, one that is abstracted from many specific instances of textual interpretation, one that defines the conditions of literary response.

Now, the usual contrast to an "ideal reader" is the "actual reader": a reader with the ability to read vs. readers actually

15. Wolfgang Iser, *The Implied Reader* (Baltimore: Johns Hopkins University Press, 1974), pp. 101–120. In another place, Iser writes that the implied reader "is a construct and in no way to be identified with any real reader. . . . The real reader is always offered a particular role to play [by the text], and it is this role that constitutes the concept of the implied reader" (*The Act of Reading,* p. 34).

16. Culler, *Structuralist Poetics,* pp. 123–24.

reading. The mistake here is to assume that ideal readers are interpretive constructs while actual readers are not critical constructions at all and that the reading experiences of ideal readers are critical fictions while those of actual readers are "really there" independent of any reader-response critics's interpretive framework. The self-analyses of Fish and Holland help correct this misconception.

In looking back on the claims of his affective stylistics, Stanley Fish now admits that his description of the reader's experience was really an interpretation creating the content of that experience. The concept of the informed or ideal reader was merely a device for generalizing that content. For example, Fish argued that the reader of Milton or Bacon or Herbert made certain epistemological moves (took stands, made judgments, reversed himself); and thus the informed reader was someone capable of performing these activities when reading these authors. Fish now sees that the epistemological moves that he described over and over again were constituted by the interpretive strategies of his critical discourse and were not independent of them.[17]

Reader-response critics who discuss actual readers do not escape this interpretive problematic. Norman Holland, for one, realizes this fact. Using the concept of an "identity theme," Holland's transactive criticism examines what actual readers say about their reading experiences. However, "identity themes" are themselves interpretations. As Holland says in one place: "*Identity* is the *unity* I find in a *self* if I look at it as though it were a *text*"; and in another essay he adds, "*Interpretation is a function of identity*, identity being defined operationally as what is found in a person by looking for a unity in him, in other words, by interpretation."[18] In Holland's approach, then, actual readers are translated into identity themes. Indeed, no critic who uses actual readers can avoid similar translations; all reading must be seen through some interpretive framework that in fact constitutes the reading experience described.

17. See Fish, *Is There a Text in This Class?*, pp. 12–13, 147, 163–64, 344–45.
18. Norman N. Holland, "Unity Identity Text Self," *PMLA*, 90 (1975), 815, and "Transactive Criticism: Re-Creation Through Identity," *Criticism*, 18 (1976), 340.

Like Fish, Holland denies that there is an independent, preexisting reading experience directly available for neutral description. Thus he too believes that all descriptions (including those of and by actual readers) are interpretations, creating what they claim to represent. The constitutive mechanism for Holland is identity themes; for Fish it is shared interpretive strategies. The lesson to be learned from Fish's and Holland's self-analyses is certainly clear: the portrayal of an actual reader's response is as much the result of a critical interpretation as the description of an ideal reader's experience.

What then is the status of my own discourse on readers reading? A look back at my theory and practice again demonstrates the constitutive power of interpretation. Chapter 4 on textual scholarship posits a dialectic between intention and convention: in order to recognize authorial intention, the reader must share the author's communicative conventions, and to know the specific conventions being invoked, the reader must recognize the author's intention. This version of the hermeneutic circle provides constraints on literary interpretation, and for textual scholarship I believe it is a useful model. It is, however, a model based on interpretive assumptions rather than some independent objective reality. These interpretive assumptions include beliefs about autonomous authors as origins for texts and about the availability of authorial intention through shared conventions. The first of these beliefs has a well-established place in the institutional enterprise of textual scholarship. But as secure as its position is, it could be displaced in favor of other interpretive assumptions.[19] The second belief about shared conventions is not as deeply entrenched in the institutional apparatus but gains its persuasive force as a proposal because it can be closely tied to intention (through an appeal to communication-intention theories in the philosophy of language). What I have done is to argue for a view of reading that has a social model of intention and convention as its foundation, and the case I have made is persuasive only insofar as it appeals to assumptions already held by textual scholars and literary critics. This is not to say that my

19. Indeed this is what has already happened in the arguments of Morse Peckham and Hans Zeller cited above in Ch. 4, n. 41.

proposal is based on an interpretive "fiction," for calling it a "fiction" suggests that there is a "nonfictional" basis, an uninterpreted given, that I could have used instead. But all we have are interpretive grounds for our proposals, and their acceptability must be judged in pragmatic terms—results that are evaluated according to beliefs already in place.

The extended analysis of "Rappaccini's Daughter" in Chapter 3 is another case of discourse performing interpretive work by producing the object of its description. I claim (and believe) that I have described the intended structure of the reader's response to Hawthorne's tale. I posit certain formal units in the text that cause the reader to perform certain actions. However, these textual elements and reader activities are not discovered but constituted by my interpretive conventions, which resemble those of Fish's and Iser's practical criticism. If I had not proceeded with the conventions of this type of reader-response criticism, I would have proceeded with *other* interpretive conventions based on different assumptions about readers (perhaps like Holland's transactive criticism) and about texts (perhaps like traditional holistic criticism). This is simply to say that there are no basic facts of reading available independent of interpretation.[20]

My conclusion has posed a series of questions that I believe all reader-response critics must face. But my own answers to these questions must, for the time being, remain incomplete because

20. An appeal to the empirical research in psycholinguistics does not change the situation. First of all, psycholinguists themselves disagree over models of reading: see Eleanor J. Gibson and Harry Levin, *The Psychology of Reading* (Cambridge: MIT Press, 1975), pp. 438–81, and James F. Ross, "On the Concepts of Reading," *Philosophical Forum*, 6 (1974), 93–141. Second, psycholinguistic data about reading derives from interpretive models; different research paradigms produce different "facts" about reading: see the disagreements over interpreting the experimental data in Gibson and Levin and cf. my discussion of a maximally constitutive view of Kuhn's paradigm theory in Ch. 1 above. And finally, when a literary theorist uses psycholinguistic models or data to support his own literary reading model, he necessarily does so in an interested way; as Fish writes: Rather than citing psycholinguistic evidence, reader critics manufacture it "by stipulating in advance that a scrutiny of the materials will reveal just the kind of activities that [they] claim readers to be performing. In short, for the 'evidence' to be supporting, it requires the addition or superimposition of the very hypothesis it would test": "Interpreting 'Interpreting the *Variorum*,'" in *Is There a Text in This Class?*, p. 178.

the proposed constitutive hermeneutics requires a much more detailed and systematic presentation. In this conclusion I have only tried to suggest some of the hermeneutic problems inherent in all reader-response theory and practice, including my own. However, even if all discourse does constitute what it claims to describe, the reasons for choosing a reader-oriented approach remain. What does such discourse allow you to do? What problems can it solve? What goals can it help achieve? This book offers my response to these pragmatic questions.

Reader-Response Criticism
and Teaching Composition

Are rhetoric and poetics separate and discrete fields of study? Although rhetorical theorists from Aristotle to Kenneth Burke have pointed out the overlap between these two areas, detailed discussion usually centers on showing their distinctiveness. The common ground of rhetoric and poetics is a "no man's land, the limbo of the faithless, for no self-respecting esthetician will vulgarize his subject by glancing, even momentarily, at rhetoric, and the rhetorician, though generally much more comprehensive in his viewpoint than the esthetician, is so busied with the 'practical' discourses of history (both past and present) that he seldom has time to concern himself with poetry."[1] Extended entry into this no man's land is long overdue, and especially so now that English departments are becoming more aware of their dual responsibility to teach composition and promote literary study. A sharp distinction between rhetoric and poetics encourages us to view these duties as two completely separate functions. Actually, the study of literature and the teaching of writing are closely related and mutually illuminating. In fact, recent trends in literary criticism suggest that a rapprochement may be taking place between literary and composition theory; shared paradigms are now emerging. In this Appendix I will outline these developing areas of shared theory and practice, emphasizing the role of reader-response criticism as a growing bond between rhetoric and poetics.

Observation and interpretation always proceed within ac-

---

1. W. Ross Winterowd, "Beyond Style," *Philosophy and Rhetoric,* 5 (1972), 110. My enormous debt to Professor Winterowd's insights in composition theory will be evident from my many references to his work below.

cepted paradigms, whether in physics, medical research, composition study, or literary criticism.[2] Since the 1940s, New Critical formalism has clearly served as the dominant paradigm in American criticism and theory. This "objective" approach (in its purest form, at least) viewed a literary work as an artifact, cut off from both authorial intention and reader response. It rejected "external" criticism and restricted its analysis to the work in and of itself. Many New Critics spacialized the text, viewing its parts in relation to the artistic whole, a tightly organized network of structures. This American New Criticism provided little of interest to rhetoricians. It not only ignored the audience, a central concern of rhetoric; it also actively discouraged talk about readers through its condemnation of the Affective Fallacy.

In recent years there have been many reactions against New Criticism. In one such reaction, a model of literature as communication challenges the established model of literature as aesthetic product. Those critics using this revitalized communication model practice the Intentional and Affective Fallacies with impunity. This new paradigm of criticism has much more to offer the composition teacher than did the old formalist paradigm, and it is here that we can begin to see the recent overlap of rhetoric and poetics most clearly. Two contemporary critical approaches that work within the model of literature as communication are textual-biographical and reader-response criticisms.[3]

Recent textual-biographical critics view art as process, not as product. This may at first seem contradictory to our usual notion that textual editors are interested only in establishing a product, the intended text for a critical edition. But such a portrayal is incomplete. As we saw in Chapter 4, the scholarly editor establishes his text based on the "author's final intention," and

2. See Thomas S. Kuhn, *The Structure of Scientific Revolutions*, 2d ed. (Chicago: University of Chicago Press, 1970), esp. pp. 10, 187–91. Cf. Patricia Bizzell, "Thomas Kuhn, Scientism, and English Studies," *College English*, 40 (1979), 764–71, and Grant Webster, *The Republic of Letters* (Baltimore: Johns Hopkins University Press, 1979).

3. For another vigorous advocate of the communication model for literature, see Mary Louise Pratt, *Toward a Speech Act Theory of Literary Discourse* (Bloomington: Indiana University Press, 1977), especially her attack on the a-contextual formalist model assumed by intrinsic criticism and structuralist theory, pp. 72–75.

Appendix

this criterion must be viewed not only in terms of the textualist's interpretation of the intended conventional responses but also in light of his historical knowledge of the author's whole composing process. In fact, the textualist sees the literary work itself as a process, a series of intentional acts by the author. When a critic studies a work from this textual-biographical perspective, when he practices what has been called the "New Scholarship," he revels in the Intentional Fallacy, bringing to bear his total knowledge of the author's composing process (including extant forms of the text) and the relevant biographical events that affect that process.[4]

From a complementary perspective, recent reader-oriented critics have also viewed art as communicative process. As M. H. Abrams puts it: "Since the late 1950's . . . there has been a strong revival of interest in literature as a public act involving communication between author and reader, and this has led to the development of a rhetorical criticism which, without departing from a primary focus on the work as such, undertakes to analyze those elements within a poem or a prose narrative which are their primarily for the reader's sake."[5] Abrams cites the work of Wayne Booth in his *Rhetoric of Fiction* (1961) as an example of this type of criticism. During the 1970s, reader-response critics extended (and transformed) this rhetorical approach: Wolfgang Iser in phenomenology, Jonathan Culler through his theory of reading conventions, and Stanley Fish in his affective stylistics. *Whereas the textual-biographical critics view literature as a series of acts by the author, reader-response critics view it as a series of acts by the reader.* Fish's criticism, for example, is "an analysis of the developing responses of the reader in relation to the words as they succeed one another in time,"[6] and, as we saw in Chapters 2 and 3, this temporal reading model emphasizes the series of acts that

4. See Brian Higgins and Hershel Parker, "The Chaotic Legacy of the New Criticism and the Fair Augury of the New Scholarship," in *Ruined Eden of the Present: Hawthorne, Melville, and Poe,* ed. G. R. Thompson and Vergil Lokke (West Lafayette, Ind.: Purdue University Press, 1981), pp. 27–45.
5. M. H. Abrams, *A Glossary of Literary Terms,* 3d ed. (New York: Holt, Rinehart and Winston, 1971), p. 148.
6. Stanley Fish, "Literature in the Reader: Affective Stylistics," in *Is There a Text in This Class?,* p. 27.

the text requires the reader to perform: judging, questioning, finding answers, assuming perspectives, solving puzzles, and so on. Or as Iser writes: we "look forward, we look back, we decide, we change our decisions, we form expectations, we are shocked by their nonfulfillment, we question, we muse, we accept, we reject; this is the dynamic process of recreation" in reading.[7] By describing these actions, reader-response critics discard the Affective Fallacy and join the New Scholars in rejecting the chief proscriptions of American New Criticism.

Whereas the old New Critical paradigm was hostile to any synthesis of rhetoric and poetics, the new paradigm that views literature as a temporal act of communication provides much encouragement for a rapprochement between literary criticism and composition theory. Like textual-biographical critics, composition theorists stress the importance of viewing the composing process as a series of acts by the writer.[8] And like reader-response critics, these rhetoricians suggest paying considerable attention to the reader while writing and analyzing discourse.[9] These shared concerns and perspectives should encourage more exchanges between current rhetoric and poetics, exchanges that will benefit both disciplines and English studies as a whole.

A simple view of the composing process based on the traditional rhetorical categories—invention, arrangement, and style—will further illustrate the fit between composition theory

7. Wolfgang Iser, *The Implied Reader* (Baltimore: Johns Hopkins University Press, 1974), p. 288.

8. See Janet Emig, *The Composing Process of Twelfth Graders* (Urbana, Ill.: NCTE, 1971); and the survey of "Invention and Conceptions of the Composing Process" in Richard Young, "Invention: A Topographical Survey," in *Teaching Composition: 10 Bibliographical Essays,* ed. Gary Tate (Fort Worth: Texas Christian University Press, 1976), pp. 33-40.

9. See, for example, W. Ross Winterowd, *The Contemporary Writer* (New York: Harcourt Brace Jovanovich, 1975), p. 30; William F. Irmscher, *The Holt Guide to English,* 2d ed. (New York: Holt, Rinehart and Winston, 1976), pp. 172 ff.; Ruth Mitchell and Mary Taylor, "The Integrating Perspective: An Audience-Response Model for Writing," *College English,* 41 (1979), 247-71; Fred R. Pfister and Joanne F. Petrick, "A Heuristic Model for Creating a Writer's Audience," and Russell C. Long, "Writer-Audience Relationships: Analysis or Invention?" *College Composition and Communication,* 31 (1980), 213-20 and 221-26; and Jim Corder, "Rhetorical Analyses of Writing," in Tate, pp. 223-40, passim.

and recent literary criticism (primarily reader-response approaches). In what follows I will oversimplify the composing process and fall into such heresies as implying a form-content split. My point, however, is simply to provide a clear framework for examining some additional parallels between literary criticism and composition.

The goal of the composition teacher is to give the student writer alternative choices at every stage of the composing process. For example, in the area of invention (the generation of subject matter), the student has at least two alternatives: brainstorming and heuristics. Brainstorming is an unsystematic way of asking questions about a topic, while heuristics are systematic ways of asking questions.[10] Literary critics often use heuristics in their analyses of literature, and such "critical" heuristics can be employed in teaching composition. For instance, Fish's heuristic "is simply the rigorous and disinterested asking of the question, what does this word, phrase, sentence, paragraph, chapter, novel, play, poem *do*?"[11] The student writer can use this same question to generate comments about any piece of discourse, including his or her own essays. An even more powerful heuristic can be found in the critical method of Kenneth Burke (whose writings have found an admiring audience among recent literary critics). Students can easily use the terms of Burke's Pentad—act, agent, agency, scene, and purpose—to generate questions about any human action.[12] Clearly, then, literary criticism can provide resources for the composition teacher at the stage of invention.

Once subject matter is generated, what choices of form are available to the student? Again, literary theory provides some useful models for the composition teacher. To Burke, form is "the psychology of the audience"; it is "an arousing and fulfillment of desires. A work has form in so far as one part of it leads a reader to anticipate another part, to be gratified by the se-

10. See Winterowd, *Contemporary Writer,* p. 82.
11. Fish, "Literature in the Reader," pp. 26-27.
12. See Winterowd, *Contemporary Writer,* pp. 82-90; Irmscher, pp. 30-40; and Young, pp. 13-16. Also cf. Kenneth Burke, "Questions and Answers about the Pentad," *College Composition and Communication,* 29 (1978), 330-35.

quence."[13] In its emphasis on the reader and temporal sequence, Fish's "structure of the reader's experience" is similar to Burke's theory of form.[14] Fish describes the specific ways the author arranges his reader's activities, what acts the reader "is being moved to perform" and the order in which he is moved to perform them.[15] At the level of arrangement, a temporal reader-oriented criticism encourages the composition teacher to make student writers aware of the expectations they set up in their essays and sensitive to their own ordering of the reader's responses.

The level of style provides another area where literary and composition theory interact. Again, the notion of choice can serve as our central concept: what sentence structures are available to the student writer? Two kinds of stylistics are relevant here, pedagogical and aesthetic. "*Pedagogical stylistics,* as the term implies, deals with teaching students to develop style," for example, using sentence-combining exercises; *aesthetic stylistics* refers to the study of style within literature.[16] When we view style as choice, pedagogical stylistics becomes a matter of providing students with syntactic alternatives. Aesthetic stylistics, on the other hand, becomes a method of analyzing a text in terms of alternative choices among available structures. Empirical studies have shown that pedagogical stylistics can improve a student's syntactic fluency, his or her ability to combine syntactic units into more complex forms.[17] No such strong claims are made for aesthetic stylistics. However, some aspects of aesthetic stylistics do have contributions to make to composition.

13. Kenneth Burke, *Counter-Statement,* 2d ed (1953; rpt. Berkeley: University of California Press, 1968), pp. 31, 124. See Richard E. Young, Alton L. Becker, and Kenneth L. Pike, *Rhetoric: Discovery and Change* (New York: Harcourt, Brace, and World, 1970), p. 323.

14. But see the contrast drawn above in Ch. 3, pp. 69–70.

15. Stanley E. Fish, "What Is Stylistics and Why Are They Saying Such Terrible Things About It?" in *Is There a Text in This Class?*, p. 92.

16. W. Ross Winterowd, *Contemporary Rhetoric: A Conceptual Background with Readings* (New York: Harcourt Brace Jovanovich, 1975), p. 17. For a persuasive critique of many approaches to aesthetic stylistics, see Fish, "What Is Stylistics?" pp. 69–96; also see his "What Is Stylistics and Why Are They Saying Such Terrible Things About It?—Part II," *boundary 2*, 8 (1979), rpt. in *Is There a Text in This Class?*, pp. 247–67.

17. See Frank O'Hare, *Sentence-Combining: Improving Student Writing without Formal Grammar Instruction* (Urbana, Ill.: NCTE, 1973).

Take the following example from one of the most informed composition texts now available:

> As we shall see, a major problem in student writing is the tendency not to put separate ideas together via the syntactic devices of the language. Here is a beginning paragraph from a freshman essay:
>
> 71 My greatest love is the love of my possessions. I feel like a king when I am amongst my possessions. But my possessions are not material possessions such as a beautiful new automobile or an enormous new house. Rather, my possessions are the wonders of nature: the beautiful, snow-capped mountains and the deep, crystal-clear lakes.
>
> I think most readers would say that 71 is either immature or awkward or both. One alternative to it is the following:
>
> 72 I feel like a king when I am amongst the wonders of nature, for they are my greatest love and my greatest possessions: snow-capped mountains and deep, crystal-clear lakes rather than material things such as a new automobile or an enormous house.
>
> I would argue that 72 sounds more mature, perhaps even more intelligent, than 71, and yet the idea content of both of them is essentially the same.[18]

Winterowd's purpose here is to illustrate the usefulness of pedagogical stylistics (in this case, embedding propositions within propositions). As he further argues: "The reason that most readers would prefer 72 over 71 is simply that in 72 the grammatical possibilities of the language have been used to put closely related ideas together in the neat syntactic package of a sentence."

By focusing on the syntactic choices, however, Winterowd ignores larger rhetorical strategies. If we examine 71 and 72 from the perspective of reader-response criticism, a form of aesthetic stylistics, we see that the structure of the reader's experience is radically different in each case. Though 71 may sound syntactically "immature," it is certainly more rhetorically "sophisticated" than 72. In 71 the freshman writer (consciously or not) has withheld the specific name of his "greatest love." After the first sen-

18. Winterowd, *Contemporary Writer*, pp. 308–09.

tence, the reader naturally jumps to the conclusion that "possessions" refer to material things. The second sentence offers nothing to contradict such a conclusion; it suggests the image of a king in his treasure room. (I distinctly remember my impression at this point during my first reading: not only does this student lack syntactic fluency but, more important, his values are clearly superficial and undeveloped.) The contrastive *but* begins the rhetorical reversal. The third sentence contradicts the reader's previous conclusion: the writer's greatest love is not *material* possessions. The final sentence not only provides a new equation (possessions = nature), but it also forces the reader to repudiate his previous condescending attitude toward the writer's value system. Such a reversal makes a rather commonplace statement into a rhetorically forceful corrective. Winterowd's "more mature" rewrite of 71 manifests none of these rhetorical strategies: because no information is withheld, the reader jumps to no false conclusions and makes no mistaken judgments about the writer. Does 72 have more embedded propositions than 71? Yes. Is it more rhetorically sophisticated? No.[19]

In terms of their controlling paradigms and in view of shared models for invention, arrangement, and style, rhetoric and poetics are becoming more closely related in current theory and practice. This statement implies a theoretical justification for a historical point I made at the beginning of this Appendix: literary criticism and composition theory can be parts of one homogeneous discipline of English. Indeed, literature specialists have the potential to be the best qualified teachers of composition. But I would like to stress a further point. Not just any English professor can teach writing, even if he or she *has* accepted the model of literature as communicative act. It is clear that compostion teachers are becoming specialists within the English Department (not just second-class citizens). There is now a growing empirical and rhetorical body of knowledge that all

19. Brook Thomas provides further arguments for the use of reader-response criticism in the teaching of writing—see his "Re-Reading, Re-Writing," *CEA Forum*, 11, No. 3 (1981), 1–6.

serious teachers of composition must master.[20] Nevertheless, as I have tried to show, composition and literary study need not be antithetical functions within our discipline. A synthesis of rhetoric and poetics will go a long way toward curing the English Department's split personality.

20. See Tate's collection of bibliographical essays cited in n. 10 above.

Bibliographical Note

In addition to the works cited in the footnotes, the following should prove helpful for further investigations of the topics discussed in this book. The best place to begin a study of reader-response criticism is with Jane Tompkins's *Reader-Response Criticism: From Formalism to Post-Structuralism* (Baltimore: Johns Hopkins University Press, 1980). This anthology reprints influential articles by Walker Gibson, Gerald Prince, Michael Riffaterre, Georges Poulet, Wolfgang Iser, Stanley Fish, Norman Holland, and Walter Michaels, and important chapters from studies by Jonathan Culler and David Bleich. Besides a helpful introduction and her own excellent essay, "The Reader in History: The Changing Shape of Literary Response," Tompkins provides the most extensive annotated bibliography yet published on reader-response criticism. The largest collection of original essays using reader-oriented criticism and theory is Susan Suleiman and Inge Crosman's *The Reader in the Text: Essays on Audience and Interpretation* (Princeton: Princeton University Press, 1980), which includes pieces by Culler, Holland, Iser, Prince, Tzvetan Todorov, Christine Brooke-Rose, Robert Crosman, Peter Rabinowitz, Louis Marin, Vicki Mistacco, and others. Suleiman provides a very good introduction and Inge Crosman concludes the volume with an annotated bibliography. I should note that these two major collections assume different definitions of reader-oriented criticism. Tompkins restricts her selection, introduction, and bibliography primarily to the kind of reader-response criticism I discuss in Chapters 1 and 2; while

Suleiman and Crosman also place the work of the "new Yale critics" (including deconstruction) in the category of audience-oriented criticism.

For additional discussions of the assumptions, strategies, or concepts in reader-response criticism, see David Bleich, *Subjective Criticism* (Baltimore: Johns Hopkins University Press, 1978), Ch. 4; Steven Mailloux, "Learning to Read: Interpretation and Reader-Response Criticism," *Studies in the Literary Imagination,* 12, No. 1 (1979), 93–108; Peter Rabinowitz, "Truth in Fiction: A Reexamination of Audiences," *Critical Inquiry,* 4 (1977), 121–41; and W. Daniel Wilson, "Readers in Texts," *PMLA,* 96 (1981), 848–63. An extensive summary and bibliography of empirical research on readers reading can be found in Alan Purves and Richard Beach, *Literature and the Reader: Research in Response to Literature, Reading Interests, and the Teaching of Literature* (Urbana, Ill.: NCTE, 1972). Also see David Bleich, with Sandor J. Vargyai, "The Reader's Activity and Response," *Style,* 12 (1978), 172–79; this is Section XIV of "The Psychological Study of Language and Literature: A Selected Annotated Bibliography."

Periodical volumes of reader-oriented criticism and theory include: *Bucknell Review,* 26, No. 1 (1981) on "Theories of Reading, Looking, and Listening" with an introduction by Mailloux and articles by Bleich, Iser, Mistacco, Rabinowitz, Louise Rosenblatt, Ellen Schauber and Ellen Spolsky, Roland Champagne, William Cain, Wendy Deutelbaum, and Erdmann Waniek; *Cahiers,* 4 (1977), with a section on "Lecture et lectures"; *Comparative Criticism,* 2 (1980), with a section on "Text and Reader" which includes Iser's "The Indeterminacy of the Text: A Critical Reply"; *L'Esprit Créateur,* 21, No. 2 (1981), on "The Reader and the Text," including essays by Suleiman, Prince, and Inge Crosman; *Genre,* 10 (1977), with a section on "Reading, Interpretation, Response" including articles by Bleich, Holland, Mailloux, and Susan Horton; *James Joyce Quarterly,* 16, Nos. 1–2 (1978–79), "Structuralist/Reader Response Issue," with essays by James Sosnoski and Brook Thomas; *New Literary History,* 8, No. 1 (1976), on "Readers and Spectators: Some Views and Reviews"; *Oeuvres & Critiques,* 2, No. 2 (1978), on "Contributions allemandes récentes à une nouvelle approche critique: L'esthétique de la réception"; *Poétique,* No. 39 (1979), on "Théorie de la réception en Allemagne"; and *Poetics Today*, 1, No. 4 (1980), with review essays on theories of readers and readings. Also, *Reader: A Newsletter of Reader-Oriented Criticism and Teaching* began publication in 1977.

Useful introductions to German aesthetics of reception are Rien T. Segers, "Readers, Text and Author: Some Implications of Rezeptionsästhetik," *Yearbook of Comparative and General Literature*, 24 (1975), 15–23; and D. W. Fokkema and Elrud Kunne-Ibsch, *Theories of Literature in the Twentieth Century: Structuralism, Marxism, Aesthetics of Reception, Semiotics* (New York: St. Martin, 1977), esp. ch. 5; both surveys include helpful bibliographies. Also see Peter Uwe Hohendahl, "Introduction to Reception Aesthetics," trans. Marc Silberman, *New German Critique*, No. 10 (1977), pp. 29–63. Collections of essays in reception aesthetics include Gunter Grimm, ed., *Literatur und Leser: Theorie und Modelle zur Rezeption literarischer Werke* (Stuttgart: Reclam, 1975), and his *Rezeptionsgeschichte: Grundlegung einer Theorie: mit Analysen und Bibliographie* (Munich: Wilhelm Fink, 1977); Peter Uwe Hohendahl, ed., *Sozialgeschichte und Wirkungsästhetik: Dokumente zur empirischen und marxistischen Rezeptionsforschung* (Frankfurt: Athenäum, 1974); Hans Robert Jauss, *Ästhetische Erfahrung und literarische Hermeneutik* (Munich: Wilhelm Fink, 1977); and Rainer Warning, ed., *Rezeptionsästhetik: Theorie und Praxis* (Munich: Wilhelm Fink, 1975).

Jauss remains the most influential theorist of reception aesthetics. His work is discussed by David Bathrick, "The Politics of Reception Theory in the GDR," *Minnesota Review*, N.S. 5 (1975), 125–33; Jonathan Culler, "Comparative Literature and Literary Theory," *Michigan Germanic Studies*, 5 (1979), 173–75, and "Semiotics as a Theory of Reading" in *The Pursuit of Signs* (Ithaca: Cornell University Press, 1981), pp. 54–58; John Neubauer, "Trends in Literary Reception: Die neuen Leiden der Wertherwirkung," *German Quarterly*, 52 (1979), 69–79; Stephen G. Nichols, Jr., "A Poetics of Historicism?" in *Medievalia et Humanistica*, N.S. 8 (1977), 93–95; Hans Norbert Fügen, "Literary Criticism and Sociology in Germany," trans. Ruth Hein, *Yearbook of Comparative Literature*, 5 (1973), 263–67; Dieter Richter, "Teachers and Readers: Reading Attitudes as a Problem in Teaching Literature," trans. Sara Lennox, *New German*

Critique, No. 7 (1976), p. 37; Syndy McMillen Conger, "Hans Robert Jauss's *Rezeptionsästhetik* and England's Reception of Eighteenth-Century German Literature," *The Eighteenth Century,* 22 (1981), 74–93; and René Wellek, "The Fall of Literary History," in *New Perspectives in German Literary Criticism,* trans. David Henry Wilson et al., ed. Richard E. Amacher and Victor Lange (Princeton: Princeton University Press, 1979), pp. 430–31. Finally, for discussions of the reading public in the sociology of literature, see the bibliographies in Hugh Dalziel Duncan, *Language and Literature in Society* (Chicago: University of Chicago Press, 1953; rpt. New York: Bedminster, 1961), pp. 143–214, especially 175–85; and Jeffrey L. Sammons, *Literary Sociology and Practical Criticism* (Bloomington: Indiana University Press, 1977), pp. 205–230.

Index

Index

Index

Index

McCabe, Bernard, 74n
Mailloux, Mary Nell, 149
Male, Roy R., 72n
Manley, Lawrence, 130n
Manning, John J., 121n
Marcus, Mordecai, 184, 195
Martin, Jay, 187n
Marx, Leo, 165
Mathews, Cornelius, 174n
Matthiessen, F. O., 72n, 76n, 78n,
   171n
Meaning: David Bleich on, 31;
   Jonathan Culler on, 42, 57; de-
   terminate vs. indeterminate, 61n,
   142-43, 200; and effect, 98-99;
   Stanley Fish on, 21, 23; Norman
   Holland on, 25, 38; Wolfgang
   Iser on, 42, 44-45, 48-50;
   and pluralism, 53; and signifi-
   cance, 48-49. *See also* Constitutive
   conventions; Conventions, inter-
   pretive; Interpretation, general;
   Interpretation, literary
Melville, Herman, 78n, 82n, 124-25;
   Billy Budd, 115; *Moby-Dick,* 90n,
   170-78, 197, 198; *Pierre,* 82n, 96;
   Typee, 114-15, 117-18; *White-
   Jacket,* 124n
Meyer, Michael, 166n
Michaels, Walter Benn, 199n
Miller, Harold P., 120n
Miller, J. Hillis, 53, 58n, 141-44,
   146-48, 153n, 199-200
Miller, Perry, 178n
Miller, Wayne C., 162n, 187n
Mimesis, 146-47
Mode, 130-31, 139, 178, 188
Modern Language Association, 95n
Moss, Sydney P., 87n

Narrative conventions, 132, 188-89
Narrator, fictional: and reading, 76,
   82-85, 102, 116-17
National Endowment for the
   Humanities, 95n
New Criticism, 20, 21, 24, 50-51, 58n,
   64, 66-68, 93, 113, 209-11

Nietzsche, Friedrich, 142, 192, 199n
Nishida, Guy, 93
Norman, Liane, 90n
Norris, Frank: *McTeague,* 122n; *A
   Man's Woman,* 121-24, 197

Objectivity, 21, 23, 25n, 27, 29, 31,
   37-38, 167, 209
Ohmann, Richard, 133-34, 138n
Olsen, Stein Haugom, 100n, 136n

Paradigms, 33-36, 150n, 209
Parker, Hershel, 82n, 87n, 96, 112n,
   115n, 118-19, 124-25, 162, 173n,
   210n
Pearson, Norman Holmes, 160n
Peckham, Morse, 94n, 107n, 135n,
   136n, 205n
Peirce, C. S., 145n
Perception, 20, 24, 26, 30, 34, 43
Perlocutionary acts, 104-7
Perry, Menakhem, 68n, 90n
Persuasion, 35, 106, 205-6
Phenomenology, 20, 21, 37n, 43, 51,
   55, 148
Pizer, Donald, 161n, 181-82, 184,
   187n, 188, 195
Pluralism, critical, 53
Poirier, Richard, 68n
Pratt, Mary Louise, 102n, 103n, 107n,
   132n, 134, 158n, 209n
Price, Sherwood R., 85n
Prince, Gerald, 57n
Pritchett, V. S., 180
Proairetic code, 79n-80n; in reading
   "Rappaccini's Daughter," 79-81

"Rappaccini's Daughter" (PBS film),
   81n
Rawls, John, 129n
Reader-response criticism: apolitical
   nature of, 41; vs. deconstructive
   criticism, 58n, 60n-61n; defined,
   20; kinds of, 22, 40, 57; limitations of, 38-39, 41, 61n, 62-65,
   192; and phenomenology, 20, 43;
   status of discourse of, 202-7; and

Index

Steiner, George, 140, 145n
Stewart, Randall, 81n
Stewart, Susan, 135n, 177n, 199n
Strawson, P. F., 100n, 103n, 152n-53n
Strier, Richard, 71
Structuralism, 21, 42, 56n, 57, 59, 93, 209n
Structure of the reader's response, examples of, 73-89, 115-24, 214-15
The Sun Also Rises (Hemingway), 104

Tanselle, G. Thomas, 96-98, 107n, 108-13, 115, 142n
Textual-biographical criticism (the New Scholarship), 209-11
Textual scholarship. *See* Editing
Tharpe, Jac, 74n
Thomas, Brook, 215n
Thorpe, James, 97n
Thorpe, Willard, 171n
Tolstoy, Leo: *Sebastopol,* 163
Tompkins, Jane, 194n
Traditional conventions, 129-33, 137-38, 150-52, 153n, 154-55, 157-58, 160-65, 174-91; defined, 126-28
Twain, Mark. *See* Clemens, Samuel

Understanding, 104. *See also* Interpretation, general; Interpretation, literary
Unity. *See* Holistic interpretation
Uroff, M. D., 87n

Vodička, Felix, 168n

Wadlington, Warwick, 90n
Waggoner, Hyatt H., 72n, 75n
Walcutt, Charles, 187-89, 191, 195
Warren, Austin, 51, 132-33
Warren, Robert Penn, 67
Watson, George, 112n
Webber, Charles Wilkins, 81n
Wellek, René, 51-53, 55, 94, 132-33, 159-60, 165n, 166
Whitman, Walt: *Leaves of Grass,* 116
Wiley, John, 118n
Wimsatt, W. K., 19, 66n, 93
Winterowd, W. Ross, 208n, 211-13nn, 214
Winters, Yvor, 71n, 76n

Zeller, Hans, 107n, 205n
Ziff, Larzer, 184, 191

INTERPRETIVE CONVENTIONS

Designed by Richard E. Rosenbaum.
Composed by The Composing Room of Michigan, Inc.
in 10 point Baskerville V.I.P., 2 points leaded,
with display lines in Baskerville.
Printed offset by Thomson/Shore, Inc. on
Warren's Number 66 Text, 50 pound basis.
Bound by John H. Dekker & Sons, Inc.
in Holliston book cloth.

Library of Congress Cataloging in Publication Data

Mailloux, Steven.
   Interpretive conventions.

   Bibliography: p.
   Includes index.
   1. Reader-response criticism.   2. Criticism—United States.   3. American
fiction—History and criticism.   I. Title.
PN98.R38M3   801'.95'0973   81-70712
ISBN 0-8014-1476-8   AACR2